DIRECT FROM
IRELAND

SOUTHWEST IRELAND

Kerry & West Cork

DIRECT FROM
IRELAND

SOUTHWEST IRELAND
Kerry & West Cork

Patricia Levy and Sean Sheehan

PASSPORT BOOKS
a division of *NTC Publishing Group*
Lincolnwood, Illinois USA

This edition was first published in 1995 by Passport Books, a division of
NTC Publishing Group, 4255 West Touhy Avenue, Lincolnwood (Chicago),
Illinois 60646–1975 U.S.A.

Originally published in Ireland by
Gill & Macmillan Ltd
Goldenbridge
Dublin 8
© Patricia Levy and Sean Sheehan 1995
© maps Gill & Macmillan 1995
Print origination by Design Image, Dublin
Printed in Ireland by ColourBooks Ltd, Dublin

ISBN 0–8442–9711–9
Library of Congress Catalog Card Number 95–67858

FOR ALICE WEST

CONTENTS

INTRODUCTION TO THE GUIDE

This guide is divided into five sections, one for each of the peninsulas that jut into the Atlantic. Each has an introduction giving a brief history of the area, an ecotour, useful information, suggested excursions by car and by bicycle, activities for children, activities for rainy days, daytime and evening entertainments, where to eat, where to shop and where to stay. In short, we try to emphasise practical things throughout.

Thus, for example, the 'where to eat' sections are not good-food guides. The information given is to assist visitors locate suitable or convenient places to eat. Similarly, the 'where to stay' sections are not evaluations of the accommodation. A list of hotels, rented accommodation, hostels and caravan parks is given for each area. The bed and breakfast establishments are not listed in detail as there are many homes offering this type of accommodation in the regions. Displayed outside a house offering bed and breakfast will be a sign indicating 'Bed and Breakfast', 'B/B', 'Guests', 'Room and Breakfast' or 'Accommodation'. In Gaeltacht areas the word 'Lóistín' is displayed.

The Irish Tourist Board, Bord Fáilte, advises visitors to stay only in those homes which are registered with the Board. Registered houses may display a shamrock or say 'ITB approved' on their sign. Visitors can be confident that houses registered and approved by Bord Fáilte provide a high standard of comfort and hygiene. All registered homes may be booked in advance for a small fee through local tourist offices.

Many guest houses provide en-suite bathroom/shower facilities. Many will prepare an evening meal or direct guests to local restaurants. Most houses and hotels levy a surcharge on single guests using double rooms. Some will have single accommodation at single rates. Some homes have family rooms, with extra beds put in for children, at a moderate extra cost that will suit every pocket.

If travelling around without having made reservations during the high season (July and August) it is probably wiser to book into your accommodation by 6 p.m. or 7 p.m.

You may ask to look at the accommodation without obligation to stay, but once you have entered into a verbal agreement to stay you will be expected to take up the accommodation and pay the stated rate. Currently, this is around £15 for room and breakfast, although this is not a compulsory charge, and the rate varies.

Usually you will be offered a traditional Irish breakfast of cereal, fried bacon/eggs/sausages, brown bread and toast. Some hostesses/hosts offer a menu. If you prefer a 'continental style' or vegetarian breakfast you should say so. If you want breakfast at an earlier time than stated, you should ask if this is possible. Your hostess/host will be anxious to make you feel at home. In some homes you will be offered a key if you intend to be out late. If you wish to prolong your stay in any one house tell your hostess/host at breakfast. Sometimes a cheaper rate can be agreed for longer stays.

The rate for self-catering accommodation is not given or indicated in this guide as it varies throughout the year. During the winter months the rates are modest, but they are, of course, high during June, July and August. Many of the cottages sleep up to nine people so they can be an economical way to stay in the region. Everything is provided in the rented cottages and homes down to the last details like aluminium foil and paper towels. Visitors only have to provide their food and pay for the electricity consumed. Only groups of purpose-built self-catering cottages or apartments have been listed. Bord Fáilte publishes a descriptive list of many registered houses, bungalows, apartments and cottages to let throughout the region.

Hostels throughout the region charge a nightly rate of around £6 per person. More and more hostels are offering private rooms and, with the free use of a kitchen, they offer an alternative to bed and breakfast places that is well worth considering.

ACKNOWLEDGMENTS

We would like to thank all the individuals who have contributed to the writing of this guide. Bord Fáilte local offices, and Tim Magennis in Dublin, have been unfailingly helpful and co-operative. Jack Sheehan of Raferigeen deserves special mention for his wealth of local knowledge and special thanks are also due to Mike, Joseph and Danny for the countless ways in which they helped to make this book possible. A final thank you to Fergal Tobin of Gill & Macmillan.

Patricia Levy & Sean Sheehan

INTRODUCTION TO THE ECOTOURS

The purpose of the Ecotours is to provide readers with non-technical guides to the natural attractions of Kerry and West Cork. Each ecotour sets out to cover a specific route that can be comfortably accessed by car or bicycle, with the presupposition that the visitor is keen to periodically abandon their vehicle and walk, wander or climb in order to fully appreciate the place they are exploring. An ecotour by car is, frankly, a contradiction and the natural beauty and wonder of Kerry and West Cork cannot be enjoyed through the windscreen of a motorcar.

A good map is essential for these ecotours. A useful map of the whole country is the Michelin Map of Ireland No. 405 (1:1,000,000) but the Kerry and West Cork area is covered in more detail in the South map of the North, South, East and West series that make up the Ordnance Survey Holiday Map series. Their scale is 1:250,000 (one inch to four miles). For greater detail the Ordnance Survey series of 25 maps covers the whole country and Maps 20 and 24 cover the ecotours in this book. They are not, however, a pleasure to use and are based on information collected many, many decades ago. If the choice is available, always look for the new series of 98 maps with a 1:50,000 scale (two cm to one km, as opposed to the half-inch to one mile scale of the older Ordnance Survey maps). These maps are superb and add a great deal to the pleasure of exploring an area. At the time of writing, only Map 70, covering the Dingle peninsula, and Map 78, covering the MacGillycuddy Reeks, are available. Special maps for the Kerry Way and the Dingle Way are available from Bord Fáilte offices and, at a pinch, they will suffice.

Very useful tools for the ecotours are a pair of binoculars, a bird identification book and a good flower guide book. (See Further Reading, pages 216-17.)

THE WEATHER

Plan for a wet day — a wet week — and if the sun shines instead, revel in the glory of it. The climate of Kerry and West Cork is mild and frequently damp and there is no part of the year when dry and sunny days can be assured. The influence of the warm Gulf Stream in the Atlantic ensures that temperatures rarely drop to freezing levels and 4-7°C is the norm for January and February, the coldest months of the year. The warmest months — July and August — boast average temperatures of 14-16°C, but even then a run of four to five wet days together is not unusual, especially along the coastal areas. The good news is that the weather in Kerry and West Cork rarely reaches the kind of extremes that make ecotouring inadvisable. The only exception is hill walking in Kerry or along the Beara peninsula when thick mists make any kind of mountaineering a potentially hazardous undertaking. Be guided by common sense and take sensible precautions like letting someone know where you're going and when you're due back.

There can be glorious weather in Kerry and West Cork; equally, it can be be wet and grey. It is foolish to come badly prepared. Wet gear is essential, including leggings if possible, and a sanguine disposition is the next best asset.

LIST OF PHOTOGRAPHS

WEST CORK

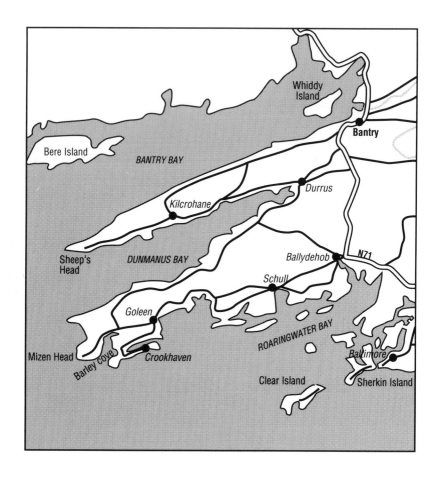

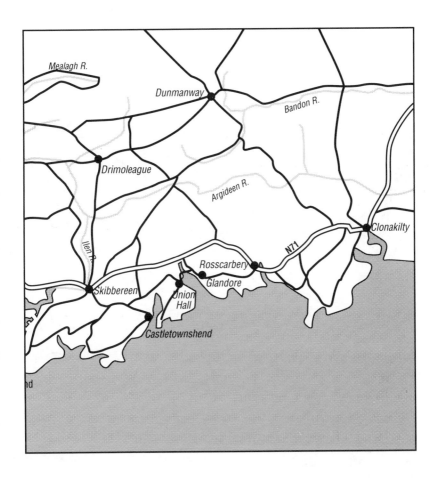

BEARA PENINSULA

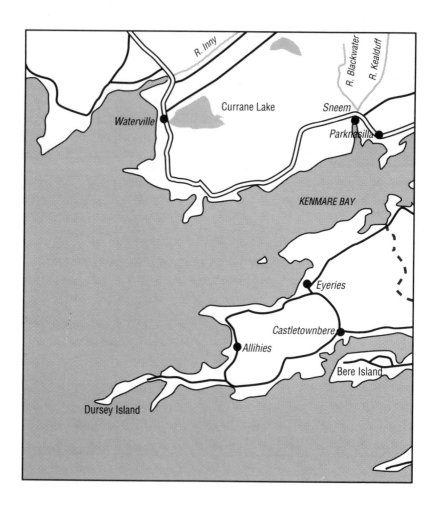

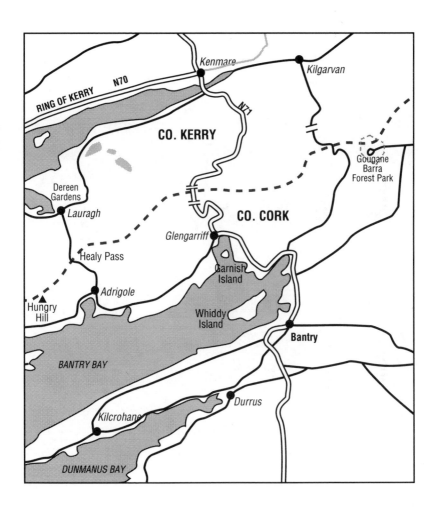

IVERAGH

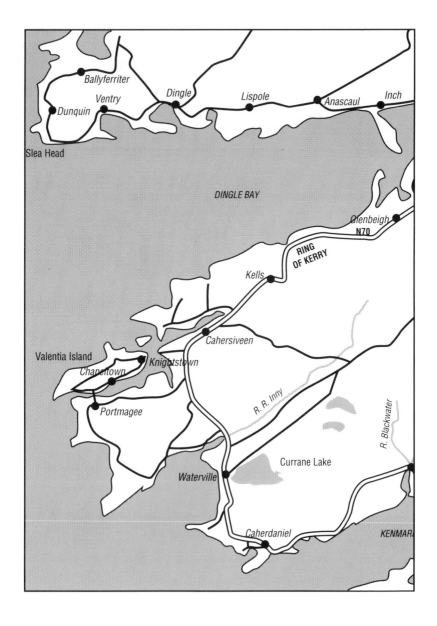

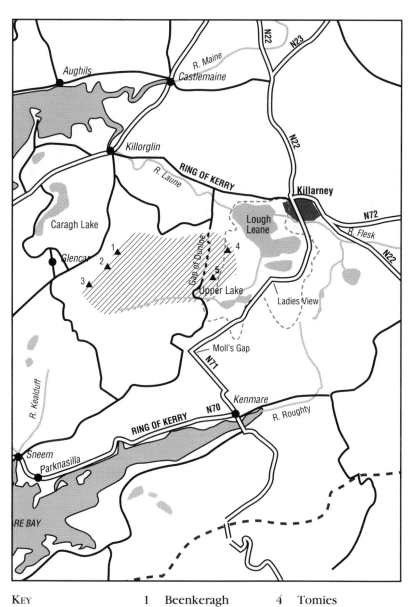

KILLARNEY AND ENVIRONS

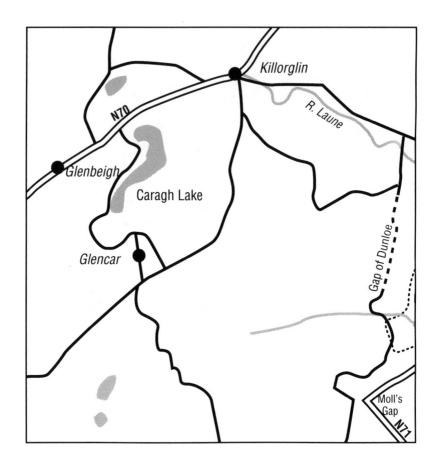

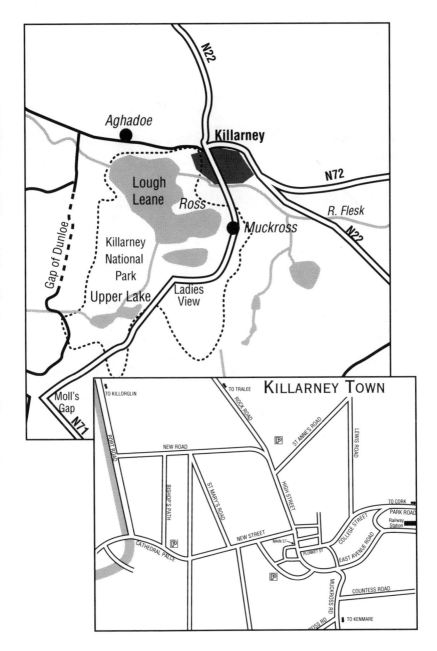

DINGLE PENINSULA

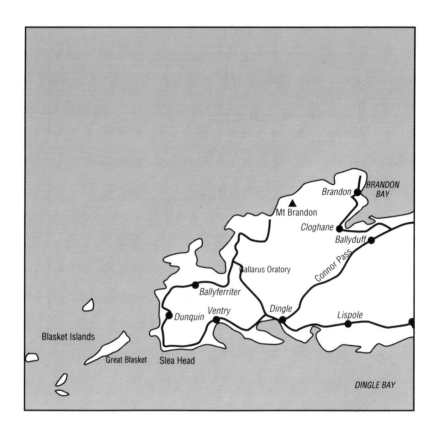

Brandon
BRANDON BAY
Mt Brandon
Cloghane
Ballyduff
Callarus Oratory
Connor Pass
Ballyferriter
Ventry
Dingle
Lispole
Dunquin
Blasket Islands
Great Blasket
Slea Head
DINGLE BAY

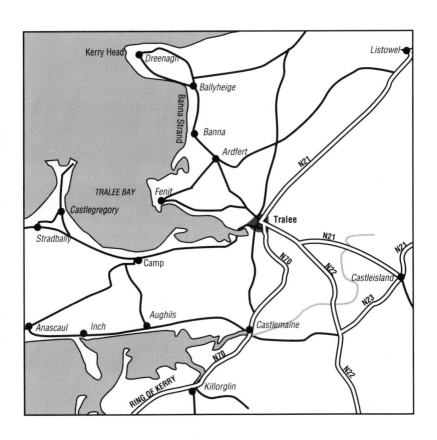

WEST CORK
INTRODUCTION

West Cork is a cosmopolitan place. In summer, travelling around the pretty little brightly coloured villages, you will see foreign names over shop doorways and the yachts of the wealthy moored in the harbours: you could almost be on the continent or in some Cornish village. West Cork has always provided suitable territory for settlers and invaders alike.

There is ample evidence of the past in this region. The fields are littered with ring forts, standing stones and stone circles dating back to the Bronze Age. In medieval times most of Cork was a part of the semi-independent territory of the FitzGeralds of Desmond (an anglicised form of Deas Mumhan, meaning West Munster), one of the great Hiberno-Norman families. Their power, like that of their Gaelic aristocrat neighbours, was broken by the English crown in the second half of the sixteenth century. Of the Gaelic families, the O'Sullivans held out the longest before leading the great march of 1602 from the Beara peninsula all the way to Leitrim in an effort to save their way of life and Gaelic identity.

In the seventeenth century a new landlord class was settled in the area and their very English names are still easy to discern in the names of streets and towns in West Cork. They built huge homes like Bantry House and Castlefreke. This new Ascendancy class dominated Irish social life for over 200 years. The first major challenge to their position came as a consequence of the disastrous Great Famine of the mid-nineteenth century. Although some of the people who owned the huge houses were absentee landlords, most were not and they were severely shaken as their starving and impoverished tenants could no longer pay rent. All of them felt the pinch financially; many were bankrupted.

West Cork suffered particularly badly during the Famine and the

1

countryside is still littered with unhappy reminders of that time — mass famine graves, the broken-down walls of workhouses and, at the village of Durrus on the Sheep's Head peninsula, the ruins of a grainstore which once held corn that might have kept the people alive. It was later used as an orphanage for the children of those who had died. Roycroft's bicycle shop in Skibbereen was used to feed soup to those of the poor who had been given meal tickets by the gentry. The Famine was a crisis for the gentry, but for the ordinary people it was a disaster on a biblical scale.

The Famine passed. West Cork grew wealthier with the development of copper mines and the expansion of mackerel fisheries. Now those have gone as well and local farmers depend on subsidies to keep their tiny farms functioning; the new boom industry is tourism.

West Cork has much to offer the discerning visitor. Sandy beaches, model farms, heritage centres, shops, all the watersports you could imagine, empty winding green roads disappearing into the hills — just waiting to test out your mountain bike — wild flowers and birds in abundance, live music every night of the week, good conversation and friendly people.

ESSENTIAL INFORMATION

BANKS

Ballydehob
AIB Main Street, telephone 028–37151. No cash dispenser. Usual banking hours.

Bantry
AIB The Square, telephone 027–50008 and *Bank of Ireland,* The Square, telephone 027–50377. Usual banking hours and both have cash dispensers.

Clonakilty
There are branches of both the *Bank of Ireland*, telephone 023–33375 and the *AIB*, telephone 023–33320 in Clonakilty with cash dispensers. Usual banking hours.

Schull
AIB sub branch with cash dispenser, 3 Upper Main Street, telephone 028–28132.

Skibbereen
AIB Bridge Street, telephone 028–21388 *Bank of Ireland*, telephone 028–21700 Market Street, hours Mon, Tues, Thurs, Fri, 10 a.m.–3 p.m. Wednesday 10 a.m.–5 p.m. At 13 Bridge Street there is also an ACC Bank, telephone 028–21218 and on Main Street there is a TSB Bank, telephone 028–21950.

BICYCLE HIRE AND REPAIR

Bantry
Carrowell/Kramer, Glengarriff Road, telephone 027–50274.

Clonakilty
MTM cycles, Ashe Street, telephone 023–33584.

Goleen
Barley Cove Holiday park, telephone 028–35302.
Schull
Cotter's Yard, telephone 028–28165. Mountain and touring bikes, from 10 a.m. to 12 noon.
Sherkin Island
Garrison House, telephone 028–20185.
Skibbereen
Roycroft's Stores, Ilen Street, telephone 028–21235.

BUREAUX DE CHANGE
Bantry
As well as the town banks the post office also has an exchange facility and is open on Saturday.
Clonakilty
Trustee Savings Bank, Rossa Street, telephone 023–33910 Open 10 a.m.–5.00 p.m.. Closed for lunch 12.30–1.30. Half day Wednesday.
Goleen
Harrington's Newsagents has a limited exchange facility.
Schull
James Lyons O'Keeffe, Main Street.

CAR HIRE/REPAIRS/24 HOUR PETROL
Bantry
Barry's Garage, Cork Road, telephone 027–50023.
Hurley's Garage, Bridge Street, telephone 027–50092.
O'Leary's Garage, Glengarriff Road, telephone 027–50127.

Skibbereen
Donelan's, Townsend Street, telephone 028–21948.

CHURCH SERVICES
Ballydehob
Catholic, Sunday, 8.30 a.m., 11.30 a.m.
Church of Ireland, Sunday, 11.30 a.m.
Clonakilty
Methodist, Kent Street, Sundays, 10.30 a.m.
Church of Ireland, Patrick Street, Sundays noon.
Catholic, Oliver Plunkett Street, daily Mass 8 a.m.,10 a.m., Saturday Mass 7.30 p.m., Sunday, 8 a.m., 10 a.m., 11 a.m., noon.
Crookhaven
Church of Ireland, Sunday 8.30 p.m.
Durrus/Kilcrohane
Durrus, Catholic, Saturday Mass 8 p.m. Kilcrohane 7.30 p.m. Sunday 11 a.m., Kilcrohane 11 a.m. or 12 noon.
Durrus, Church of Ireland, Holy Communion 11.45 a.m., 1st and 3rd Sundays of the month. Morning prayer 2nd and 4th Sundays.

Rosscarbery
Catholic, Saturday 8 p.m., Sunday 8.30 a.m., 11 a.m., noon.
Church of Ireland, Holy Communion 8.30 a.m., Morning prayer 11.30 a.m.

Schull
Catholic,Saturday 8 p.m., Sunday 10.30 a.m.
Church of Ireland, Sunday 10 a.m.

Skibbereen
Catholic, North Street, Saturday Vigil 8.00 p.m., Sunday Mass 8 a.m., 9.30 a.m.,
10.45 a.m., noon.
Church of Ireland, Bridge Street, June, July, August, 8 a.m., the Eucharist.
Methodist, Bridge Street, noon.
Gospel Hall, Townsend Street, 11 a.m. breaking of bread, Gospel meeting Tuesday,
8.30 p.m.

GARDAÍ (POLICE)
Ballydehob Telephone 028–37111.
Baltimore Telephone 028–20102.
Bantry The Square, Bantry, telephone 027–50045/50465.
Clonakilty MacCurtain Hill, telephone 023–33202.
Rosscarbery Telephone 023–48162.
Schull Schull barracks, telephone 028–28111.
Skibbereen Telephone 028–21088, 21026.

HOSPITALS
Bantry Accident and Emergency, telephone 027–50133.
Schull Hospital, telephone 028–8268.
Skibbereen, telephone 028–21677.

LAUNDERETTES
Bantry
Bantry Cleaners, Main Street.
Wash Tub Launderette, The Square.

Clonakilty
Moderne Cleaners, Pearse Street. Dry cleaning and launderette. Sam's Cross, 3 miles
from Clonakilty. Pub next door to sit in while you wait.

Schull
Schull Watersports Centre, Pier Road.

Skibbereen
Bubbles and Suds, North Street.
Hourihane's Launderette, Ilen Street, beside the Busy Bee takeaway.
West Cork Cleaners and Launderette, Bridge Street. Dry cleaning and laundry service.

PHARMACIES
Bantry
Michael Coen, The Square, telephone 027–50531.

Clonakilty
Bluett, Pearse Street, telephone 023–33124.
Forristal, Pearse Street, telephone 023–33393.

Harrington, Ashe Street, telephone 023–33318.
Hoskin Pharmacy, Pearse Street, telephone 023–33361.

Rosscarbery
Kingston's, telephone 023–48255.

Schull
McCarthy's, Main Street, telephone 028–28108.

Skibbereen
Dennehy's Chemist, telephone 028–21389.
M.O'Brien, telephone 028–21543.
McCarthy's Pharmacy, North Street, telephone 028–21587.

POST OFFICES

Baltimore, telephone 021–20181, in Abbey Stores.
Kilcrohane, telephone 027–67001, half day Wednesday.
Skibbereen, telephone 028–21046, open Mon–Sat 9 a.m.–5.30 p.m.,
Fri 9 a.m.–6 p.m.
Durrus, telephone 027–61001, Mon–Sat 9 a.m.–5.30 p.m., half day Wednesday.
Rosscarbery, telephone 023–48161.
Schull, Newman's, telephone 028–28110.

TAXIS

Bantry
Telephone 027–50023.

Clonakilty
T. Barry, 55 Pearse Street, telephone 023–33179.
P. O'Neill, Ashe Street, telephone 023–33125.

Schull
George Swanton, telephone 028–37127.

Skibbereen
Mr Michael Hegarty, Bridge Street, telephone 028–21258.
Mrs K.O'Donovan, Bridge Street, telephone 028–21632.
Donelan's, Townshend Street, telephone 028–21312.
Fahy Taxi Service, telephone, 028–21458.

TOURIST OFFICES

Baltimore
Tourist information is available from an office on the pier.

Bantry
The Square, telephone 027–50229 (29 June–3 Sept).

Clonakilty
Ashe Street, telephone 023–33226. Open July–August.

Schull
A portacabin opposite the Spar supermarket. Open June to August inclusive, Monday to Saturday 2–6 p.m., Sunday 12–2 p.m.

Skibbereen
Telephone 028–21766. Open all year. July–August, Mon–Sat 9 a.m.–7 p.m.

TRAVEL AGENTS

Bantry
Bantry Travel, Barrack Street, telephone 027–50658.
West Cork Travel, High Street, telephone 027–50341.

Clonakilty
West Cork Travel, telephone 023–33220.

Skibbereen
West Cork Travel Agency, Bridge Street, telephone 028–21525.

FESTIVALS AND SPECIAL EVENTS

MAY
Bantry Mussel Fair. A long weekend of music and mussels.

JUNE
Union Hall Regatta

JULY
Glandore Harbour Regatta. Usually in late July or early August, the three day regatta includes some old boats such as Galway hookers.
Fastnet International Schools Regatta. International youth sailing dinghy event. Trophies and prizes, social events.
Annual Festival of Classical Music. St Barrahane's Church, Castletownshend.
Festival of West Cork. Clonakilty. Lots of music, funfair, activities, street entertainers etc.
Skibbereen Welcome Home Week. Includes the Maid of the Isles festival, a kind of Rose of Tralee only less well known. Lots of music and activities.
Kilcrohane Festival. Discos, races, activities.

AUGUST
Skibbereen Fishing Festival. Contact Nick Dent at 028–37406.
Schull Regatta. First Sunday in August. Swimming, sailing and rowing competitions.
Ballydehob Festival. One week, early August. Annual show, ballad sessions, karaoke, duck races, raft races, horse races. Discos in community hall, talent competitions, sports night, tennis competitions, soccer tournaments.

WHAT TO SEE

BALLYDEHOB
The name of this picturesque village comes from the Irish *Beál Átha dá Chab,* meaning 'the ford at the mouth of two rivers'. The approach from Skibbereen in the east brings into view the brightly coloured cluster of houses that makes up this small village. When entering Ballydehob from this direction look out on the left for the old 12-arched tramway viaduct. Until the 1930s Ballydehob was a market village for islanders from Roaringwater Bay. Nowadays, one is more likely to encounter a north European 'blow-in' than an islander, for the village and surrounding area have become especially popular with expatriates.

The picturesque village of Castletownshend, Co. Cork

BALTIMORE

This is a tiny village whose population swells alarmingly in summer when the sailing fraternity arrive. The village harbour is the departure point for visits to Clear and Sherkin islands and also for sea fishing trips. It has an ancient ruin, lots of restaurants and pubs with music every night in summer and some pretty coastline.

Baltimore is famous for the fact that some of its inhabitants were spirited away to Algeria to join the white slave trade. In 1631 a shipful of Algerian pirates landed here and took away 100 people. Their descendants can still be traced in Algeria through the family names of those who were kidnapped.

Long before the leisure yachts arrived, Baltimore was a serious fishing and boat building area. In the dim past the O'Driscoll family ruled the area and dominated both the land and the fishing. They held three castles, one on each of the islands of Sherkin and Clear, and what is now the ruin in the middle of the village. Boats from Spain and France fished here for the plentiful shoals of mackerel and pilchards that swam offshore and each boat paid a levy to the O'Driscoll family. Their control of the area was particularly envied by the people of Waterford who in 1413 sneaked into Baltimore and kidnapped the head of the clan and his family. The feuding continued for centuries and in 1537 Fineen O'Driscoll seized a Waterford ship with its cargo of Portuguese wine. The people of Waterford retaliated by sending a small fleet of ships which bombarded Baltimore, sacked Sherkin Island and captured a 30-oar galley. The fortress in Baltimore was burned down.

Today's ruin is a later version built in the early seventeenth century by the last O'Driscoll who cleverly juggled his allegiances through the wars against Queen Elizabeth I and was able to prevent all his land being confiscated.

In the seventeenth century a new wrangle began between Sir Walter Coppinger and Sir Thomas Crooke over the rights to the area. In the middle of that, the Algerians struck, led in to Baltimore harbour by a Waterford sea captain. In 1649 an English emissary was sent to Algeria to buy back the slaves but only two of them were given their freedom. The kidnapping incident resulted in a system of beacons being put up around the coast, each one visible to the two on either side, so that the whole coast could sound the alarm should another attack take place. Many people moved inland to Skibbereen and O'Driscoll left his castle to live on the island in Lough Hyne, his last stronghold. Over the next century English peers of one complexion or another squabbled over the rights to the town and seaport until by the eighteenth century its chief use to them was as a rotten borough that could return an unchallenged Member of Parliament.

Baltimore made its living as a safe harbour for fishing fleets. The pilchards fished in the surrounding seas provided the staple diet for the local population as well as oil used for lighting, and for curing the leather. Some time in the eighteenth century the pilchards disappeared to be replaced by mackerel and herring which were salted and put into barrels. A huge export industry developed all along the coast of West Cork sending salted mackerel to the US. Women from as far away as Scotland arrived in Baltimore for the mackerel season — July and August — and during the early years of this century as many as sixteen trains a day left Baltimore loaded with mackerel. The industry collapsed when the US imposed tariffs to protect its own fishing industry and the terms negotiated for Ireland's entry to the EC ensured that, for the immediate future at least, no fishing industry will develop here again.

BANTRY

A splendid approach to Bantry on the Cork road leads to narrow streets and shopfronts that have remained basically unchanged since the nineteenth century. The large town square gave ample space for the monthly open air market on the first Friday of each month but, while the tradition remains, the horses and cattle have now mostly been replaced by stalls selling shoes and tools. The only colour lent to the Friday market now comes from the presence of 'hippies' who play the odd tune on the street and sell second-hand bric-a-brac.

The real attractions of the region lay further west al[ ]
peninsulas although Bantry is a good supply centre for those [..]
off elsewhere. There are decent shops, restaurants and amenities and
just outside of town Bantry House and the French Armada Exhibition
are well worth visiting.

Bantry House

From 1820 to 1840, Viscount Berehaven spent much of his time
travelling around Europe and periodically sending back many
wonderful works of art and other artefacts to his family home in Bantry.
Visitors walk over them — literally — for the entrance porch contains
four tile panels taken from Pompeii. Each room open to the public is a
strange blend of the functional and the exotic: wonderful fireplaces,
carpets and furniture share the space with items like a sixteenth
century mosque lamp or a Tibetan water ewer.

Architecturally, the house is unremarkable but the location lends it
an eighteenth-century grandeur. The two drawing rooms have
magnificent views and the library is all light and grace on a fine day.
The dining room seems heavy and dark by comparison and its
baroqueness is a little forbidding.

It costs £2.50 (£1 for children) to view inside the house but a walk
outside and in the gardens can be had for free. The formal garden
overlooking the bay is well worth a stroll. The house and garden are
open all year around, except Christmas Day, from 9 a.m. to 6 p.m.
(8 p.m. in summer) and shares with the town supermarket the
distinction of not closing for a lunch hour.

How to get there Bantry House, telephone 027-50047, is on the main
Cork–Bantry road. Coming from Cork the house is on the right just
before the town. A car park and entrance are clearly marked. There is
another entrance 200 metres further on but this won't allow cars.

1796 French Armada Exhibition, Bantry

An excellent exhibition devoted to the story of a planned invasion
which, if successful, would have changed the entire course of Irish
history and Anglo-Irish relations. In December 1796 almost fifty
warships left France with some 15,000 soldiers, their aim being to
rouse the peasantry to revolt against their English overlords with the
help of the Irish patriot Theobald Wolfe Tone and the United Irishmen.
Nineteen ships reached Bantry Bay but the weather, unfortunately, was
against them and when the decision to return to France was made the
veteran frigate *la Surveillante* was scuttled off Whiddy island.

Money permitting, the ship will one day be raised from the bottom
of Bantry Bay. In the meantime this exhibition tells the story of the
planned invasion in graphic detail and there is a fine 1:6 cross-sectional
model of *la Surveillante*.

Opening hours for the exhibition, telephone 027-51796, are 10 a.m. to 6 p.m. Price of admission is £2.50 for adults and £1 for children.

How to get there The Exhibition Centre is located in what were once the stables of Bantry House. See above for directions.

Bantry Museum

The museum is built on the line of the old Cork to Bantry railway. The museum is run by the Bantry Historical Society which is an active group of local people who meet regularly and go in search of forgotten pillar stones, wedge graves and the like. The museum is open at odd hours but the key can be got from Mr Donald Fitzpatrick at the Super Valu supermarket. Opening hours are Wednesday 10.30 a.m.-1 p.m. and Friday 3-5 p.m. It has an interesting collection of bits and pieces relating to the town and its history.

Kilnaruane Pillar Stone, outside Bantry

This is interesting because of its representation of a boat — the kind that St Brendan may have used to reach America — only rarely found on pillar stones. It is signposted for a left turning just past the West Lodge Hotel on the road to Cork. The stone is on the right side of the road that goes down past the hotel. It cannot be seen from the road, look for a faded pink corrugated tin roof and a gateway through to a field. The signpost pointing the way has been interfered with and the name of the stone is missing.

BARLEY COVE

The best beach in West Cork. It's a good job it's so cold here for most of the year or this would be in the same sorry state as parts of the coast of Spain. There are pleasant walks around the sand dunes, especially in the evening when the rabbits come out. There are tennis courts at the hotel and caravan park, which also hires out bicycles and the hotel has an indoor heated pool if the beach gets too cold.

Three Castle Head, near Barley Cove

This amazing thirteenth-century O'Mahony castle, which sits on the edge of sheer cliffs with a lake in front, must have been impregnable in its day. It comprised three towers with the main one in the middle linked to the outer two by a wall. It was the seat of Dermot of Dunlough, who became chieftain of the O'Mahonys in 1535.

How to get there Just past the Barley Cove Beach Hotel car park turn right. At the next T-junction turn left. At the next junction, which is signposted left for Ocean View B&B, go right. At the end of the road there is a farm gate to be climbed: *permission must be sought from the farm owners* who don't mind people wandering about as long as they don't bring dogs. They will also point you in the right direction, since the castle cannot be seen from the road.

Mizen Head

Set on a tiny promontory of land and accessible only by a cast iron bridge, the lighthouse is now automatic. There are some wild walks around the edges of the cliffs, not to be undertaken by anyone with a poor head for heights. Going west past the lighthouse along the cliffs there is a cliff walk to Three Castle Head but it is rarely done and the path is not well trodden. The lighthouse has recently been opened to the public.

How to get there Mizen Head is signposted from the Barley Cove Beach Hotel.

MIZEN HEAD SIGNAL STATION

Opened to the public in 1994, eighty-four years after the station was completed. It was designed to complement the Fastnet Lighthouse and add to the safety of ships crossing the Atlantic. The station is on a small island, connected to the peninsula by a superb suspension bridge that offers exciting views of the rock formations in the vicinity. The station was automated in 1993 and the various rooms are now open to view from June to September daily. Check in advance, telephone 028–35225, for opening times between October and May. Entry is £2.50, students £2 and children £1.50, 10 a.m. to 6 p.m.

How to get there Follow the road past Barley Cove, signposted for Mizen. There is a car park where the road ends and it is a short walk to the suspension bridge. No wheelchair access.

CASTLETOWNSHEND

This is not a typical Irish village. It developed in the late seventeenth and early eighteenth centuries when English families settled here. In 1859 one of these families, the Somervilles, returned to the area from Corfu. Mr Somerville had been serving as an officer in the British army on the Greek island and when he returned he brought with him his young daughter Edith. Edith Somerville was to spend most of her life here, finding a setting for her fiction, and died unmarried in 1949 at Drishane House, Castletownshend.

In 1886 Edith Somerville met her cousin from Galway, Violet Martin (who took the pen-name 'Martin Ross'), and their unusual literary partnership began. Their most famous works are *Experiences of an Irish R.M.*, *Further Experiences of an Irish R.M.* and *The Real Charlotte*. The two authors were very close and after the death of Violet in 1915 Edith claimed she was able to communicate with her partner's spirit.

Drishane House is still in the Somerville family. Its gates stand at the top end of the village. Edith and Violet are buried in St Barrahane's church which can be reached by turning left at the bottom of the village and climbing the steps. Their graves lie behind the altar end of the church. The church interior includes a stained glass window by Harry Clarke, and an oar from one of the *Lusitania's* lifeboats that was washed up nearby after the sinking. The *Lusitania*, a passenger liner, was torpedoed by a German submarine off Kinsale in 1915; almost 1,200 people drowned.

Approaching the village of Castletownshend, there is a sign pointing the way to the Knockdrum ring fort, which was restored by the Somerville family in the nineteenth century.

CLEAR ISLAND, OFF BALTIMORE

This island is accessible from Baltimore, boats taking about 45 minutes to cover a beautiful piece of seascape, weaving about between rocks and the coast and taking the route that the Algerian pirates must have taken when they sacked Baltimore in 1631. The island itself has no good beaches but is a great day out, wandering around the narrow lanes and dodging the ancient clapped out cars that grind their way around the island. A good day's fun is spotting the rustiest car. The island has about 150 Irish speaking inhabitants, one shop and three pubs. It is 3 miles/5 km and 1 miles/1.5 km wide.

Clear Island is one of the most significant spots in Europe for bird watching, particularly in October when rare American migrants get blown in regularly. At the pier is a coffee shop which serves snacks and light meals but a packed lunch might be a good idea if planning a long visit. See the Ecotour section (page 41) for more details about the bird and plant life of the island. There is also a cheese farm on the island and some ceramic artists selling their wares.

How to get there Boats leave from Baltimore regularly.
Departure Times (Telephone 028-39135/39119)
May: 11 a.m. and 5.30 p.m.
June & September: 2.15 p.m., 7 p.m. (Returning 9 a.m., 6 p.m.).
July & August: 10.45 a.m., 2.15 p.m., 7 p.m. (Returning 9 a.m., 12 noon, 6 p.m.). There may be extra boats on Sunday.
October to May: Monday to Thursday 2.15 p.m. (Returning 9 a.m.).
Friday 10.30 a.m., 5.30 p.m. (Returning noon).
Sunday 5 p.m.
The cost is £7 per adult, £3.50 per child, £16 family ticket for two adults and two children. No extra charge for bicycles.

CLONAKILTY

This is a lively and prosperous town which is particularly lively during the annual festival week with fun fairs, street performers, pub music and lots more.

The town received its royal charter in 1615 and in 1620 the core of its population arrived from Somerset: about twenty families, one of them bearing the name Spillers whose descendants presumably run the hardware store of the same name in the centre of town.

West Cork Regional Museum, Clonakilty

A pleasantly organised little museum with lots of material relating to Clonakilty's industrial, political and social past. The material on Michael Collins is particularly interesting. Entrance is £1 (children 50p)

How to get there The museum is in Oliver Plunkett Street at the east end of town.

Lisnagun Ring Fort, near Clonakilty

This is a restored ring fort, a structure occupied by wealthy farmers well into the tenth century A.D. For centuries after, including the first part of the twentieth, they were considered magical places, which is why so many of them are undisturbed. Its souterrain, or underground passage, was found fairly intact and has been made usable again. The excavators also found the midden with the remains of the food the tenth-century farmer and his family ate. This fort has a double bank outside it, indicating that he was a particularly wealthy man. It is thought that the cattle and slaves lived in the ditch between the earth banks while the man himself and his wives and family slept inside in a daub and wattle hut. A copy of what one probably looked like has been reconstructed.

The exhibit is supported by good information and a guide will explain the ins and outs of it. It is open from 1-6 p.m. daily. Admission is £1.50 (children 50p).

Darrara College, the local agricultural college which excavated the ring fort, has also set up a small animal park with the typical domestic animals of a farm of the early years of this century. Each type is in its own enclosure. The park has a picnic area and gift shop. It is open from May to September. Admission £2 (children £1)

How to get there The fort and animal park are signposted from the road to Bandon about a mile out of town.

Model Village, near Clonakilty

This is a new venture that opened in 1994. It is about a quarter of a mile on the road to Inchydoney beach.

Birthplace of Michael Collins, near Clonakilty

This is the spot where Michael Collins' family lived for a time and where he was born in 1890. The building has been restored as a cottage but actually spent some time as a shed after the family built a larger house in front around the turn of the century. Little of the newer building remains: the Black and Tans (a ruthless and cruel police auxiliary force which terrorised the civilian population) burned it down during the War of Independence in 1921.

Michael Collins emigrated to England in 1906. After working as a post office official in London for ten years, he returned to Ireland in 1916 and took part in the Easter Rising, fighting in the General Post Office in Dublin. He was arrested afterwards and imprisoned in Wales with about 560 other rebels, all without a trial. Following an amnesty he was released within a few months and was back in Dublin by Christmas, determined that the next battle would be longer and more effective.

Collins was strongly critical of the leaders of the Easter Rising for the bungling way he felt it had been handled. Within four years this formerly unknown man from West Cork was the most effective organiser of armed rebellion in Irish history. He organised the IRA as a guerrilla army and he was responsible for highly effective assassination squads. His men also infiltrated the British security apparatus, he himself even spending one night inside the headquarters of the Dublin detective force reading secret papers! He inspired awe among Irish and British alike for his ability to stroll past police and army checkpoints. There was a high price on his head. The effectiveness of his troops and his system of spies helped to drive the British to the negotiating table in 1921.

Collins was one of five people chosen to negotiate the treaty in London. Eamon de Valera, the political head of the independence movement, did not go, preferring to remain in Ireland to help reconcile people to the compromise that would inevitably be negotiated in London. But when the treaty was signed by Collins and the others de Valera himself repudiated it. A civil war followed, fought out between those who accepted the terms of the treaty and those who didn't. Collins himself was assassinated outside Macroom, Co. Cork less than two months before his 32nd birthday.

How to get there Take the N71 west from Clonakilty and look for the signposts on the left at 3 miles/5 km and 4.3 miles/7 km from town. Both lead to the site. Entrance is free.

Castle Salem, near Clonakilty

Following the signs to this well preserved fifteenth-century castle you will be surprised to find yourself drawing up in a modern working farmyard. This is because the farmhouse, sixteenth century in origin, is built into the front of the castle. The only way into the castle now is through what looks like a broom cupboard at the top of the stairs in the farmhouse. The castle still has its roof and floorboards, although it is no longer safe to walk into the building. The passages built into the walls are still safe and you can have a look at a fifteenth-century multi-storey toilet. In any other European country this place would have a preservation order and millions spent on its upkeep. See it before it crumbles away. It was originally called Benduff castle and was owned by a Florence McCarthy from whom it was confiscated after the rebellion of 1641. It was given to one of Cromwell's soldiers, Major Apollo Morris, who later became a Quaker and renamed the castle Shalom (which in time became Salem). He removed the top storey of the tower and built a slate roof which is just giving way today. Morris had six children, Fortunatus, Tribulation, Appolos, Temperance, Phoebe, and Patience. The eldest son, Fortunatus, built the present farmhouse in 1682. A whole colony of Quakers developed here and a graveyard can be seen on the left of the entrance gate as you are leaving. Quakers from all over Cork were buried here until 1763 when William, grandson of Apollo, was buried in a tomb, offending Quaker belief that gravesites should be as simple and unostentatious as possible. William Penn spent some time in the modern farmhouse and the owners will point out the bed he slept in.

How to get there 9 miles/15 km west of Clonakilty on the N71 (Skibbereen) road. The castle is signposted. Entrance is £2 (£1 children).

Lisselan Estate
This is a model dairy farm which includes pedigree cows such as the Holstein. Viewing is by appointment only, telephone 023-33249, fax 023-34605. There are also gardens full of unusual species of plants and varieties of rhododendrons. It is open from April to September, Thursdays only, from 10 a.m. to 5 p.m. Admission £3 (children £1). The house also allows shooting in its woods by appointment only from September to January. Also fishing by appointment.

CROOKHAVEN
This is a tiny crook of land that was once a thriving centre for fishing fleets. In the eighteenth and nineteenth centuries it had its own large fleet of fishing boats and provided shelter for the many West Indian and other transatlantic ships that called in here to report their safe arrival across the Atlantic. The Protestant church here was built specifically for sailors. Marconi built the first transatlantic telegraph station here in 1902 moving it to Valentia in Co. Kerry in 1906.

As you will see on your drive into Crookhaven, the land across the water was the site of a large stone quarry, the remains of which still scar the rugged scenery. As late as the 1930s a hundred men worked here. Nowadays Crookhaven is saved from annihilation by the new pastime of leisure sailing. In July and August the sailor caps are thick on the ground and the village is positively crowded. There are several pleasant walks to take in the area, notably up to the old transatlantic cable station.

DURRUS AND THE SHEEP'S HEAD PENINSULA

Durrus is a small village at the fork in the road where the route to the Sheep's Head peninsula goes off from the road that connects Bantry with the Mizen peninsula. The Protestant church of St James was built in 1792 and was visited by President Mary Robinson on its bicentennial anniversary. Across the water from the church is the old grain store and orphanage.

Ten miles west on the road to the Sheep's Head is the very small village of Kilcrohane, famous for its early potatoes and daffodils. Down by a lake near the sea is the site of an ancient school where it is said that the King of Spain's sons attended. From Kilcrohane it is a brief drive out to Sheep's Head, feeling the land slip away from you on either side until you stand on a high rocky promontory feeling you're at the end of the world. Look down and there below you — where you expect to see an open expanse of water — are farmhouses snuggled into the side of the rock, with tiny fields above and around them.

While Bantry Bay and the town of Bantry are well known, the Sheep's Head peninsula is the least visited region in West Cork. This is mainly due to the fact that attractions to be found along the neighbouring peninsulas — castles, beaches, hills and mountains — are noticeably missing here. A survey once reported that the area was 'rocky and frequented only by eagles and birds of prey — never to be inhabited by reason of the rough incommodities'. The advantage, of course, is that the commercialisation is less obtrusive. Everything about the Sheep's Head peninsula is low key. There are places to visit, beautiful seascapes and enjoyable trips to experience on foot, by cycle or in a car but they are not aggressively advertised.

See page 25 for details of the scenic Goat's Path route that heads north from Kilcrohane, to a point where both Bantry and Dunmanus Bay are visible, before travelling east to Bantry.

GLANDORE

This is a tiny fishing village and harbour. It claims to be the first holiday resort in Cork as well as being the first harbour to organise a regatta in 1830. Pretty for a drive through or a brief visit to one of the bars, the village also has two men in its history who deserve mention. William Thompson was a noted socialist who inherited an estate at Cargoogarriff, a few miles outside Glandore, where he attempted to implement many of his progressive principles. He introduced radical reforms on his estate and his socialist ideas appeared in print and predated Marx by fifty years. He supported mass education, equality for women and birth control and condemned the existing marriage laws as unfair for women.

Another notable character from Glandore was James Redmond Barry, also a landlord. He was born at Barryroe in 1789 to a family of Norman descent. They were one of the few Catholic families that had retained some of their wealth during the penal days of the eighteenth century. He was personally responsible for reviving the fishing industry in West Cork in the early nineteenth century, was responsible for many of the tiny quays and wharves which abound in the area and supervised the building of boatyards at Baltimore and Union Hall. Barry set up model farms, roofed his tenants' cottages with slate at a time when most landlords were busy knocking roofs in, and gave them stock, equipment, and household furniture. He built free schools for both boys and girls in Glandore and an industrial school, where boys learned farming and craft skills. He was prominent in relief work during the Famine.

Union Hall, near Glandore

This town was named after the Act of Union which abolished the Irish parliament in 1801. Its original Irish name, *Bréan Trá*, means 'foul beach', although it must have improved a little since it was originally named. There is a small museum just outside town called Ceim Hill Museum run by the owner of the farm of the same name. There are exhibits of Stone Age and Iron Age artefacts as well as more recent documents. Entry is £2 (children £1). Open from 10 a.m. to 7 p.m.

How to get there Just outside Union Hall on the road to Castletownshend.

GOUGANE BARRA

> *There is a green island in lone Gougane Barra*
> *Where Allua of song rushes forth as an arrow,*
> *In deep vallied Desmond — a thousand wild fountains*
> *Come down to that lake from their home in the mountains.*
>
> J.J. Callanan

This is the most picturesque part of inland Cork. The mountain lake is the source of the river Lee and is surrounded by mountains and numerous streams which trickle or flood down to it, depending on the weather. St Finbarr, the founder of Cork, came here in the sixth century and established a monastery. He had a hermitage on the island in the lake which is now approachable by a short causeway. There is now a modern chapel built on the island.

A road runs through the park in a loop but it is easy to escape down any of the meandering paths that lead off from it. There is a map on a notice board in the park and it is worth using this to head for Bealick's summit from where good views of the surrounding landscape can be enjoyed. The land is owned by the Forestry Commission and the walks pass through sitka spruce, larch, douglas fir and pine trees. Remnants of the original oak forests still cling to the edges of the sharp cliffs that surround the valley.

The island is often in use as a pilgrimage centre, particularly around the time of St Finbarr's Day on 25 September.

How to get there Take the road to Glengarriff from Bantry and after 3 miles/5 km turn right at the bridge, signposted for Macroom. Along this road there is a signposted turning to the left for Gougane Barra before Macroom.

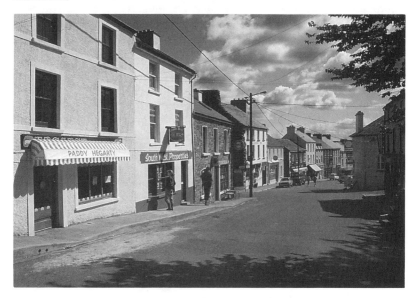

A view down the main street in Ballydehob, Co. Cork

ROSSCARBERY

This is a small town, just off the Clonakilty–Skibbereen road. It has an interesting twelfth-century Romanesque church with an elaborately carved doorway and a pleasantly domestic interior. This town was once the home of O'Donovan Rossa, a founder of the Fenian movement, who was born here in 1831. The town stands at the head of a landlocked inlet of the sea and is a good spot for bird watching. The tourist office in Rosscarbery has a leaflet which highlights the many local antiquities and historical sites in the area.

How to get there Coming from Clonakilty, Rosscarbery is signposted right off the N71 just beyond the estuary/bridge.

Castlefreke
Although the house at Castlefreke, once the home of the earls of Carbery, looks ancient, this Gothic extravaganza was built in the 1860s to a design by the Cork architect Sir Richard Morrison. In its original state it contained ornamental carvings, stained glass windows and elaborately patterned ceilings. The earls of Carbery owned huge tracts of land in Cork, much of which was lost under the Land Acts from 1870 onwards. These allowed tenant farmers to buy their smallholdings from the landlords by putting up a proportion of the price and paying the rest off in instalments.

The last Lord Carbery was a flamboyant figure, marrying three times, racing around the countryside in a car, showing off at local fairs by looping the loop in his plane and finally, when things began to look very difficult for Irish landowners, walking out the front door of his castle and never returning. The entire castle and contents were left intact, with tiger skins on the walls and valuable artefacts in the rooms. One story tells of how he shot out the eyes of the portrait of the first earl of Carbery before he left. The oakwoods disappeared except for one small tract which had been claimed by the Land Commission and preserved. The rest is planted out now with the depressing conifers that seem to be creeping all over the country like a fungal disease. The Irish army occupied the house during the 'Emergency' (as World War II was called in Ireland), dances were held there from time to time, and the leaded roof went during the 1950s. It is still a very atmospheric place and some of the stone carvings can still be seen.

How to get there 3 miles/5 km from Clonakilty on the coast road going west or 1.5 miles/2.5 kms from Rosscarbery going east. From the N71 follow signs for Ownahincha beach, and once there take a left fork at the end of the caravan site. This road leads up to a car park in some woods where you should look for an old No Entry sign. Ignore it and walk up the path to the castle.

Drombeg Stone Circle, near Rosscarbery
This is a well preserved group of seventeen standing stones (two missing and one fallen) dating back to about 150 B.C. On the surface of the largest stone are two shallow cup-marks, one surrounded by an oval carving. The portal stones and the flat stone are aligned to the winter solstice. Like other stone alignments in West Cork the circle stands on elevated ground overlooking the western horizon. When it was excavated the remains of a cremated adolescent male body were found in the centre of the circle. The remains had been ground to dust

and placed in a pot covered in cinders. Charcoal from the burial yielded a radiocarbon dating of around A.D. 600. Some sixty yards to the west are two interlinked stone huts containing a roasting oven. A stone road led from the huts to a cooking place with a hearth, a well and a water trough which was used to heat water. Hot stones would be dropped into the trough of water to bring it to the boil. They could keep the water hot for up to two and a half hours. The cooking place is about 200 years older than the other remains and the whole site is thought to have been a seasonal resting spot for hunters. The best time to visit is at the summer solstice when New Age folk come out to play.

SCHULL

This pretty little village, lying beneath the slopes of Mount Gabriel with its two golf ball-shaped aircraft tracking dishes, comes alive for the summer tourist trade. It has a picturesque harbour which in the early years of this century was crowded with French fishing boats. The village itself is good for a wander up and down with lots of shops aimed at summer visitors and some interesting pubs. There are a number of holiday villages here but they have done no real damage to the prettiness of the place. From Schull pier a ferry leaves for Clear Island. Ferry times are: July and August 10 a.m., 2.30 p.m., 4.30 p.m. Adults £6 (children £2). Sometimes there is also a service in May and June.

Boats go to Long Island from Colla Pier which is to the west of town. The island is still inhabited but is a bleak place.

Schull Planetarium

Schull is home to the Republic's only planetarium. It has an eight-metre dome and can display the current night sky or any configuration of stars that could have been seen from the northern hemisphere at any time in past history. Its opening hours vary with the seasons. In July and August the planetarium is open Tuesday to Friday from 11 a.m. to 1 p.m. and from 2 p.m. till 8 p.m.. There are demonstrations and simulations all day. Public shows take place at 7 p.m. and special shows are advertised. The planetarium can be booked for private showings for £25. Telephone 028–28552. Admission £1 (children 50p); shows £2.50 (children £1.50). From April to June the planetarium is open Wednesday to Friday and in September and October on Wednesday and Saturday.

Mount Gabriel, near Schull

A pleasant drive to the top or a strenuous walk or cycle. Walking or driving up the access road to the tracking station the remains of ancient copper mines can be clearly seen. Walkers should be careful to avoid some of the hidden mine shafts which are not fenced off. From the top of the road a walk to the south brings you to the summit of the mountain. From here to the west can be seen the peaks of Seefin on the Sheep's Head peninsula and beyond it Sugarloaf and Hungry Hill on the Beara. To the south, Fastnet Rock may be visible while south-east and spread before you will be the coastline of West Cork with Sherkin and Clear islands and tens of other smaller ones. The mountain was once home to Neolithic people who lived in raths and mined for copper. They used large round stones from the beaches below which they cut and shaped into axes, sometimes with grooves cut into them for handles. A fire would be lit by the rock face to expand it and then cold water thrown over it to crack it. The hand axes would then be used to chip out the pieces of ore.

Up until the eighteenth century wolves lived on the mountain. In 1652 a bounty was offered for each female wolf caught and killed; many skins were exported to England.

SHERKIN ISLAND, BY BOAT FROM BALTIMORE
Like Clear Island this is accessible from Baltimore harbour, a fifteen minute journey from the mainland. It has a few pleasant beaches to choose from, the best and biggest being Silver Strand on the far side of the island while Trabawn and Cow Strands are also very sandy and pleasant. It takes about twenty minutes to reach the nearest beach on foot but the pubs are only a short sprint from the harbour. There are the ruins of a fifteenth century Franciscan Abbey and some B&B accommodation if you choose to stay. The island has several pubs with generous opening hours and there is a post office where tourist information can be found, telephone 028-20181.

How to get there In summer ferries leave every half hour from the pier in Baltimore. Out of season there are about seven ferries a day. Adults £3 (children £1).

SKIBBEREEN
Skibbereen is both a centre for tourism in the area and a working agricultural town. It is one of the few places left which is able to support a weekly mart and farmers from a huge area around bring animals here to sell. An interesting few minutes can be spent in here trying to make sense of the auctioneer's words, delivered at machine-gun pace. The town has gone through many different phases in its time. It is thought to have originated when the survivors of the Baltimore raids moved inland in 1631. Originally owned by the McCarthy clan the land around here was confiscated by various English rulers during the seventeenth century and planted by two major Anglo-Irish families, the Townshends and the Beechers.

In the Famine years Skibbereen was hard hit and, because the railway made travel to this area relatively easy, was visited by many reporters from London newspapers. Three miles west of town is the Abbeystrowery graveyard, once the site of a fourteenth-century Cistercian abbey. Here is the 'Pits', where a mass grave for Famine victims was kept open so new bodies could be added each day. When Thackeray visited Skibbereen in 1842 he described the huge numbers of people who lived in this area. It was one of the most heavily populated parts of Ireland. The Famine was all the worse for that, taking the very young and the old. Thousands died around Skibbereen but only those who came to the town to seek aid from the workhouse had their deaths recorded. The workhouse was supposed to house 900 people but during 1846 thousands of people came here. Roycroft's bicycle shop, then a steam mill, was used as a charity soup house. Each of the landed families of the area, the Somervilles, the Townshends, the Hungerfords, the Donovans and so on, contributed to the soup house enabling it to issue two tickets per day to the needy which they could exchange for soup. The workhouse is now gone, burnt down in 1921, but its walls still stand around the town's hospital.

Inside Roycroft's cycle shop can be seen signs from the emigration years that followed the Famine: advertisements for emigration boats, even luxury liners with steam power which for £29 would take the hopeful to a new life.

In town the Maid of Erin statue pays tribute to various people and bodies who died or suffered in the cause of Irish independence: Wolfe Tone, Robert Emmet, the Phoenix Society and the Young Ireland Society.

Lough Hyne, near Skibbereen

This unusual seawater lake was once freshwater but some time in the geological past it sank below sea level and became flooded with sea water. The lake is tidal and through some strange quirk of nature is very warm compared to the sea that feeds it. It contains marine life more commonly found in Mediterranean waters. The channel which links the sea with the lake is only accessible by some stiff and difficult climbing but there are pleasant walks around the lough in the nearby Knockomagh Wood.

How to get there 4 miles/6 km south of Skibbereen. Take the road from the 'Maid of Erin' monument that passes the post office on its left. Well signposted.

Fastnet Lighthouse

The lighthouse can be seen from a number of vantage spots in West Cork which pick out the large rock on which the lighthouse is built. It is ten miles out to sea and the first lighthouse built on the rock in 1854 only lasted for eleven years before being blown away in a gale. The lighthouse which can now be seen was finished in 1906 after granite blocks were imported from Cornwall. They have stood the test of time.

Road Bowling, West Cork

A rare leisure activity that is unlikely to be encountered outside of a Sunday afternoon or public holiday. It is played along quiet public roads and the first sign of a game in progress will be a group of men on either side of the road waiting for your bike or car to pass them by. Ahead of them will be a smaller group whose job is to chart the progress of the bowled steel ball. The object of the game is to cover a set distance of winding road in as few throws as possible, and this can include lofting the ball over a piece of adjoining field so as to shortcross the bend in the road. Bets are usually taken on the eventual winner or even individual bowls of the 7 in (18 cm) 28 oz (794 g) ball. Occasionally, big games will be played with a visiting team from the north of Ireland, for apart from the south-west the game is only played in Armagh. Regular games are played just outside the village of Kilcrohane.

CYCLE TOURS

CLONAKILTY TO UNION HALL 15.5 miles/25 km.

This tour heads out of Clonakilty on the main N71 road to the west and meanders down to Rosscarbery and then across to Glandore, taking in Coppinger's Court and the Drombeg stone circle. At Glandore a causeway crosses to Union Hall from where one can either retrace the route back or rejoin the N71 and return east to Clonakilty or west to Skibbereen. It is broken down into two sections below.

Clonakilty to Rosscarbery

Take the N71 west towards Skibbereen but after 3 miles/5 km take the left turn signposted to Rosscarbery, the Coastal Route, Long Strand and Rathbarry. Follow this road south to Ownahincha, with the option of stopping off to visit Castlefreke (see page 23), before rejoining the N71 for the short distance west to Rosscarbery. After crossing the causeway do not turn off right for Rosscarbery but look for the junction with a road off to the left signposted for Coppinger's Court and B&Bs. This is the R507.

Rosscarbery to Union Hall

After turning left follow the road, ignoring the first small turning to the left, for 0.9 miles/1.5 km until reaching an unmarked road to the left, just 200 metres after a sign for Vicky's Frames. A short distance down the road cross a bridge and turn right at the T-junction. A little way down this road Coppinger's Court is in a field on the right. Carrying on to a junction turn right to rejoin the R507. The next turn off to the Drombeg stone circle is clearly marked. Carrying on again the road leads to Glandore.

Glandore is built around a semi-circular harbour and the two small islands in the estuary are called Adam and Eve ('avoid Adam and hug Eve' was old sailing wisdom). From Glandore an estuary bridge crosses to Union Hall where Jonathan Swift came in 1723 to stay while grieving over the death of Vanessa.

From Union Hall either retrace the route back to Clonakilty or take the road north to the N71.

SKIBBEREEN TO CLEAR ISLAND
A return journey of 15 miles/24 km
Depart from outside the post office in Skibbereen and head south on the R595 to Baltimore. A longer but more picturesque route to Baltimore could be enjoyed by taking the left turn off this road — signposted for Lough Hyne — and threading your way through the narrow country roads.

In Baltimore take a ferry to Clear island (see page 12). Off the boat, turn left at the end of the pier to ascend the road up the hill. Keep to the left, following the sign for the youth hostel but just before the hostel take the turning to the left. Keep on this road, passing a post office on the left, until another main road is reached at a junction. Turn left here for the road back to the harbour, passing the heritage centre on the way and enjoying spectacular views across the water.

Plan your time to catch a ferry back to Baltimore and return to Skibbereen.

SCHULL TO GOLEEN, VIA COAST ROAD AND RETURNING ON THE R591 AND R592
A return trip of 19 miles/31 km
Leave Schull on the main road to Goleen but just outside of Schull take the left turning signposted 'Coastal Route'. Go straight across two minor junctions, with the way to Goleen signposted, and after 3 miles/5 km an old tower comes into view on the left as the road climbs gently for more than 0.6 miles/1 km. The narrow road passes farms but very little traffic will be encountered.

At 4.7 miles/7.7 km from Schull, at a T-junction, the main Schull–Goleen road is met. Turn left here and after 1.4 miles/2.3 km a church is passed on the right and a small inlet on the left. Just after this, at Toormore, there is a road signposted for Durrus going off to the right. Ignore this and carry on for 3.7 miles/6 km to Goleen passing

Sylvan Connell's knitwear shop and café on the right.

From Goleen, a land once described by a local TD as consisting of 'briars, bullocks and bachelors', the tour could be extended for another 5 miles/8 km to Crookhaven, or you could return to Schull keeping to the main road (the R591 to Toormore and then the R592 to Schull).

BANTRY TO THE SHEEP'S HEAD VIA THE GOAT'S PATH AND BACK TO BANTRY VIA DURRUS
A return journey of 42 miles/67 km

Head out of Bantry on the main road to Cork and, just after the West Lodge hotel on the left, take the right turning signposted 'The Goat's Path'. At first the road is uninteresting but as Bantry Bay comes into view the scenery becomes progressively more exciting and after about 12 miles/20 km the road climbs to a 650-feet pass with commanding views of Bantry and Dunmanus bays. It then descends into the village of Kilcrohane where a right turn leads out for 6.5 miles/10 km to the Sheep's Head, the end of the peninsula.

Return to Kilcrohane and continue straight on. You pass the hamlet of Ahakista and then Durrus where you keep to the left for the final inland leg of the tour back to the main Bantry–Cork road. Turn left when the N71 T-junction is met and return to Bantry.

AN ECOLOGICAL CYCLE TOUR
From and to Kilcrohane via the Goat's Path and north side of Sheep's Head peninsula

This is a 10 mile/16 km cycle trip for those who like solitude and scenery. A mountain bike is essential as part of the route traverses a very green road.

Leave the church in the village of Kilcrohane and climb to the top of the Goat's Path to the north. At the top of the Goat's Path locate an old disused turf road that heads out to the west: standing near the marble statue and facing Bantry Bay you will see the old road about 100 metres to the right. The road is hardly ever used nowadays and is well overgrown; it is recognisable still, however, by a low wall of slate on the sea-facing side. Take this road and cycle west.

After about ten minutes of cycling, having reached a horseshoe bend, the road is beginning to disappear but there is no danger of losing the way.

This road was built in 1891, ten years after the Goat's Path was completed, for the purpose of accessing the peat bog at this end of the peninsula. Before the roads were built the turf was carried across on the backs of donkeys and, although turf is no longer dug here, it is still there in plentiful supply and can easily be seen on this journey.

The bog growth began some ten thousand years ago when the first temperate plants appeared around lakes and rivers after the last ice age. In time the fens and floating masses of lake vegetation spread to take in woodland and the native pine was well preserved in the anaerobic environment. Centuries later farmers came across the wood when digging out the turf and it was still good enough to use. Most of the farmhouse hearths in this area have been modernised but the ones that retain the old style fireplaces could well have the mantelpiece made from a solid piece of wood taken from the bog and still smelling of pine.

The best place to view the bog is about half an hour's walk on from the horseshoe bend. A junction with a surfaced road can be seen ahead but before reaching it there are fine exposed bog cuttings, unused now for over twenty years.

At the junction with the surfaced road there is a choice of routes. The first choice involves turning to the right, and cycling for five minutes, would bring in view the remains of the North Kileen copper mines on the left side of the road. A row of roofless miners' cottages can be clearly seen and easily reached by just climbing over the ditch and walking down. Before doing this, the remains of a small lake can be seen on the right of the road. Here the miners dammed the stream coming down, in order to create enough water flow to turn the pumpwheels that drained the mines of seawater. Down near the miners' cottages little remains of the mine works, though the shaft is there. In front of the crumbling miners' cottages are the remains of a small building with a tall chimney still intact. The water from the dam was channelled down the chimney to turn the wheel that powered the pump.

This tour continues back at the junction where the second choice involves turning left to continue a cycle that keeps the majesty of Bantry Bay in full view for nearly an hour. Birds are few, just the occasional lark or seagull. Eventually the road has another horseshoe turn that brings a small green valley into view. Ignore a surfaced road to the right that appears a short while after and carry on to the left. The road climbs and brings Dunmanus Bay into view. This stretch of the road, known as the Crimea for some unknown reason, was built in 1847, supposedly at the rate of ten miles in eleven days.

Where the road meets the main road from Kilcrohane to Sheep's Head a fine stone building stands. From here it takes less than fifteen minutes to cycle back east to Kilcrohane, and the vegetation is noticeably different from the exposed north side. There are more flowers in the ditches, cranesbill and speedwell for instance, and hedges of blackthorn and hawthorn. Fuschia, honeysuckle and campion grows wild by the side of the road.

DAYTIME ACTIVITIES AND SPORTS

BEACH GUIDE

Inchadoney (Clonakilty)
This is a lovely wide beach just south of Clonakilty and there is a pub nearby. The only drawback is that a riptide can make it unsafe for swimming at times. If lifeguards are on duty a red flag will indicate that it is unsafe. Wheelchair access, facilities and food in pub behind the beach.

How to get there The road to the beach is signposted from the Fax roundabout at the east end of Clonakilty.

Dunnycove (Clonakilty)
This is a small cove, only sandy when the tide is out. It is, however, quite safe and rocks to the left can be clambered over and explored by children looking for sandy spots. No wheelchair access. It is rarely crowded.

How to get there. Leave Clonakilty on the road to Ardfield village, 3.7 miles/6 km away, crossing a causeway along the way. Just beyond Ardfield turn left at the churchyard where a small sign points the way to Dunnycove. After 0.3 miles/5 km turn left at an unmarked road, just before the road bends sharply to the right (ignore the unsurfaced road that goes straight on here). After 250 metres the road bends to the right where a left turn is an unpaved lane leading up to a farmhouse. After the road bends to the right, turn right again immediately off the road you were on. Follow this road downhill for 0.4 miles/0.7 km then, after passing three white bungalows on the left, turn sharply to the right. If you pass a few caravans in a field you have gone too far. The beach is 0.3 miles/0.5 km on this road. The road comes to a dead end and if there are more than a couple of cars parked at the bottom it is better to find space on the road above.

Ownahincha (Rosscarbery)
A decent beach only marred by the ugly caravan site and dilapidated amenities nearby. Sometimes the waves are too rough for bathing and children need supervision. Lots of facilities, good wheelchair access.

How to get there
From Clonakilty or Rosscarbery the left turning that leads to the beach is signposted on the N71. It is 6.8 miles/10.9 km from Clonakilty.

Long Strand (Rosscarbery)
A terrific 1 mile/1.6 km beach, pounded with huge Atlantic waves, but unfortunately not suitable for swimming. There are restaurants and toilets at Ownahincha. Wheelchair access.

How to get there Follow the directions above for Ownahincha and continue on the road past this beach. Long Strand is basically a continuation of Ownahincha.

Warren Strand (Rosscarbery)
Smaller and safer than either Ownahincha or Long Strand. No facilities, wheelchair access possible.

How to get there The beach is signposted from Rosscarbery on the N71.

Glandore Beach
A small attractive beach accessed from the road entering Glandore from the east.

Tragumna
Situated 4 miles/6.5 km from Skibbereen. This is a very popular but small bathing spot with fine sand and safe bathing.

How to get there From Skibbereen take the road to Baltimore and at 4 miles/ 6.5 km the beach is signposted.

Barley Cove

Glorious sand and sea. There are safe spots to swim and lifeguards patrol the area in summer. Toilets and food at the Barley Cove Hotel beyond the sand dunes. Wheelchair access with difficulty.

How to get there Follow the main coast road from Schull. Barley Cove is well signposted.

Close by to Barley Cove are two smaller beaches, *Galley Cove* and *Cockle Beach*. Neither have any facilities but are pretty strands. Both are visible from the road as you approach Barley Cove.

FISHING

Deep Sea Fishing

Near Clonakilty
Possible at Ring. Contact P. Houlihan at Blackbird's Pub in Connolly Street, or Fin's Tackle Shop off Emmet Street, telephone 023–34377.
Glandore Day trips and chartered boats for longer periods are available from the Marine Hotel (telephone 028–33366, fax 028–33600) or deep sea fishing and shark fishing.

Baltimore
Several operators charter boats for deep sea fishing from Baltimore.

The Baltimore Sea Angling Association, telephone 028–20145, will book a boat for you or individual skippers can be contacted. Michael Walsh at Baltimore Marine Services can be contacted at the Angler's Inn telephone 028–20145, or Nick Dent at *Fastnet Charters*, telephone 028–37406. Both men operate boats which will take eight persons, will take individual bookings at about £20, and have a minimum charge of around £80–£100 per day. Teddy Brown at The Cove, telephone 028–20319 and Sean O'Brien at the Marine Hotel (telephone 028–33366) in Glandore have smaller six-person boats for hire. Individual rate £15–£17, minimum charge £60. The area has several wrecks close at hand and these can provide large pollock, ling and conger eel while the open sea has blue shark. Schull Watersports Centre, telephone 028–28554, can arrange a boat with Mr F. Reilly.

At *Crookhaven* Bear Havinga, telephone 028–35240, has a 36 ft boat for hire for around £60 per day or £15 per person. Mike Roach of Schull, telephone 028–37256, charges more at £110 per day. For more information contact Schull SAC at the Marine Bar Schull, telephone 028–28455.

Shore Fishing

Near Clonakilty
Starting east of Clonakilty and travelling west, good places for shore fishing are Bar Rock, Ring Harbour and Clonakilty estuary, where bass and flounder are to be caught, drift lining in the harbour and bottom fishing at Bar Rock and the estuary. At Muckross Head flounder and bass again can be got by bottom fishing. At Ownahincha beach, at the east side of the Long Strand, surf fishing for flatfish and bass is possible. The river mouth itself is the best at low tide. Around *Rosscarbery* there are several good spots, on the bridge itself, on the boat slip and along the strand on the west side of the inlet. From the bridge floats are used for mullet while on the beach and at the boat slip bottom fishing gets flounder and bass. Ray and dogfish have been caught at night. Enquire at Derhams (telephone 023–48111) in the village for fishing tackle and information.

At *Glandore* the road bridge and the shore east of it are good spots for dogfish, flatfish and mullet. Further along the coast towards Toe Head but still close to the road are some good spots. Ask at Skibbereen for directions. Around the shores of *Lough Hyne,* particularly the western shore there is very deep water and conger eel, pollock, dogfish, wrasse and gurnard can be caught. The tidal stretch of the Ilen, as it flows into Skibbereen, is also good for sea fish, especially mullet. The best bet in this area,

Schull in West Cork

where there are any number of good places, is to ask locally. Everyone has their own favourite spot, bait and fish.

Along the Mizen Head peninsula *Ballydehob Harbour* around high tide produces flounder and bass. Bottom fishing, using a spinner, sea trout can be caught. At *Toormore* where the road comes close to the shore as it travels around an inlet, shore fishing from the rocks can provide wrasse, dogfish, bull huss, and flounder. Around *Rock Island* lighthouse at the mouth of Crookhaven rock fishing produces ray, codling, and dogfish while spinning for mackerel and pollock is possible. At *Galley Cove*, where the road comes close to the shore, it is possible to fish for pollock or coalfish from the rocks. *Barley Cove* has some good fishing spots for codling and plaice while Barley Lake, the stretch of water behind the beach fed by the tidal river flowing across the beach, provides eels, mullet, and sea trout. Best spots are those from the road crossing the river.

In Dunmanus Bay there are fewer good places and it might be a good idea to ask in the bars at Durrus about fishing in the area. On the south shore of Bantry Bay are two good spots for mackerel and pollock. One is at *Glanroon*, off the main Goat's Path road and along the northern tip of the Sheep's Head peninsula. Fishing off the rocks west of the small pier at Glanroon is popular with locals but can be dangerous. People have lost their lives there in high winds. Back on the Goat's Path road at *Collack* mackerel and pollock can be caught off the rocks.

Game Fishing

Most of Cork's large rivers lie north of the West Cork area and so there are few places in the region where fishing for sea trout or salmon is possible. But there are many lakes in the area which are stocked by the fisheries board with rainbow trout and which have their own natural stocks of small brown trout.

Starting from east of Clonakilty and moving west game fishing areas are: *Arigideen River* From 15 Feb to 30 Sept, sea trout and brown trout. Visitors' tickets from: South Western Fisheries Board, 1 Neville Terrace, Masseytown, Macroom, telephone 026–41222.

Corrin Lake The only coarse angling in this area is pike here.

Shepperton Lakes Open season from 1 April to 30 September. 3 miles east of Skibbereen. Boats for hire and permits from N. Connolly, Shepperton, Skibbereen, telephone 028–33328.

River Ilen Open season 1 Feb–30 Sept; the river flows south to meet the tide at Skibbereen. Spring salmon around March and grilse in June. Sea trout July. Fishing rights are owned by several different people. Contact Tony Kelly, Fallon's Sports Shop, North Street, Skibbereen, telephone 028–31514.

Schull reservoir Open season 15 June–31 August. Small brown trout and stocked rainbow trout, some rudd and eels. Permits from Ms K. Newman, Schull. Boats available.

Lough Bofínne Open season 1 April to 30 September. Three miles east of Bantry. Rainbow trout. Permits and boat hire Mrs Spillane, Lough Bofinne, Bantry (telephone 027–51546).

AQUA SPORTS

Self drive hire boats from The Stone House, Baltimore, telephone 028–20157. Courses of instruction on sailing from Baltimore Sailing School, telephone 028–20141.

Glenean's Sailing School, Baltimore, telephone 01–611481.

Schull Watersport Centre Ltd. Windsurfing lessons at the pier, Schull, telephone 028–28554 or 028–28351.

Windsurfing lessons at Cockle Strand, Crookhaven. Enquire for Guiney at the local pubs.

Schull Community College Summer Sailing School. Telephone 028–28315, fax 028–28467.

Rossbrin Yacht Charters. Fifteen-ton sailing boat takes up to five people. Telephone 028–37165.

Scuba diving at *Dunmahon Country House,* Kilcrohane, telephone 027–67092.

GOLF

Skibbereen Golf Club, 9 hole course, visitors welcome, telephone 028–21227.

Dunmore House Golf Course, Clonakilty, telephone 023–33352.

Coosheen Golf Links. 9 hole golf links at Coosheen near Schull. Green fees £6. Entertainment in lounge at weekends.

Colla House Hotel. 9 hole golf links, bar and restaurant.

Barley Cove Golf Links. 9 hole golf links on sand dunes at Barley Cove. Telephone 028–35234. Green fees £3.50.

DEEP-SEA DIVING

Schull Watersports, telephone 028–28554. Boat, compressed air equipment, weights and bottles for hire.

HORSE RIDING

Rosscarbery Riding Centre, telephone 023–48232. Open all year. £10 per person for 90 minutes. The centre is off the N71, on the right if coming from Clonakilty (11 km), opposite the signposted turn off for Ownahincha beach.

Limbo, Creagh, Baltimore, telephone 028–21683. Cross country rides and treks around Lough Hyne, and surrounding countryside. Horse and trap rides, and riding lessons. Open all year.

Keamore Pony Trekking, Leap, telephone 028–33307.

O'Connor's Riding School, Goat's Path Road, telephone 027–50011.

Swiss Riding School, Coomanore South, telephone 027–51412.

Animal Farm & Aviary, Goat's Path Road, telephone 027–50011.

John Hughes, Colla, telephone 028–28185. One-hour pony trekking sessions taking in local views.

Highland and Harbour Pony trekking, Goleen, telephone 028–35416. Michael Goggin. One-hour sessions.

Kingston's Riding School, telephone 023–33793. Beginners and advanced lessons, trekking along scenic trails.
Schull Riding Centre, Colla Road, telephone 028–28185.

PITCH AND PUTT

Fernhill House, Clonakilty, telephone 023–33258,
The Warren, Rosscarbery, telephone 023–00000.

SEA CRUISES

Innisfree Fast offshore cruiser, Baltimore, telephone 028–20192. Sea trips, fishing diving.

SNOOKER

De Barra's, Clonakilty.
Snooker Club, Main Street, Schull. No membership needed. Pool tables, video games, snooker. Teen hang out.

SWIMMING

Barley Cove Indoor swimming pool, Barley Cove Hotel, telephone 028–35234. Adults £2.75, children £1.50.
West Lodge Hotel, Bantry, telephone 027–50360. Indoor heated swimming pool, recently enlarged and renovated.

SQUASH

Schull Community College, Colla Road. Booking at shop.
West Lodge Hotel, Bantry.

TENNIS

Community Centre, Clonakilty,
Courtmascherry Hotel
Rosscarbery Sports centre
East End Schull
Barley Cove Hotel. Adults £2.75, children £1.50
Barley Cove Holiday park.
East End, Ballydehob.
West Lodge Hotel, Bantry.
Durrus, just west of village on the road to Goleen.

EVENING ACTIVITIES

Discos for teenagers and under 14s in the parish hall Goleen entrance £1–£2. Under 14s, 8.30 to 10 p.m. Teens, 10.30 to midnight. Tuesdays and/or Thursdays.
The Parish hall, Schull has discos for under teens and teenagers. Check noticeboards. Under 14s, 8 to 10.30 p.m., teenagers 11 p.m. to 1 a.m.

Ballydehob

Foróige Club. Meets in parish hall on Fridays at 9 p.m. Soccer, volleyball, pool. Occasional concerts.
Horse Races held occasionally through the year.
Coughlans' Bar. Main Street. Entertainment Wednesdays, Fridays and Sundays in summer.
The Irish Whip Bar. Irish music most nights.

Baltimore

Brendan McCarthy's Bar has traditional Irish and folk music most nights in the summer and on Sunday afternoons in the beer garden. *Bushe's Bar* in front of the pier attracts nautical enthusiasts and has lots of tables and chairs out front for those long sunny evenings. Lots of old ships' bits and pieces, admiralty charts and all that. The *Algiers Inn* has live music sessions, bar food and a beer garden. *Declan McCarthy's* (not to be confused with Brendan's!) is on the corner in front of the pier and also has several nights of music a week.

Bantry

The West Lodge Hotel. Discos at weekends.
Crowley's. From the front it looks like a grocer's but go round the back and there's a big dance hall and bar. Ballad sessions every weekend.
Other bars have occasional music nights so you should watch out for them.

Barley Cove

The *Barley Cove Hotel* has occasional music.

Clear Island

There is no regular music planned at Clear Island but the pubs get pretty lively at night. Look locally for notices of music.

Clonakilty

O'Donovan's Hotel. Music on Monday, Wednesday, Friday and Saturday.
Dunmore House and Golf club. Traditional music on Tuesday nights. Small golf course.
Tally Ho Bar and Lounge. Music on Saturday nights.
Courthouse Tavern, Connolly Street. Karaoke on Friday nights. Live music Thursdays, Saturdays, Sundays.
Emmet Hotel. Discos most weekends. Often has big bands appearing.

Crookhaven

O'Sullivan's Bar. Music every night.

Durrus

No regular music evenings are organised but look locally especially around the time of the Durrus festival. At **Kilcrohane,** the village festival in July brings musicians in and there are special occasion events. At the bar in **Ahakista** there is often music on Friday nights.

Glandore

The *Glandore Inn* has music at weekends.
Casey's Bar at the top of the hill in Glandore is worth a call for the often unusual and spontaneous entertainment it seems to generate.
The *Marine Hotel* puts on entertainment nightly during the summer. At **Union Hall** are three pubs all of which put on music in the summer and should be checked out in passing. *Dinty's Bar, Nolan's Bar* and *Casey's Bar* have music from time to time.
Leap Inn on the main road to Skibbereen from Clonakilty has a traditional Irish music session on Wednesdays and dancing on Sunday nights. In the same village there are two more places that organise musical nights, *Connolly's* and *The Morris Arms.* Check local shop windows or newspapers.
Lil McCarthy's, Castletownshend. Bar food. Music at weekends. Barbecues in beer garden.

Schull

The tourist office, which is in a portacabin opposite the Spar supermarket and is open from June to August, lists all music venues.
The Black Sheep Inn. Occasional entertainment. Look in window for information.
Courtyard Pub has live music ranging from jazz to traditional music and ballads. Sometimes there is an admission charge.
Arundel. Music on Thursdays.

Sherkin Island
The *Jolly Roger* has live music and does bar food as does *Garrison House.*

Skibbereen
Most pubs have some kind of music night in the summer season, particularly during the town's annual festival, usually in late July/early August.
Sean Óg's in Market Street is a pub which has music on most weekends.
Kearney's in North Street has music at weekends.
At Caheragh, on the road to Drimoleague is the *Stag's Head* which has an open-air dancing space where set dancing takes place to live accompaniment on Sunday afternoons.
The *West Cork Hotel* has a cabaret on Tuesday nights from June to September with an admission charge and ballroom dancing Sundays, price £2.50.
Annie May's in Bridge Street, has music at weekends and every night in July and August and does bar food.
Sheehy's in the square has music weekends and occasional Wednesday sessions.
Carroll's Bar, Ilen Street. Live entertainment every weekend.
Perhaps the best bet is to wander around from pub to pub looking for the best music. Many of the bands that play in these pubs are local and do a different pub each night so you might ask around which bands are good and find out where they are playing.
Five kilometres out of town at Tragumna is the *Old Court Inn* beside the water's edge with pretty gardens overlooking the sea. It also has music nights.
Also in Tragumna, the *Skibbereen Eagle Inn.* Bar food, traditional Irish music at weekends, snooker and pool.

Rosscarbery
The Leap Inn. The bar and restaurant are situated at Leap, on the main road (N71) from Rosscarbery to Skibbereen. Traditional Irish music on Wednesdays in summer. Dancing on Sunday nights.
Connolly's, Leap. Advertises in local papers and shop windows.

WHERE TO STAY

HOTELS
A price guide is provided by identifying each establishment in ascending order of cost as either economy, budget, moderate, or high. Rates vary with the season and the number of persons staying. It is always worth enquiring about special deals if staying more than one night.

Baltimore
Beacon Park Hotel, telephone 028–20361, satellite TV & video, gardens, nightly entertainment. One Star. Rating: economy.

Bantry
Seaview Hotel, Ballylickey (a few miles outside Bantry, on the road to Glengarriff), telephone 027–50462, fax 027–51555. TV, gardens, child meals. AM, AE, DE, VB. Pretty views, close to golf course, the hotel has a good reputation. Four Star. Rating: moderate.
Dromkeal Lodge, Ballylickey, telephone 027–51510, fax 027–51510. TV, gardens, child meals, dog friendly. Sea views and close to golf course. AM, AE, DE, VB. Two Star. Rating: budget.
Reendesert, Ballylickey, telephone 027–50153, fax 027–50597. TV, gardens, child meals, dog friendly. AM, AE, DE, VB. Two Star. Rating: moderate.
West Lodge Hotel. Telephone 027–50360, fax 027–50438. TV, swimming pool, gardens, games room, tennis, wheelchair friendly, child meals. AM, AE, DE, VB. Three Star. Rating: economy.
Bantry Bay Hotel, Bantry, telephone 027–50362. TV. VB. One Star. Rating: economy.

Barley Cove
Barley Cove Beach Hotel, Goleen, telephone 028–35234. En suite rooms, swimming pool, 9 hole golf course, playground, games room, tennis, self-catering chalets. Two Star. Rating: moderate.

Clonakilty
Imperial, Wolfe Tone Street at the east end of town. Child meals. Closed 24 to 31 December. Telephone 023–34185. AM, AE, DE, VB. One Star. Rating: economy.
O'Donovan's, Pearse Street. Telephone 023–33250. Closed from Christmas Day until the New Year. AM, AE, VB. One Star. Rating: budget.
Fernhill House, just outside town off the main N71 road. Gardens, TV, child meals. Telephone 023–33258. AM, VB. Two Star. Rating: budget.
Inchydoney, close to Clonakilty's fine beach, 2.7 miles/4.5 km from town, open from 23 May to 20 September. Telephone 023–33143. VB, AM. One Star. Rating: budget.

Glandore
Marine. Telephone 028–33366, fax 028–33600. Open from March to October. VB, AM, AE, DE. Two Star. Rating: moderate.

Rosscarbery
Ownahincha. By the beach of the same name, 2 miles/3 km from Rosscarbery. Telephone 023–48104. Close to the sea but a run-down look to the area. AM. One Star. Rating: economy.

Schull
East End. Main Street, telephone 028–28101. AE, VB. One Star. Rating: budget.
Colla House. Telephone 028–28105, fax 028–28105. TV, dog friendly, gardens, child meals, 9 hole golf course and pitch and putt. AM, VB. One Star. Rating: economy.

Skibbereen
West Cork Hotel. Ilen Street, telephone 028–21277, fax 028–22333. Family run, TV, babysitting, child meals, pet friendly. AM, AE, DE, VB. Three Star. Rating: moderate.
Eldon Hotel. Bridge Street, telephone 028–21300. Family run hotel, TV, gardens. AM, VB. One Star. Rating: budget.

SELF–CATERING

Ballydehob
The Forge Apartments. Self–contained flats with courtyard and patio, telephone 028–37353.

Baltimore
Baltimore Holiday Homes. Telephone 023–33220, fax 023–33131. Three-bedroomed cottages, washing machines, multi–channel TV, tennis courts, bed linen supplied.
Killeena Self-catering apartments. Creagh, telephone 028–21029.

Clonakilty
West Cork Holiday Homes, telephone 023–33544, fax 023–34393. Purpose built terraced cottages, 3- or 4-bedroomed, washing machines, electric heating, TV, bed linen supplied, babysitting.
Cashelfean Holiday Houses. Four-star holiday homes, stone built, 2 to 7 bedrooms, overlooking Dunmanus Bay. Also Glengarriff. Contact Eleanor O'Reagan, telephone 027–61208, fax 027–61175.

Crookhaven
Crookhaven Holiday Apartments, telephone 028–35344, fax 028–35392.

Rosscarbery
Celtic Cottages, telephone 021–772370 or write to Nora M. Wycherly, Camp Hill, Kinsale, Co. Cork, telephone 021–772370, fax 021–774482. The cottages, which are not Celtic in any obvious way, are situated close to one another within walking distance of Rosscarbery village.

Schull

James K. Lyons O'Keeffe, 48, Main Street, Schull, telephone 028–28122 is the agent for several sets of holiday cottages in Schull.

Celtic Cottages. Two-, three- and four-bedroomed cottages. Bookings from Nora M. Wycherly, Camp Hill, Kinsale, Co. Cork, telephone 021–772370, fax 021–774482.

West Cork Holiday Homes. Purpose built cottages, each accommodates 5-7 people. Includes servicing, linen, satellite TV, grocery delivery, babysitting. Contact West Cork Travel, 26–27 Rossa Street, Clonakilty, telephone 023–33220, fax 023–33131.

The Moorings. Houses and apartments, adjacent to pier, all mod cons, conservatories, moorings for boats. Telephone 027–50525, fax 027–50016.

HOSTELS

Baltimore

Rolf's Hostel. Telephone 028–20289. Open all year. Dormitory accommodation only, no private rooms. Laundry, bike hire.

Bantry

Bantry Independent Hostel. Bishop Lucey Place, telephone 027–51050. Dormitory accommodation and two private rooms. Laundry facilities and bike hire.

Clonakilty

There is no An Óige or IHH hostel but in nearby Timoleague *Lettercollum House* hostel, telephone 023–46251, there is dormitory accommodation and private rooms.

Clear Island

An Óige Hostel. Telephone 028–39114. A short uphill walk from the pier. Open from April to the end of October, 48 beds. This is a pretty hostel close to the sea with swimming and fishing spots nearby. Boats for hire.

Bird Observatory. No telephone, can be booked through Kieran Grace, telephone 01–785444, 84 Dorney Court, Shankill, Dublin. Small and often booked up by birdwatchers, especially in October.

CAMPING AND CARAVAN SITES

Bantry

Eagle Point Caravan and Camping Park, Ballylickey, telephone 027–50630. Open all year, four star, laundry TV room, playground.

Clonakilty

Desert House Caravan & Camping Park. Within walking distance of the town. Heading out of Clonakilty for the N71 to Bandon there is a roundabout with a road off to Ring. The campsite is on the left just a couple of hundred metres down this road. Telephone 023–33331, fax 023–33048.

Clear Island

Cuas An Uisce Camping Park has space for 20 pitches. Telephone 028–31149. Open from June to Sept.

Crookhaven

Barley Cove Caravan Park. telephone 028–35302. Launderette, washing–up area, shop, takeaway restaurant, playground, playroom, bike hire, barbecue area, baby sitting. Very large site of mostly permanently sited caravans and mobile homes which are for hire. No dogs.

Glandore

The Meadow Camping Park. Two star site, telephone 028–33280. Small site, open from March to October.

Rosscarbery

O'Riordan's caravan and Camping Park. Two star, TV room, playground, no tents. Open all year. Telephone 021–541825.

Timoleague/Clonakilty

Sexton's Caravan and Camping Park is on the main Timoleague/Clonakilty road, some 5 miles/7 km from Clonakilty. Open all year, telephone 023–46347.

WHERE TO EAT

This is a guide to places to eat in West Cork. It is not a good food guide. The price rating is similar to that for accommodation and is intended as a rough indication of cost. Again, it is in ascending order: economy, budget, moderate, high.

Ballydehob

Annie's is a tiny restaurant where the owner cooks seafood and steaks and can do vegetarian food. Open for lunch and dinner. Rating: high. AM, DE, VM. Closed October. In high season booking ahead is essential. Telephone 028–37292.
Teach Dearg is a little way out of town at Scarteenakilleen and does steaks, salmon, game and vegetarian dishes. Open for lunch and dinner Tuesday to Sunday. Reservations necessary. Telephone 028–37282. AM, AE, DE, VM. Rating: economy.
The *Ballydehob Inn* does bar food and has a restaurant. Rating: economy.
Duggan's is inexpensive and does light meals and takeaways. Rating: economy.
Vincent Coughlan's Pub. Bar food. Soup and sandwiches. Rating: economy.

The beach at Barley Cove, Co. Cork

Baltimore

There are a number of restaurants in this tiny seaport, catering both to sailing enthusiasts and the passing trade en route to the islands.
Chez Youen, the Pier, telephone 028–20136, is actually a French restaurant run by a French person specialising in fresh seafood. Ethnic pine interior, meat and vegetarian alternatives. Open Easter to September for lunch and dinner, closed for long periods in winter so phone ahead. AM, AE, DE, VB. Rating: high.

The *Harbour Restaurant* has budget meals, mostly fish, and does child meals and breakfast.

The *Lifeboat Restaurant* is another place doing budget type food, and is open from 9 a.m. to 6 p.m.

Declan Mc Carthy's Bar does bar food all day and has a restaurant called the *Pride of Baltimore* which does a set dinner for around £10. It is open from 6.30 p.m., and offers free range meats as well as organic vegetarian choices. Rating: budget.

Casey's Cabin, just as you arrive in town from Skibbereen, is a large bar with a restaurant doing mostly seafood items with a vegetarian choice. Busy at lunchtimes with the tourists, its prices change daily and are chalked up on the menu at the door. Open all year. AM, VM. Rating: budget.

The *Captain's Table* is a restaurant above a B&B, specialises in seafood. Rating: economy.

The *Customs House* is quieter, does lunches and dinners, and has a reasonable wine list. Rating: moderate.

Bantry

Larchwood House. Pearson's Bridge near Ballylickey. Not easy to find but well worth the effort. This tiny restaurant rarely advertises but is usually full. Open from 6.30 p.m. Closed Sundays. Telephone 027–66181. AM, DE, VB. Rating: high.

Sea View Restaurant. In hotel of same name at Ballylickey on road to Glengarriff. Has won lots of awards. Open from late March to November. Closed on Wednesdays. Telephone 027–50073. Rating: high. AM, AE, DE, VB.

Ballylickey Manor House. Poolside restaurant, open for lunch and dinner. Telephone 027–50071. AM, VB. Rating: high.

West Lodge Hotel. Fish and meat restaurant in '60s hotel on Cork road. Large helpings. Open for breakfast, lunch and dinner. Very large dining room. Telephone 027–50360. AM, AE, DE, VB. Rating: high. Closed Christmas week.

O'Connor's Seafood Restaurant. Reservations must be made at this small but very popular restaurant. Fresh seafood including oysters and Bantry mussels. Steaks and lamb too. Open from 6 p.m. to 10.30 p.m. Also for lunch when it gets very busy. Telephone 027–50221. AM, AE, DE, VB. Rating: high.

Vickery's. Bar food all day is good in this popular inn. Tourist menus and lunch specials in the restaurant. Potatoes predominate. AM, AE, DE, VB. Rating: budget.

O Siocháin. Café and restaurant doing mainly lunchtime business. Homely food. Lunch specials. Rating: budget.

Tra Amici. Another of the Ballylickey cluster. it is well signposted from Ballylickey. Recently purpose built restaurant run by Italian Americans. It has its own bakery and makes beautiful bread. Good selection of dishes including vegetarian. Rating: high.

Several of the other pubs do bar food; they have notices outside.

Clonakilty

The *Sandlighter.* Strand Road, telephone 023–33247, concentrates on seafood with steak and vegetarian alternatives. The menu depends on what fish is available that day. Moderately priced tourist menu while the a la carte would work out in the high bracket. AM, VB. Open till midnight. Tourist menu till 8.30 p.m.

An Súgán. Opposite the Sandlighter, has a restaurant and a bar menu. Specialities are lobster and oysters. Try some black pudding which is often served as a starter. Same price tourist menu as its neighbour, slightly cheaper a la carte. AM, VB. Tourist menu till 8.30 p.m.

An Chistin. Pearse Street, light lunches at around £3 and dinner. Rating: budget.

Emmet Hotel. Does bar food at lunch time — toasted sandwiches grills, etc. It also has a beer garden and a TV lounge near to the bar. Rating: budget.

Fionnula's, 30 Ashe Street. Old style Italian restaurant and wine bar. Nice interior, with a bare stone wall and candles in bottles. Wednesday and Saturday nights. Sunday mornings: live music. Lunch and brunch noon to 3 p.m., dinner 6–10 p.m. Rating: budget.

Imperial Hotel. Hotel lunches and dinners, tourist menus. Rating: budget.

Jade Garden Chinese Takeaway. Restaurant inside. Main dishes around £5. Open 5 p.m. to 1.00 a.m. Rating: economy.

Karen's Country café. Pearse Street. Snacks and coffee. Rating: budget.
O'Donovan's Hotel. Hotel food, lunch from 12–3 p.m., dinner from 5–9 p.m. Children's menu. Rating: economy.
Rossa Grill. Fast food to take away — pizzas, fried chicken etc.
The Whistle Inn. Bar and Lounge does pub food.

Crookhaven

Marconi House. Eat in the spot where Marconi erected a radio mast in 1902. Seafood and steaks. Rating: moderate.
The Crookhaven Inn. Bar food. soup, sandwiches. Rating: economy.
Journey's End. Just before the village of Crookhaven. Lunches and dinner. Reservations 028–35183. Rating: moderate to high.

Durrus

Blair's Cove Restaurant. Highly acclaimed restaurant on the edge of the sea. Excellent views. Buffet-style starters, meat and seafood in French style, very attractive interior. Reservations necessary in summer, telephone 027–61127. Open March to November. Closed Mondays. AM, AE, DE, VB. Rating: High.
Shiro Japanese Restaurant. Reservations are essential at this two-table restaurant. Has rave reviews from food writers on expenses. Ordinary mortals will love the food but wince at the prices. Set in pretty gardens at Ahakista, 7 miles/11.3 km from Durrus on Sheep's Head peninsula. Rating: high. AM, AE, DE, VB. Telephone 027–67030.

Goleen

Barley Cove Beach Hotel. Bar food, breakfast, lunch and evening meals from 6 to 9.45 p.m. Irish cuisine. Telephone 028–35234. AM, AE, DE, VB. Rating: moderate.
Heron's Cove Restaurant. Set in a cove near Goleen harbour where herons do actually fly about. Open for breakfast, lunch and dinner. Tourist menu. Dinner from 6 to 9.45 p.m. Good seafood selection including lobster picked from a tank. AE, AM, DE, VB. Open June to September. Telephone 028–35225. Rating: moderate.
The *Altar Restaurant* is out of town at Toormore, does seafood and has a wine bar but the premises are cramped. Customers can bring their own wine. It has live music on Wednesdays. Vegetarian dishes. Reservations necessary in high season, telephone 028–35254. AM, VB. Rating: moderate.

Kilcrohane

Dunmanus House. Kilcrohane. Well cooked food by a local escargot breeder. Phone for a reservation, 027–67092. Rating: moderate.
Fitzpatrick Sandwiches and light snacks at this very friendly pub, just north of the church on the Goat's Path road.

Rosscarbery

Roisin's in the main square is a teashop which does light snacks while *Clanan's* pub opposite does inexpensive bar food all day.
Marine Hotel in Glandore does moderately priced bar food at lunchtime and evenings. Nice sea views, seafood dominates the menu.
Mary Anne's at Castletownshend, telephone 028–36146, does bar food from 12.30 to 3 p.m. and 6 to 7.30 p.m. It also has a restaurant open from 6.30 p.m. AM, VM. Reservations necessary in summer. This is an ancient pub with lots of charm and a similar amount of tourists in July and August. Four-course dinner, mainly seafood with meat alternatives. Eat in the wooden beamed restaurant or out in the garden but beware the Sunday evening rock bands. Rating: high.
The Leap Inn. Bar menu and dinner. Sunday lunch. Restaurant open for dinner from 6.30. Situated at Leap on the road between Rosscarbery and Skibbereen. Rating: .

Schull

La Coquille. Lunches and dinners, local seafood, simply decorated. Open Monday to Saturday, last orders 9.30 p.m. Rating: moderate.
Colla House Hotel. A la carte dinner menu 6 to 9 p.m. Situated 2 miles/3 km out of Schull on Colla Road. Bar lunches 12 noon to 6.30 p.m. Telephone 028–28497. Rating: moderate to high.

Ard na Gréine. A mile west of Schull. Restaurant with beer garden. Lunches and dinners.

Black Sheep Bar and Restaurant. Seafood and steaks a la carte. Children's menu. Rating: moderate.

Bunratty Inn. Bar menu of toasted sandwiches, hot dishes. Restaurant, fish and meat menu. Small. No children in restaurant or in bar after 8 p.m. Rating: moderate.

East End Hotel. Big spacious dining room and food in the bar all day. Bar food mostly fish dishes. Sunday lunches. Rating: moderate.

Cotter's Yard. Café and coffee shop.

The Courtyard Restaurant. Interesting menu including ray, garlic scallops, duck. Country kitchenish with open fire. Bar food of high quality. Rating: moderate.

The Greyhound Inn. Barfood. Rating: budget.

Pizza and Cream. Main Street. Open from 11 a.m. Freshly cooked takeaway pizzas at £2 to 5 with 60p toppings. Also ice cream. Rating: economy.

Sylvia Connel Designs. Ballyrisode. Coffee shop, hot lunches, cakes. Open 10 a.m. to 7 p.m. Sunday 2 p.m. to 7 p.m. Rating: economy.

Adele's. Main Street, snacks and cooked light meals. Rating: economy.

Sherkin Island

There is a limited selection of food on the island, although the two pubs both serve barfood. There is a little coffee shop by the pier which does light meals. There is also a tiny shop on the island where you can get chocolate or biscuits. A picnic lunch is recommended

Skibbereen

The *Eldon Hotel* does bar food all day until 9 p.m., serving steaks and seafood at moderate prices.

The *West Cork Hotel* is open for lunch and dinner (6 to 9 p.m.) Prices are moderate, helpings vast, particularly in the potato department, and tastes simple. AM, AE, DE, VB.

The *Windmill Tavern* in North Street serves seafood. It is open for breakfast and lunch as well as dinner on weekdays and just for dinner on Sundays. Rating: moderate. AM, VM.

Sean Og's has barfood.

Annie May's good bar food until late on nights when there is no music and around 9.30 p.m. on music nights.

Backroom in North Street does Indonesian food at budget prices.

The *Hi–Style* is open all day till 11 p.m., does caff type burgers, grills etc. It has a takeout section which is open until 1 a.m. Rating: budget.

The *Busy Bee.* Fast food joint in Ilen Street. Rating: economy.

Foley's. Bridge Street. Bar lunches and restaurant during summer. Mostly seafood. Rating: moderate.

SHOPPING FOR GIFTS & SOUVENIRS

Ballydehob

Keltic Knot. A small craft shop with the usual range of pots and things.

Castaways Curiosities. Bric-a-brac and crafts, old books. The shop also sells wine. Opposite the Texaco garage.

Baltimore

The Islands Crafts and Information Centre, the pier, sells pottery knitwear and other items made on the two islands. It also offers information about accommodation on the islands.

Bantry

Bantry has a few good craft and clothes shops. Look around the shops along from the police station facing the sea and the road that heads out towards Glengarriff. If travelling between Bantry and Gougane Barra look for *Future Forests* on the left side of the road about 8 miles/12 km from Bantry. Primarily a garden centre, there is also a shop selling local craft items.

The Round Tower. A very good selection of Irish arts and crafts including some famous names like Louis Mulcahy.

Clonakilty

West Cork Craft and Design Centre. Guaranteed West Cork crafts ranging from kites to candles to rugs, jewellery, knitwear etc. Not cheap, but good quality. The shop is situated at the top of the Supervalu supermarket at the Fax roundabout east of town.

Twomey's Butchers, 16 Pearse Street, for reputedly the best black pudding in Clonakilty, a local speciality.

Claire Ryan. Gifts and pottery. Small but nice pottery.

The Sweater Shop. Wolfe Tone Street. Wool, cotton, alpaca and linen items.

Sean O'Connell. opposite the Bank of Ireland. Jewellery and crystal.

Ceard Siopa. Western Road. Crochet workshop gifts and crafts.

John Lowney. Ashe Street, jewellers and crystal, Donegal china.

Golden Pheasant Crafts. Courtmacsherry. Set in garden and aviary. Batik, books, gardenpots, pottery, Arans, tweeds.

Durrus

Cottage Antiques. 3 miles/5 km from Durrus on the Mizen Head road. Open Monday to Saturday from 10.30 a.m. China, brass, prints, boxes.

Glandore

At Union Hall is *Union Crafts,* which makes and sells wooden toys, house signs,and other souvenirs. They will make any sign or wooden toy to order.

Schull

Schull Books will delight bibliophiles. It's a large second hand and antiquarian bookshop. Lots of Irish interest and military history. Appointment necessary. Telephone 028–37317.

The Fish Shop. The pier, sells very fresh locally caught seafood. Open 10 a.m. to 6 p.m.

Cotter's Yard. Craft shop and boutique.

Phyllis O'Meara. Knitwear shop selling handknits and Arans.

Sylvia Connell Designs. Ballyrisode. Factory outlet, knitwear and crafts.

Bizzy Lizzie. Antique furniture.

Skibbereen

West Cork Arts Centre, opposite the library, has a craft shop and exhibitions of local art which is also for sale.

Trag Knitwear. On the road out to Baltimore from Skibbereen, selling lots of local handknits plus some weird and wonderful knitted and sewn garments. As in all knitwear shops, though, you should try the jumper on before you buy it.

Jugs and Reels, North Street. Irish music and instruments and some fascinating pottery from Corsett's potteries such as a kinky Victorian sink unit in the shape of a bending woman.

Designs. Main Street. Everything from big pots to tiny candles.

Fastnet Candles. Hand made candles in various Celtic designs. Showroom is in the factory at the old railway station on Bantry Road beyond the West Cork Hotel.

CHILDREN'S ACTIVITIES

- Visit the Schull Planetarium (see page 20)
- Enrol on one of the canoeing or sailing courses available in Schull, Bantry and Crookhaven during the summer. See local shop windows for times and other details.

- Visit the Mizen Head lighthouse (see page 11)
- Make a visit to the atmospheric Three Castle Head near Barley Cove (see page 10)
- Visit the animal farm and the model village outside Clonakilty (see page 13)
- Hang out in the snooker hall in Schull.
- Go pony trekking.
- Visit Barley Cove Beach Hotel for a swim in the heated pool.
- Visit Barley Cove Beach and make sandcastles.
- Hire bicycles and go for a ride.
- Have a game of pitch and putt. (see golf page 30)
- Go to a disco. There are several in the church halls around Schull, Goleen, Kilcrohane during the festival period.

RAINY DAY ACTIVITIES

- Visit a cheesemaking plant. West Cork Natural Cheese is at Dereenatra, telephone 028–28593 for an appointment. Durrus Cheeses at Coomkeen, Durrus is also open for visits from 10 a.m. to 2 p.m. Phone for an appointment, 027–61100.
- Visit and join, as a temporary member, the Clonakilty public library. A returnable deposit of £10 (£5 for children) is required.
- Visit the West Cork Regional Museum in Clonakilty.
- Visit Bantry House and the adjoining French Armada Exhibition.
- Visit the small Bantry museum.
- Visit the Schull Planatarium
- Visit the Mizen Head lighthouse.
- Find a bar with a pool table and hang out.
- Find a bar with a big screen TV and watch it.

ECOTOUR

CLONAKILTY–CLEAR ISLAND VIA ROSSCARBERY/SKIBBEREEN/ LOUGH HYNE/BALTIMORE

Link 8 miles/13 km from Clonakilty on the N71 west.

The signpost, on the left, for Owinahincha is 6.8 miles/11 km west of Clonakilty on the main road. Follow the road through a run-down caravan park and take the right fork at the first junction. The sea is on the right behind the sand dunes. At the second junction also bear right, following the sign to the Galley Tea House. Carry on for about 0.6 miles/1 km and stop beside a single-storey stone cottage on the left with pine trees behind it.

Walk across the road to the sand dunes and beach.

The dunes are covered with marram grass, a perennial with tightly rolled leaves that helps resist the wind and salt. The plant's rhizome grows down through the sand and binds together otherwise loose sands and in this way it helps stabilise the dunes. And these dunes need stabilising, for they receive a terrific buffeting from the Atlantic waves that crash on the beach. Even on a sunny day the waves here are fierce and wild and the beach hardly requires a sign warning of the dangers to reckless swimmers.

Walk back across the road, near where the river flows into the sea, to the stone cottage.

Follow the laneway that goes up by the side of the cottage. Kilkeran Lake soon comes into view on the right. Shags, not to be confused with cormorants, can sometimes be seen resting near the reeds. The laneway eventually comes out onto a road and on the other side is the old lodge entrance to what was once the Castlefreke estate. Walk through the pillars and after 600 metres, ignoring the track to the right, there is a car park area. Ignore the old sign prohibiting access and walk up the pathway to Castlefreke. This is a mixed wood of beech, oak and bamboo plants with the ubiquitous rhododendrons growing unheeded.

Link Castlefreke to Lough Hyne. 15.5 miles/25 km.

After returning to the N71 the road is uneventful until the causeway at Rosscarbery is reached. This gives picturesque views on both sides and wading birds can often be seen along the shores of the water. The main road continues on through the village of Connonagh and after passing a couple of pubs on the right look for the picnic spot on the left at Dromillihy Wood. On the opposite side of the road are the remains of the last flax factory in West Cork. The next village is Leap — pronounced Lep — so called because of the gorge that is now hardly noticed if whizzing through in a car.

At Skibbereen, a thriving market town, take the road for Baltimore. After another 2.5 miles/4 km take the turnoff on the left for Lough Hyne.

Stop in the Lough Hyne car park.

This is the only inland sea lake in Europe. Once in the distant past it was a freshwater lake but it is thought that due to subsidence it fell below sea level and instead of draining continually into the sea as other lakes do it spends half its time being filled by sea water. A curious system has evolved where at high tide the surface of the lough is below sea level and sea water flows into it. As the tide recedes water begins to flow out again. At the mid point of the tide the water in the channel stands still for a few seconds and then alters direction. In the open sea the tide alters about 1 cm between high and low tide while at Lough Hyne the water levels change by about 30 cm.

The lough is 0.6 miles/1 km long and 0.4 miles/0.75 km wide. Because of its unusual geography it is home to a very strange flora and fauna and a marine station has been set up here to study the life of the lough. Basically its marine life is more typically that of the Mediterranean although of course it is much shallower. Among the unusual species found here are the red-mouthed goby fish, which looks like it should be in someone's fish tank rather than sea water in southern Ireland. There are also sponges and sea squirts which normally live in much warmer climates. Another inhabitant is coral, usually associated again with hotter places. The lough has been designated a marine nature reserve and in order to dive in it a permit must be sought from the government. To the north of the car park and surrounding the road is Knockomagh Wood, one of Ireland's few remaining aboriginal oakwoods. The oaks are interspersed with beech and the usual holly trees that have found a niche in older oakwoods of this sort. The beech were probably planted some time in the eighteenth century. Around the edges of the wood are conifers. The wood is healthy — many woodland flowers survive in its shelter. It also contains some spindle trees which are really small shrubs rather than trees. In autumn its bright pink fruits distinguish it as well as its orange leaves. There also occasional Irish yew trees here.

Link Lough Hyne to Baltimore. 9 miles/15 km.

Follow the small road from Lough Hyne to Baltimore or retrace the 2.5 miles/4 km back to the main Skibbereen/Baltimore road and turn left to continue on to Baltimore. Bear in mind the departure time for boats to Clear Island, 7 miles/11.3 km south of Baltimore.

Cape Clear Island is the most southerly point in Ireland. Together with Sherkin Island it forms the south-eastern arm of Roaringwater Bay. It is three miles long and about a mile wide at its broadest. At its narrowest it is a matter of a few metres. It was once the tip of a peninsula of land and its old red sandstone has folded and been eroded to form an amazing coastline of stacks, caves, blowholes and many offshore jutting rocks, perfect for birdlife. Closer inspection of the rocks around the coast will show that many of the rocks are slate or shale with small veins of quartzite material running through.

The island's mild climate but high rainfall makes farming a difficult business and it relies heavily on the tourist trade in summer. Cows and goats are kept and a few vegetables are grown but in winter salt spray reaches almost everywhere on the island, affecting the vegetation. A few imported pine and alder trees provide a little shelter but as the population dwindles less and less of the land is cultivated and more of it moves into bracken-filled rough pasture. The rocky nature of the island can be seen in the many stone walls which divide the tiny fields, many of which are no longer cultivated. The walls are the result not of the need to divide up the land so much as the need to clear the soil of rocks. Flax was once grown on the island and the shores of the lake still bear the rings of stones used to wash the flax.

Boat to Clear Island
Departure Times (telephone 028-39135/39119)

May: 11 a.m. and 5.30 p.m.
June & September: 2.15 p.m., 7 p.m. (Returning 9 a.m., 6 p.m.).
July & August: 10.45 a.m., 2.15 p.m., 7 p.m. (Returning 9 a.m., 12 noon, 6 p.m.). There may be extra boats on Sunday.
October to May: Monday to Thursday 2.15 p.m. (Returning 9 a.m.).
                    Friday 10.30 a.m., 5.30 p.m. (Returning noon).
                    Sunday 5 p.m.

£7 per adult, £3.50 per child, £16 family ticket for two adults and two children. No extra charge for bicycles.

WALK/CYCLE

Turn left at the end of the pier and follow the path up to the café and pub. Ignore the turning left to the Heritage Centre and continue on uphill to the shop. At this junction the right turn leads to the camping site and Blananarragaun (see below) where the seabirds are best seen. For this walk, however, bear left instead and follow the road that leads to the youth hostel. Look along the ditch on the left for the Hairy Birdsfoot Trefoil. This flower is rarely found in Ireland: this is one of the few places where it can definitely be seen. It is a peaflower and can be spotted by its bright yellow flowers and hairy stems. Wood sage, wild thyme and scentless mayweed are also easy to find. Another rarity to Ireland is the pale butterwort and in May this can be spotted in the boggy spots. It is a scaled-down version of the more common butterwort but really is very small, only an inch or two in height, and has to be searched for on all fours. Of the 931 different plants in Ireland this island has over one-third of them, so it is advisable to bring along a flower identification book.

On the other side of the road South Harbour is clearly in view and choughs are often to be seen along this walk. Shoals of dolphin and even the occasional hump-backed whale visit the island's waters but a sighting is still a lucky occurrence.

Just before the youth hostel turn left and follow the road that passes a lane to the post office. On the right the island's windmills are clearly to be seen. For the past four years the island's electricity has been mostly provided for by wind power thanks largely to a German company and EU funds. Now, due to increased energy demands in the summer when the wind is not at its strongest, the system needs upgrading. The ESB (Electricity Supply Board) is not interested, claiming that it is more economic to lay an underwater cable to the island. Meanwhile the 150 inhabitants continue to benefit from a wind power system that produces surplus electricity during the winter months. If the ESB receives funding from the EU the wind station will be dismantled.

Continuing past the windmills the road comes to a T-junction. Turn right to head out to the eastern edge of the island or left to head back to the pier, passing the Heritage Centre on the way. The Centre opens from 3.30 to 5.30 p.m. daily between June and August (£1 for adults, 50p for children) and contains an interesting collection of artifacts relating to the island's history and culture.

The real ecological treat of Clear Island is at Blananarragaun, a tip of land in the south-west of the island. To reach it take the turning at the shop that is signposted to the campsite and carry right on to the end of this road and then keep going to the end of the southern spur of land. From this point it is possible to experience something wonderful. During the summer months seabirds fly out regularly from their nests in the Blasket islands and other westerly outposts. They head east looking for food in the Irish Sea and in the evening they fly back, always skirting this tip of Clear Island. Thousands of large seabirds — Manx shearwaters, gannets, fulmars and kittiwakes — can be seen. In late July as many as 35,000 shearwaters fly past in one hour, skimming over the water where the slight air current caused by the waves enables them to minimise the use of their wing power. The shearwater is easy to spot, being a large bird black on top and white underneath, and heavily outnumbering all the other birds.

The shearwaters do not breed on the island because the presence of rats could quickly wipe out their colonies. The only notable breeding birds on the island are the guillemots and they are identified by their black plumage with a large white area that makes them look like black and white ducks in the water.

Dedicated ornithologists are particularly drawn to Clear Island around the first two weeks of October when American vagrants are spotted. At this time the bird observatory hostel is booked up well in advance. Other times of the year, especially the summer, anyone interested in birdwatching should visit the Bird Observatory. On reaching the end of the pier turn right and head for the two-storey white-fronted building. Enquire about trips to Blananarragaun, for an hour spent in the company of an ornithologist is well worth it.

CLEAR ISLAND TO DURRUS VIA BALLYDEHOB, SCHULL, GOLEEN, CROOKHAVEN AND MIZEN HEAD

Link Skibbereen to Mizen Head. 21 miles/35 km.

Retrace your steps to Skibbereen and then take the road to Ballydehob. The road passes through rich-looking fields, dotted with some outlandish architecture with yachts set in driveways, an indication of the many people who have settled in this area in the last few decades. The area from here to Schull and beyond is full of very recent settlers and in the pubs in the evenings you are just as likely to hear German or French accents as Irish ones. Beside the road flows the river Ilen, a wide, slow moving river, popular with anglers. After a few miles the river runs south to meet the sea.

The road turns north-west towards Ballydehob and begins to follow the line of the old Skibbereen and Schull light tramway. The line carried passengers but its chief job was to move copper ore and fish to centres where they could be exported. The line was built in 1886 and closed in 1947 and for most of its lifetime ran at a loss. When the fishing industry was hit by American import tariffs at the beginning of this century and South African copper became cheaper than Irish its two main reasons for existing disappeared.

This whole area once supported a large population of fishermen, fish factory workers, copper miners and workers and their families. The old copper workings can still be seen along the fields south of the road and the slag heaps are still there. Major industries are farming and tourism. EU regulations have recently had a major effect on local farmers who for years have brought milk churns to the creamery each day after a night's storage by the cowshed. Recently every farm has had to invest in a tank with a built-in refrigerator, where the milk is stored for one or two days until it is collected from the farm by lorry. The creameries are no longer crowded with tractors and horses and carts.

At Ballydehob is the picturesque twelve-arched bridge which once carried the tramway into town. At lowtide Ballydehob harbour is an expanse of mud as the river has built up an extensive delta in the middle of the estuary.

From the brightly painted village the road travels through fairly boggy land to Schull, another retreat for well-heeled North Europeans. The town still functions as a harbour although most of the boats now are pleasure boats rather than working ones. In winter the place has a deserted feel but it comes alive in summer. A whole economy functions here for about eight weeks before it all closes down again for the next year.

The route carries on through the tiny village of Goleen with its sheltered harbour and interesting birdlife. The road continues past a deserted stone quarry until a caravan site comes into view. The road forks, the left hand fork curling round into Crookhaven while the right goes down into Barley Cove. Crookhaven was named after a developer of the area, a Mr Crook, although the idea that it might be an ancient refuge for pirates and the like is a pleasant one. Barley Cove is now a popular tourist spot but its wildlife is barely harmed by the influx of people. A walk in the dunes behind the beach reveals a healthy ecology. Typical plants of the dunes lie here such as the conspicuous sea holly with its blue flowerheads and prickly leaves. Rabbits live in an enormous colony here and the wide marsh land around the river provides a home for estuary birds. Continue on past the Barley Cove Beach Hotel to Mizen Head.

Stop At the car park at Mizen Head.

The cliffs here are 200 feet/70 metres high and from close to the edge it is possible to see the teeming birdlife of the cliffs. Although they do not nest here many seabirds pass by here as they do on Cape Clear Island and some rare birds can be spotted, especially after the October gales. Shearwaters, petrels, kittiwakes and fulmars are easily seen. Growing on the rocks and grassy banks around you are also some rare plants. The Hairy Birdsfoot Trefoil, described earlier (see page 44) may also be spotted here. Thrift is also abundant as is wild thyme; its tiny purple flowers might be mistaken for heather until you get closer and smell their rich perfume. In autumn the hills behind you will be brilliant yellow and purple with autumn gorse and various types of heather which prefer the acid soil. If you are really very lucky you can spot whales, porpoises and dolphins far out at sea migrating past this point from the northern Atlantic in autumn and from the southern oceans in spring. You are more likely, however to spot seals in the water than cetaceans. There is an exciting walk around the cliffs here for those with a head for heights or the lighthouse can be visited.

Link Mizen head to Durrus. 26 miles/39 km.

Retrace your journey as far as Toormore where you should take the left turning, signposted for Durrus. The road goes inland for a while after Toormore to re-emerge along the coast of Dunmanus Bay. To your right are the last and smallest of the mountain folds thrown up when the great hills of Kerry were formed. There are more old copper mines in the hills as well as many standing stones and raths. As you reach the end of the bay Mount Corin reaches up behind you. There is a disused barytes mine in this hill which once employed large numbers of people and had a system of overhead cables bringing the material down to Durrus. Barytes has an unusual density and was used as ballast in empty cargo ships.

DURRUS–BANTRY VIA KILCROHANE

Link Durrus to Kilcrohane. 10 miles/15 km.

At Durrus turn sharp left for the road leading west on the Sheep's Head peninsula to Kilcrohane. From Durrus to Kilcrohane the road winds its way close to the shoreline. In winter winds the sea can splash the road with seaweed and more than one unfortunate driver has taken a turn too fast and landed in the sea. The reason the road hugs the shoreline is most likely because good farmland went almost to the water's edge and roadbuilders had to be content with what was least

St Kieran's Church, Cape Clear Island, Co. Cork

inconvenient to the landowners, i.e. the smallest piece of land closest to the sea. (Having said that, though, an older inland road from Bantry to Sheep's Head can still be traced. Why this new road wasn't built over the old one is not completely clear.)

Having turned to the left at Durrus the road passes a Protestant church on the right. The church of St James was originally built in 1792 and rebuilt seven years later after the nave collapsed. It looks fairly solid now, unlike the ruined three-storey stone building that can be seen on the other side of Dunmanus Bay. This dates back to the early 19th century and was built as a wheat mill and storehouse by the local landlord. Tenant farmers brought their wheat here, in lieu of rent, to be weighed and stored and many probably continued to do so through the Famine years. Towards the end of the Famine the building was used as an orphanage for children whose parents had died in the Famine.

In the waters at the head of Dunmanus Bay can be seen the long blue lines of rope and floats that denote mussel farming. Few people make their living out of the mussels but many people are able to supplement their incomes with it.

Six miles/9 km further on, just outside Ahakista, is a memorial by the water's edge to the Air India plane disaster of 1985 when a terrorist bomb blew up a plane approaching the south-west of Ireland.

It seems unfair to villages to call Ahakista one, there being only two pubs with no shop. Having said that, there is a Japanese restaurant. The pub opposite has lovely grounds and someone here, a long time ago, had a passion for gardening. There are giant rhododendrons fronting a pine tree (*Pinus insignus*) that is the mother to all the pine trees seen west between Durrus and Sheep's Head. Enterprising farmers were led here by the village schoolmaster of Kilcrohane in the 1930s to collect the pine cones and plant the seeds after the cones softened and opened by the warmth of a turf fire.

Not that pine trees are in their multitude on this peninsula, for the terrain is bare and the deep green of the fields is due to the nitrogen-rich fertiliser poured out onto them. A fair number of the dwellings seen either side of the road are either empty or owned by English, Dutch or German folk. If the foreign owners seem reasonably smart in their appearance they are simply called 'blow-ins' but if they sport brightly coloured jumpers and drive old cars they are labelled 'hippies'.

Between Ahakista and Kilcrohane, on the water's edge, is a robust stone tower. Known as Bandon's Folly, named after the earl of Bandon, it was constructed as a Famine relief project. Standing inside it, it is obviously too small for a proper dwelling place and the three chimneys are only decorative.

Stop Just outside the village of Kilcrohane at the B&B Dunmanus sign.

A vehicle could be left here and returned to after a seaside stroll taking less than an hour.

Walk A small road leads off down to a lake by the sea.

A stroll down here, looking across to the left just before coming to a white-painted bungalow, reveals the stone wall remains of an ancient bardic seminary. This townland, *Farrannamanagh* (the field of the monks), is linked to the O'Daly clan who once ruled over this peninsula (modern O'Dalys have erected a memorial to their illustrious past outside the church in the village). The site of their bardic school, which functioned till the thirteenth century, is a short distance east of the stone remains and there is a legend that the king of Spain had his sons educated here, only to have them drown in the lake. True enough, there are two children's graves in the vicinity but they might belong to unbaptised infants refused clerical permission for a church funeral.

Having reached the water's edge it is possible to walk to the right across the stony beach and follow the shoreline for about 300 metres until a pier is reached. This is now on the other side of the village and a road leads up from the pier, past a cemetery and the remains of the original village church (fourteenth or early fifteenth century). In spring time ramsons, smelling strongly of garlic, grow abundantly on the road between the pier and the churchyard. Where this small road meets the main road again a turn to the right brings one back to the village and a few hundred metres beyond the village — on the road to Durrus — to your car parked at the B&B sign (see above).

The village of Kilcrohane consists of a church, creamery and shop, a post office and two pubs.

Link Kilcrohane to Sheep's Head, a return trip of 12 miles/20 km.

A road from Kilcrohane to the peninsula's end was originally laid by the British army, the purpose being to maintain the signal tower that once stood on a high point near Sheep's Head. The tower was blown down in a gale a few years back. For a few miles after Kilcrohane the scenery is pleasant enough and two miles out of the village one reaches a public house known locally as the White House — the last bar before Boston' as a past owner once said. Outside the pub a concreted square area still marks the community's dance hall of years long gone.

After another couple of miles there is a junction where the road to Sheep's Head carries on straight, with a right turn leading over the peninsula to the north side. The vegetation along the roads is lush, with high hedgerows and a profusion of wild flowers in the spring and summer. Often rabbits can be seen nesting in the ditch almost oblivious to the few cars that pass.

Approaching land's end the landscape becomes more and more barren, seeming to justify the name of Sheep's Head, for who or what else could possibly survive here. An answer of sorts is to be found at the end of the road for here, perched a stone's throw from the ocean, are two houses still occupied and the surrounding patch of green still farmed. There was a time when the children of this community walked daily to the abandoned school passed some miles back on the main road.

From this point there is little to do but gaze out at the Atlantic ocean or across Dunmanus Bay. Walking across the last rocky piece of headland is possible but there is nothing at the end except the wild ocean and an automated beacon. It wasn't there in 1796 to warn one of the ships of the French armada that struck a rock off this head with the loss of over 600 lives.

Link Kilcrohane to the top of the Goat's Path. 1.3 miles/2 km.

Return to Kilcrohane and turn left at the church, passing a pub on the left and heading up the Goat's Path.

With the village of Kilcrohane only half a mile behind, on the left can be seen a three-chimneyed cottage that was once boycotted after the widowed tenant was thrown out for failure to pay the rent. On the other side of the road, a few metres up, a scraggy clump of pine trees surround a rath (Celtic ring-fort). There are over 30,000 raths scattered around Ireland and this one, in the townland of Raferigeen, is a modest but typical one. From the early Bronze Age to the twelfth century raths were the homesteads of the wealthier farmers (*boáire*), a commonplace origin considering the realm of magic and superstition that surrounds them. If it wasn't for the mystical respect held for them by farmers they would have been pulled down long ago.

On the left of the road, almost opposite the first rath, is a second on the top of a low hill. This hill is a drumlin and forms one of a chain of these features around this part of Bantry Bay. The drumlins were formed when the ice of the last ice age began to melt, dropping all the material it carried in tidy piles. The whole hill is formed of debris from the ice and if it were excavated the rock layer would be somewhere on a line with the road.

The road winds gradually up the Goat's Path road and the pine trees brought from Ahakista are left behind as the landscape becomes wet and the plants change. Just at the line of the pine trees, if you look into the field at the right the marks of old potato ridges can still be seen. This area has not been inhabited since the time of the Famine and local people can point out famine graves which were laid at the sides of the fields.

Bog cotton, noticeable from its cotton puffs in early summer, grows higher up the slope as do bog asphodels, bright orange lily-like plants that carpet the area in August. Wild thyme, ling and heather are easily confused all being low-lying plants with purple flowers. If you drive up this road on a damp evening giant black slugs patrol the grass verges. In spring the lurid bright green and purple of the insectivorous butterwort grows right beside the road.

Stop at the top of the Goat's Path.

At the top of the Goat's Path, near a tacky copy of Michelangelo's Pietá (put there by relatives of a family that once left this area for America), there are tremendous views: to the south rests Dunmanus Bay with the Fastnet Rock discernible on a clear day further out to sea; to the north of Bantry Bay, Hungry Hill dominates the Beara landscape. There is room here to leave four- or two-wheeled transport and set off for a quick climb to the summit of Seefin (1,136 feet). Named after the legendary giant Finn McCool, *see* meaning 'the seat of', the smaller hill alongside is known as *Brán* after Finn's pet dog. Finn sat on top of this mountain and his feet stretched to just short of Dunmanus Bay. He literally dug his heels in anyway and created the small lake to wash his feet in. The climb to the top of Seefin is more of a stiff walk than a mountain climb. This land is commonage, land shared in common by two or three farms for grazing cattle or sheep. Few animals graze it other than rabbits. If you turn back towards Kilcrohane the patchwork of good soil stands out against the rough green of the mountains. Often in early spring the mountainsides burn with fires lit either accidently or by people wanting to clear the bracken. Fires cause enormous damage to the wildlife of the mountain. Much of the land you see at the edges of cultivation have been reclaimed by draining and fertilising.

From the top of the Goat's Path an ecological walk could be undertaken by following the suggested cycle tour (see page 25). The walk would take at least two hours to return one to this spot at the top of the Goat's Path.

Link It is 16 miles/25.7 km to Bantry from the top of the Goat's Path.

BEARA PENINSULA
INTRODUCTION

The Beara peninsula, consisting of a long spine of mountains — the Caha Range and the Slieve Miskish — with the only cultivable land between the mountain ridges and the sea, is one of Ireland's best kept secrets. Its northern shores which fall away into the Kenmare River are rarely visited and while its southern shores, which disappear in a similar fashion into Bantry Bay, are better known, the peninsula as a whole is wonderfully undeveloped and unspoiled. At its farthest tip the sea cuts off the final mountain and creates Dursey island, one of the few in Cork and Kerry that has maintained a human settlement into the present era. The scenery of the Beara is stunning and this, combined with the absence of unnecessary heritage or interpretative centres and a modest tourist infrastructure, helps to make a visit to the peninsuala a memorable experience.

Considering how far away from the rest of the world this peninsula seems it is surprising suddenly to come upon Russian being spoken in Castletownbere or discover that the proprietor of one of the town's better restaurants is German. While the native population continues to leave the peninsula in search of a supposedly better life elsewhere, other Europeans are arriving to replace them; setting up small businesses, building studios to practise their arts and crafts, establishing meditation centres, or just generally escaping from late twentieth-century life. Very few people actually make a living out of tourism, although the number of enterpreneurs catering to the summer trade is increasing.

Very recently a sustained effort has been made by a group of local people to make the area more accessible to tourists and visitors in 1994 found, for the first time, that many of the more interesting sites of historic interest were signposted, with well laid-out paths going to them. The Beara Way, a long-distance walk around the whole peninsula, complements the Kerry Way and the Dingle Way. It is 116 miles/185 km in length and largely follows green roads or secondary roads in a circuit of the peninsula, from Kenmare to Glengarriff and west to Dursey island. Enquire at the tourist offices in Castletownbere or Kenmare for maps.

Quite apart from the Beara Way, the number of walks possible on the Beara peninsula is a chief attraction, if you don't mind the occasional scramble and climbing over sheep fences. There are eight or nine walks around Glengarriff all marked out and well signposted, walks around the gardens at Dereen on the north side, any number of green roads heading up into the mountains and to isolated loughs — with the dedicated fisherman occasionally sitting by them — some exhiliarating climbs to the peaks of Sugarloaf and Hungry Hill, and island walks on Dursey and Bere.

ESSENTIAL INFORMATION

As before, the telephone number prefix need only be used if phoning from outside the prefix area.

BANKS

Glengarriff
AIB. Sub office, telephone 027–63220. June: Tuesdays 10.30 a.m. to 12.30 p.m.; July and August: same hours but Tuesday and Thursday. No cashpoint.

Castletownbere
AIB. The Square, telephone 027–70025. Regular banking hours. No cashpoint.

BICYCLE HIRE

Glengarriff
Bicycles can be hired from *Ladybird House* or *The Perrin Bar* in the village. Hire for the day or by the week.

Castletownbere
Dudley Cycles. Telephone 027–70293. Head west out of town but take the first right signposted for a stone circle. The bike hire is situated in a bungalow a few hundred yards up the road.
Supervalu Supermarket. A few cycles for hire. Opposite the pier.

Allihies
Bonnie Braes Hostel. Hires out mostly to residents so it might be worth checking first. Telephone 027–73107.

BUREAUX DE CHANGE

Glengarriff
The Spinning Wheel, Maureen's handicrafts, Eccles Hotel and *Patrick O'Shea's* foodstore all have bureau de change facilities. All currencies accepted as well as traveller's cheques.

Castletownbere
AIB bank has bureau de change facilities. Banking hours.

Allihies
John Sullivan's supermarket has bureau de change facilities.

CAR HIRE AND REPAIRS

The nearest car hire is in Bantry. See car Hire in West Cork section (page 3).

Glengarriff
Glengarriff Motor Works. Jerry O'Sullivan, near the Eccles Hotel, telephone 027–63065. Repairs and breakdowns. Petrol available here and at the *Spinning Wheel.*

Castletownbere
O'Donoghue's. Petrol station in the centre of the town. Telephone 027–70007. *O'Sullivan's Garage*, Main Street, telephone 027–70040.

Eyeries
Sullivan's. Telephone 027–74044.

CHURCH SERVICES

Adrigole
Catholic Church. One Sunday Mass, telephone 027–60006 for the time.

Allihies
Catholic Church. Mass at 8 p.m. Saturday, 9.30 a.m. or 11 a.m. on Sunday, alternating the time with the church at Cahermore 3.5 miles away.

Glengarriff
Catholic Church. Mass at 8 p.m. Saturday, 11.30 a.m. Sunday. June July and August Mass also at 8.30 a.m. Sundays.
Church of Ireland. The nearest church is at Bantry where Morning Prayer is on the first and third Sunday at 10 a.m. Holy Communion on second and fourth Sundays at 10 a.m.

Castletownbere
Church of Ireland, St Peter's. Services at 11 a.m., Sundays.
Catholic Church. Times of Masses are posted outside the church.

GARDAÍ (POLICE)

Adrigole: Telephone 027–60002.
Castletownbere: Telephone 027–70002.
Glengarriff: Telephone 027–63002.

LAUNDERETTES

The nearest laundrettes are at Bantry or Kenmare.

PHARMACIES

Castletownbere
Patrick Crowley, Main Street, telephone 027–70024.

POST OFFICES

Post Offices are open from 9 a.m. to 5.30 p.m., Monday to Friday and closed for lunch from 1 to 2 p.m. Open Saturday mornings from 9 a.m. to 1 p.m.
Glengarriff: O'Shea's foodstore, telephone 027–63001.
Castletownbere: On the main road at the west end of town, telephone 027–70011.
Adrigole: Telephone, 027–60001.
Allihies: Telephone 027–73001.
Eyeries: Telephone 027–74001.

TAXIS

Castletownbere
Bere cabs. Cametringane Woods, telephone 027–70235.

TOURIST OFFICES

Glengarriff
Tourist information is available from the office in the Eccles Hotel car park. Open July and August. Otherwise shops will give information.

Castletownbere
The tourist office is in a little shed in the town square, telephone 027–70344, open Monday to Saturday 11 a.m. to 5 p.m., closed from 1.30 to 2 p.m. for lunch.

TRAVEL AGENTS
The nearest two travel agencies are in Bantry.

WHAT TO SEE

GLENGARRIFF
The village of Glengarriff is little more than a crossroads and a string of tourist amenities. From the nineteenth century onwards it has been a noted tourist spot, primarily due to the attraction of nearby Garnish island. Famous writers like Thackeray and George Bernard Shaw stayed at the Eccles Hotel which still dominates the seafront at the side of the wide road that heads out to Bantry. In 1839 work began on blasting rock to make a road through to Kenmare, and when this was completed the village was connected with Killarney. In 1858 the Prince of Wales visited Glengarriff, following which the route from London to Glengarriff became known as the Prince of Wales Route. It cost thirty shillings (£1.50) to make the journey by ship to Cork harbour, by train to Bantry and finally by steamer round to Glengarriff.

The village lies at the most sheltered inland part of Bantry Bay. The coastline is full of little inlets and pools which make very pretty seascapes even on one of Ireland's many wet days. The area has the Blue Pool recreation ground with its pretty shoreline and swimming place. And of course there is always Garnish Island.

Glengarriff Woods
In the eighteenth century the Beara peninsula was pretty much owned by two families — the Puxleys and the Whites. Glengarriff belonged to the Whites and it owes much of the beauty of its woodlands to Richard White, the first earl of Bantry, who had the oakwoods planted between 1807 and 1810. The new trees were added to existing woodlands and complemented by rhododendrons to made good ground cover for game. The results of all this can be seen any time in May when the whole place becomes purple with the pretty but deadly plant. Later earls added Scots pines in around 1857 and larch in 1887.

In 1955 the state bought 942 acres of the woodland from descendants of the earls and began planting more pine trees as well as cedar, hemlock and beech. In 1989, 300 hectares (750 acres) of the state land became a nature reserve. There are nine excellent walks through the woods and the surrounding area, available in a leaflet from the tourist office in Glengarriff or Bantry. One of the best and least tiring walks is to Lady Bantry's Lookout, from where there are wonderful views over the whole demesne and Bantry Bay. The park also has a picnic spot with tables and can provide an enjoyable day out wandering the forests. Some of the trees here are primeval — meaning indigenous woodland that has grown on this spot since the Ice Age. At one stage an earl of Bantry had a cute Hansel and Gretel-style cottage built in the woods as a resting place, no doubt for Lady Bantry after she had looked out over her lands, but it was burned to the ground early in this century.

How to get there From Glengarriff take the Kenmare road. The entrance is signposted a few hundred yards along the road on the left and vehicles can be parked near the picnic tables.

On Garnish Island, near Glengarriff, Co. Cork

Garnish Island

The island was little more than a rock in an inlet of Bantry Bay at the turn of the last century until its owner, a man called Bryce from the north of Ireland, somehow saw its potential. Harold Pinto, an architect, was brought in to design the gardens and he used a workforce of a hundred men to bring in the materials he needed, including most of the island's topsoil, and build the pavilions, the clock tower and walled gardens. World War I put a stop to the garden's development but work resumed in 1925. It was bequeathed to the state in 1953. It is at its most colourful in May when all the varieties of rhododendron are at their best. During the summer the small island (37 acres) can become crowded if a tour bus has just deposited a group, but making the trip in the early morning usually ensures that you have the place to yourself. The walks are pleasant, with planned viewpoints of Bantry Bay and Sugarloaf mountain, and a walkway to a Martello tower which is the highest point at 135 feet/41 metres above sea level. Many of the unusual plants you notice in older gardens in the area come from cuttings furtively pinched from a day trip to Garnish.

The island is open to visitors in July and August from Monday to Saturday between 9.30 a.m. and 6.30 p.m., and Sunday from 11 a.m. to 7 p.m. Between April and June, and in September, 10 a.m. to 6.30 p.m. and 1 to 7 p.m. on Sunday. The rest of the year the hours are 10 a.m. to 4.30 p.m. and 1 to 5 p.m. on Sunday. Admission is £1.50 (children 50p).

How to get there Boats depart from the Blue Pool pier or from Ellen's rock about 1.75 miles/2.8 km further down the road to Castletownbere. The standard rate is £4 return but depending on the time of year and the number of people going this is negotiable.

Sugarloaf Mountain

Compared to Hungry Hill (see page 59) the climb to the cone-shaped summit of Sugarloaf, at 1,887 feet, is a snip. Good walking shoes are necessary, wet gear is advisable, and a drink and perhaps some food to have a picnic along the way. It takes about two hours to reach the top.

On the road to Adrigole, 8 miles/12 km from Glengarriff, look for a right turn 0.3 miles/0.5 km after a disused national school, also on the right side, and a blue Community Alert sign on the left. The unsignposted turning is just before a group of houses on the left side of the road.

After 1 mile/1.6 km park outside a new looking bungalow or a two-storey house close by with pine trees around it. The way up the mountain is behind the houses and it is only polite to ask for permission to go across the land. Climbing steadily upwards you come to an old road which should be followed for a while in order to avoid the rock faces just above. Carrying on up the shoulder of the mountain is a lot easier than going straight up. At the top there is a triangulation point and splendid views: the Caha Mountains to the north, Hungry Hill to the west, Garnish Island to the east and Bantry Bay spread out to the south.

BERE ISLAND

The island is seven miles long by three miles wide, about the same area as Manhattan. Its name comes from Irish myth. A ruler from this area, Mug Nadat, married a princess from the island. She was the goddess Etain and was able to protect Mug Nadat when he was driven out of the island to Spain. There he married again to a Spanish princess and reinvaded the area. When he succeeded in this effort he lived on the island and named it after the Spanish princess, Bere. Later, around the time that history and myth begin to merge, another ruler of Bere island was Tadg MacCéin, whose wife was carried off by Spaniards. Tadg set off after her and began a series of magical voyages which have since passed into Irish literature.

In 1796 the island was for a short time home to part of the French invasion fleet. It consisted of forty-three ships, carrying 15,000 men, with artillery and arms to distribute to the Irish people. The fleet was split up and only thirty-five ships made it to Bantry Bay, among them the *Indomitable* carrying the leading Irish Republican, Theobald Wolfe Tone. They lay off Cape Clear for some time while the commander, still handicapped by the continuing bad weather, decided what to do about the missing ships. In the middle of a fierce gale sixteen ships got as far as Bere island where they anchored. The others were blown away from shore. For two days they were trapped on the island by snowstorms before trying to get to Whiddy island near Bantry harbour. One by one their anchors broke and they were swept out to sea until only eight ships remained. They gave up all hope of an invasion and attempted to get to Clare and make a safe landing there but they were caught in a wild storm off Dursey island. They turned back for France. Two ships sank and two other were captured. The fleet spent six days almost on Irish soil but were finally beaten by the weather.

In the nineteenth century the island became a naval base for the British fleet. Its strategic importance for the imperial navy was immense. The very deep anchorage made it a valuable base in World War I; the whole Allied fleet spent some time here before the Battle of Jutland. After independence in 1921 the British continued to use the base under the terms of the peace treaty but it was finally handed back to the Irish in 1938.

Remains of the Royal Navy's presence on the island are still to be found, not least because they were used by the Irish military for training purposes long after the British departed. A signal tower and Martello fortifications still stand. Working farms are dotted around the island, there are a couple of pubs and a bed and breakfast, and a few small beaches with some sand.

How to get there The ferry leaves Castletownbere for Bere island at 9.30 a.m., 11.30 a.m., 1.30 p.m., 3.30 p.m., 5.30 p.m., 6.30 p.m. and

8.30 p.m. From Bere Island ferries return to the mainland at 8.30 a.m., 10.30 a.m.,12.30 p.m., 2.30 p.m., 4.30 p.m., 6 p.m. and 8 p.m. There are fewer services on Sundays. Adults £12 return for a car and two passengers, £3 for foot pasengers.

CASTLETOWNBERE

This is the largest town on the peninsula, the largest whitefish port in Ireland and the second largest natural harbour in the world. When its full name — Castletownberehaven — is used, it shares with Newtownmountkennedy in Co. Wicklow the honour of having the longest place name in Ireland. It mixes workaday country life with its role as a fishing port and a small tourist centre. There are growing signs of rejuvenation and the old-fashioned shops with unbuyable frocks in the window are beginning to be bought by North Europeans and converted into more profitable concerns. The town has become a part of the new dynamism that seeks to market the peninsula as a tourist destination. A nice garden shed, squashed next to the fire station in the main square, serves as a tourist office during the summer. The old schoolhouse has become an exhibition centre for local artwork and history. At regular intervals Russian fishing fleets come in to the harbour and vodka takes second place to pints of Guinness.

The town is nineteenth century in origin, blossoming as a result of the work generated by the Allihies copper mines. It also became a market centre for cattle trading and had four fairs a year for cattle, sheep and pigs. At various times the fishing fleet brought in huge hauls of mackerel or pilchards. The Famine unfortunately coincided with a serious scarcity of fish and made the suffering much worse. Quakers set up a fishing station here to scale the fish and salt them but the fishing was so poor that it closed in 1852. By 1900 the mackerel had returned, some wealth had arrived in the area and people were able to buy bigger boats and profit from their use. By this time the town was catering to the British naval base on Bere Island. Now there is a fish processing plant and a fishmeal factory; farmers have the benefits of nitrates for the grass and the tourist industry is picking up. In recent years two sea accidents have brought tragedy to the town. First a couple from Bere Island were drowned when their small boat was bringing them across from the island, and in 1994 a ferry carrying people across to the island also sank and four people died.

Hungry Hill

This is the highest point on the peninsula, at 2,251 feet/686 metres, and its dramatic dominance of the landscape is best appreciated when the mountain is viewed from the top of the Goat's Path on the Sheep's Head peninsula, above the village of Kilcrohane, on the other side of

Bantry Bay. The mountain provided Daphne du Maurier with the title of her novel *Hungry Hill* that was based on the Puxley family and the copper mines they owned at the end of this peninsula at Allihies.

The walk, or rather climb, should not be attempted if there is any likelihood of mist descending over the mountain or if the weather is likely to turn bad. Reaching the top takes somewhere between four and seven hours, depending on one's stamina and rate of walking. The descent is steep and the pathway is not very clear. Strong shoes or boots and waterproofs are required, and a compass is helpful. You should also tell someone that you intend to climb the hill. Having given these dire warnings, we should point out that many people climb the hill every year and live to tell the tale.

About 4 miles/7 km west of Adrigole there is a signpost pointing to Hungry Hill on the right. Ignore this and carry on along the road and look for a turning on the right at the gable end of a shop, just past Rosmacowan church on the other side of the road. This approach to the summit is easier than the signposted one, though a little longer.

After turning right at the shop, follow the road up to a T-junction, turn left, and continue heading northwards until the road ends at a wire sheep fence. Leave your vehicle here, bearing in mind that people are working here and need access along the road, and set off up the green road. The green road circles round in a large arc, first of all away from the mountain and then back towards it. There are turf bogs at the end of this road that are still in use and cars can go further up it. The green road is about 2 miles/3.2 km long and ascends in a very gentle slope. At the end of the road, a long time ago, the route ahead was marked with yellow paint but it has faded badly and can no longer be depended on. Just beyond the end of the road, across very boggy land, is Glas Lough which is a good spot for a rest or spot of lunch.

Keeping the water on your left, climb to the top of the ridge and continue towards the summit, heading east and following the line of the Cork-Kerry border. There is no footpath but occasionally the yellow marker dots can be seen. Keep eastwards, climbing upwards until you reach the summit. Occasionally, walls of rock are encountered which have to be negotiated and the final climb to the summit is a demanding, though ultimately rewarding, exercise.

The comprehensive views of West Cork from the top of the mountain are excellent on a fine day. The ground is surprisingly soft and there is a circle of stones on the flat summit.

Coming back down, retrace your footsteps. Don't attempt short cuts: they can be dangerous.

Dunboy Castle

Dunboy Castle was the stronghold of the O'Sullivan Beres who first came to the peninsula in the eleventh century. They found a good line in smuggling and fishing and grew wealthy from their control of the area for five centuries before the real trouble started in the first years of the seventeenth century.

In October 1601 a Spanish force arrived in Kinsale to support Gaelic chieftains in their last and decisive struggle against the English. They were defeated by the English who proceeded to turn their attention to Dunboy Castle where Donal O'Sullivan Bere (1560-1618) and the remnants of the Spanish-Irish alliance had decided to make their stand. He had built up the fortifications and had a supply of Spanish gunpowder. In May 1602, English troops under Sir George Carew marched across Co. Cork, through Bantry and along the Sheep's Head peninsula to save travelling through the difficult mountain territory of Beara. From a point on the Sheep's Head peninsula they sailed across Bantry Bay with their artillery to Bere island and surrounded Dunboy, cutting it off by sea and land. Over 140 men were besieged in the castle by 4,000 men under Carew and they held out for eleven days before finally attempting to blow up the castle rather than have it taken.

It was six months after the battle of Kinsale that Dunboy was taken and its capture put the final seal on the end of Gaelic Ireland.

The survivors assembled at Glengarriff from where Donal O'Sullivan Bere (who had managed not to be in his castle at the time of the siege) led them — in Ireland's equivalent of Mao Tse Tung's Long March — on a journey to the north where he hoped to unite with other remaining pockets of Gaelic life. They went in the midwinter of 1602-3 with little food or supplies, going via Gougane Barra and up the Coomhala Valley, crossing the Shannon by making boats out of the hides of their horses, the flesh of which they ate. By the time they reached friendly territory there were just over thirty left out of a thousand people. Here the analogy with Mao Tse Tung comes to a dismal end: Donal left for Spain where the king gave him a pension. He never returned. He was killed by his manservant in 1619 after a quarrel.

How to get there From Castletownbere follow the main coast road west for 2 miles/3.2 km. The castle is signposted on the left. Follow the path beyond Puxley Mansion to where the meagre remains of the castle can be discerned.

Puxley Mansion

Don't make the mistake of following the sign for Dunboy Castle and thinking the grand Disney-like ruin of a building constitutes the remains of a splendid Gaelic stronghold. This is Puxley's mansion, built by the Puxleys out of the profits from the copper mines. The Puxleys arrived on the peninsula in the eighteenth century. They originally settled in Galway from their native Wales. The land on the Beara had been confiscated from the O'Sullivans a century earlier but various attempts to settle had failed. The first few generations of Puxleys were more successful, mainly because they joined happily in the lucrative local pastime of smuggling in wines and silks from the continent along the little bays of the peninsula. This allowed them to get on passably well with their remaining O'Sullivan neighbours who were doing the same. Then in the 1740s one of them, Henry Puxley, foolishly decided to stamp out the smuggling. He was made a Commissioner of the Peace and given a frigate and soldiers. By this time the O'Sullivans were not only smuggling but were also encouraging French privateers to recruit men to help in the wars against England. Matters got rough, with Puxley carrying a loaded weapon wherever he went. But this didn't stop him being murdered on his way to church in 1757 by Murty Óg O'Sullivan.

The Puxleys soldiered on — as aristocrats are wont to do when they own valuable reserves of copper — and in the late nineteenth century began work on the mansion. It was designed in an eclectic manner — Elizabethan, French chateau, Italian, pseudo-Gothic — and was never finished. The Puxley family themselves spent most of their time in Cornwall. Servants kept the place going while they were away. By 1920 the IRA were training in the grounds of the castle and the immigrant English housekeepers had to be taken to safety to Bere Island. The house was burned down in 1921 by the IRA. Their excuse was that they wanted to prevent it being used as a garrison by the English but the real cause was probably local resentment against the family. The story has all the elements of a soap opera, as Daphne du Maurier realised when she began reading through the family papers and discovered she had the raw material for another novel (*Hungry Hill*).

The extensive remains of Puxley Mansion are well worth exploring and the Italian marble making up the columns that still stand, in what was designed to be the grand hallway, bear testimony to the enormous wealth that the family was able to command.

How to get there 2 miles/3.2 km west of Castletownbere, on the main road to Allihies, turn left at the sign for Dunboy Castle.

DURSEY ISLAND

The farthermost point of the Beara peninsula, Dursey Island, consists of three grass-covered hills ending in cliffs. A community still ekes out a living there based on cattle farming and some fishing. The cable car was erected in the early 1970s, and was designed to carry six passengers or one person and a cow 75 feet/22 metres up and across the 721 feet/220 metre-wide Dursey Sound. It was originally intended to be hand winched from the cabin with an alarm to call for help should the winding system jam but it was eventually electrified.

The island itself has one road through the village of Kilmichael. In 1925 this was one of the Gaeltacht areas but Irish is no longer spoken here — a curious change since there are other mainland areas that have retained the language. The road tracks across the middle of the island and ends in a pathway which goes out to a Martello tower built on the highest point of the island. There are also tracks leading around the cliffs to Dursey Head where there are great views and birds to be spotted making their way along the Irish coast in search of food. From here the three rocks off the tip of the island — the Bull, the Cow and the Calf — can be seen, with the Bull towering 300 feet out of the water. An older name for this rock is Teach Duinn. Folk legend has it that Duinn of the original Milesian invaders of Ireland was killed when his boat was wrecked on the rock and buried here. Duinn was the god of the underworld and the expression 'going to teach Duinn' meant to die. The rock became one of the entrances to the isles of enchantment in the Gaelic afterlife.

How to get there From Castletownbere follow the main coast road west to the end of the peninsula. The cable car operates Monday to Saturday between 9 and 11 a.m., 2.30 and 5 p.m. and 7 to 8 p.m. Cost is £1.

ALLIHIES

The village of Allihies, 10 miles/16 km from Castletownbere, more or less came into existence with the discovery of copper nearby, although it had been a tiny fishing village long before that. After the mines closed Allihies went into a long period of decline but has recently seen considerable growth with the increase in tourism in the area. At the beach a local group has opened a café and a New Age-style centre which collects local folklore. The copper mines give the place a derelict look but the beach is a small marvel of pretty crystalline sand and it lends considerably to the astonishing beauty of the locality when first viewed coming in along the road from Castletownbere.

Bere Island, Co. Cork

Allihies Copper Mines

The copper ore at Allihies was discovered in the early nineteenth century by a Colonel Hall of Glandore, on land belonging to the Puxley family. The story of the mines is not a happy one. The Puxleys opened up the mines in 1811 and over the next thirty years more than 88,000 tons of copper were brought up. The mines employed 1,200 people, around 400 of them miners; the rest washed the ore or operated the machinery. A whole community of Cornish miners were brought over because of their skills and experience; houses were built for them on the hill. The local people, resenting the loss of jobs that might have gone to them, boycotted the miners' families, refusing to sell food or fuel to them. Ships from Wales brought supplies to the Cornish people and took away the ore to Swansea. The expatriate community even had their own nonconformist chapel. When the writer Peter Somerville-Large visited the area in 1972 one man remained who could trace his descent from the Cornish settlers, the only Protestant in the area and the person who had dismantled the chapel roof.

At its peak of production the mines made the Puxleys an average of over £35,000 a year after they paid out some £24,000 in wages to the entire work force. Girls were paid 'thruppence ha'penny' a day, boys sixpence, and men one shilling and fourpence. The wear and tear on tools was deducted from their pay. The mines were powered by steam engines which pumped the water out and the men got to the ore by climbing hundreds of feet down rough wooden ladders.

As the price of copper fluctuated towards the end of the century, and the mines were beset by problems such as flooding from the sea, they became less profitable and finally closed in 1930, despite speculation that profitable amounts of the ore are still under the ground.

Nowadays there are grand walks around the mines and the mineshafts are still there, dangerous now but mostly fenced in. The chimney stack of one of the pumping stations remains and the mine-house entrance has been renovated and is somebody's home. The tunnels run right through the mountain and out to sea and it is said that the outwashings from the mine created the sandy strand at Ballydonegan Bay beneath.

How to get there Leave the village at the top, north, end. Go right at the first fork, ignore the next turning on the right which heads back to the village, and look for an untidy dump area on the left of the road. This is the entrance to the copper mines.

EYERIES

This photogenic little village on the northern shore of the peninsula overlooks the Atlantic. Most of its houses have been painted bright Mediterranean colours and its windows are full of flower boxes as are its tiny open spaces. A French film called *The Purple Taxi* was filmed here in 1975. A local cheese, Milleens, is made here.

How to get there From Castletownbere take the main road north. Where it meets the coast road take a left fork down to the village. From Allihies take the very scenic route north to Eyeries.

DEREEN GARDENS

Garnish is an organised set piece of sub-tropical gardening compared to the anarchic jungle growth at Dereen gardens in Lauragh. Wandering through the gardens, especially in the rain, is as close Ireland ever gets to Borneo or Malaysia. The gardens were planted about a hundred years ago by Lord Lansdowne and within a few years his gardeners spent much of their time chopping it down in an effort to control its manic growth.

The region was a part of the reward given to Sir William Petty for his part in Cromwell's wars against the Irish. The land was taken from the O'Sullivans and Petty took over and later bought up 270,000 acres. Petty had started off life as a cabin boy, rose to the position of physician to Cromwell's forces in Ireland and later secretary to the Lord Lieutenant of Ireland. He had the bright idea of mapping Ireland and was responsible for the Downe Survey which mapped out over two million acres. He did the usual range of entrepreneurial activity, opening iron mines, starting fish processing plants and introducing the seine net to the local fishermen. He is blamed for the complete eradication of the indigenous oakwoods in the area, cut down for smelting the iron ore. He did some replanting in the area but it was his descendants who created this amazing jungle of quite naturalised plants. In the eighteenth century the land was let to tenants, O'Sullivans who carried on the family tradition of smuggling by exchanging local wool for French brandy. In the mid-nineteenth century the O'Sullivan tenancy lapsed and the owners, now enobled as the Lords Lansdowne, settled there. The house was enlarged and the woodlands planted. Giant conifers from North America were introduced and are still there now, over 140 feet tall. Various descendants kept the place going and periodically chopped down the rhododendrons. The gardens are great fun to wander around. The most famous plants are the New Zealand tree ferns which seed themselves freely and are occasionally sold off to luxury hotels for their landscaping. There are also giant blue gum trees and bamboo groves. One tree, the *Cryptomeria Japonica Elegans*, grows across the rock garden walk and has to be supported. It has a girth of 10 feet/3 metres and is 60 feet/18 metres high.

The gardens have a cafeteria and a good map which explains and identifies some of the plants which are numbered.

How to get there Dereen House and Gardens are situated in Kilmakilloge harbour at the north end of the Healy Pass. They are well signposted. Admission is £2.

THE HEALY PASS
The standard recommendation for this scenic 7 mile/11 km drive is to do the journey from north to south, and on a fine day, so that the views of Bantry Bay can be appreciated. But fine views are ten a penny on this peninsula and an equally stunning journey can be made in either direction in the rain when thousands of cascades of water pour out over every rock ledge.

At the top of the pass where Kerry and Cork meet there is a flat rock. In the last century, so the story goes, if a woman from Kerry married a Cork man from the peninsula and then died childless the custom was to return her to Kerry for burial. The two families would meet at the top of the pass and the Cork men would push the coffin towards the Kerry men believing that the push would take the bad luck to Kerry along with the coffin. Not wanting the bad luck the Kerry men would shove back. Fights often broke out over who would shove furthest! The rock is situated behind the shop at the top of the pass in an open gulley known as the Eisc.

The road was opened in 1931, named after the nationalist Tim Healy who was born in Bantry in 1855. He rose to become the first Governor-General of the Irish Free State and as a retirement present he asked for improvements to be made to the existing bridle-path from Adrigole to Lauragh.

ARCHAEOLOGICAL SITES
The Beara is scattered with the leftovers of previous civilisations. They are mostly unmarked and difficult to locate but some of them are worth the scramble and are in the process of being signposted. One of the best is a stone circle at *Derrintaggart*, signposted from the road going north at the west end of Castletownbere. It is about 0.6 mile/1 km along this road. There were once fifteen stones here but only twelve remain, three having fallen.

Further along the same road a raised ring fort is signposted from the road. Why exactly it is raised in this manner is not quite clear but what is typical here is the way that generations of farmers have made no effort to clear what must have been an irritation. The present farmer plants the field around the fort.

On the left side of the road from Castletownbere to Allihies, at the junction where the road goes left for Dursey and straight on for Allihies, there is a wedge grave formed by huge overlapping slabs of rock. The site is signposted and is only a short walk across a field.

Just outside Eyeries, on the road to Ardgroom in the townland of Ballycrovane, the tallest ogham stone in Ireland is located in a farmer's field. It is near the turning for the scenic coast route to Ardgroom. The stone is over seventeen feet high and bears the inscription: 'Of the son of Deich descendant of Torainn'.

CYCLE TOURS

The best available map for these tours is the half inch to one mile West Cork Ordance Survey map No 24.

GLENGARRIFF TO BANTRY AND BACK
A round trip of 21 miles/34 km
Depart from the Eccles Hotel at the east end of Glengarriff and head out along the broad N71 road. One can stay on this road all the way to Bantry, taking a signposted sharp right turn at Ballylickey where the road ahead leads to Gougane Barra and Macroom. It is possible, though, to take a minor loop road by way of Coomhola bridge before rejoining the N71. To do this take the first turning on the left after leaving Glengarriff, just after an old school building on the left. This road leads to a T-junction at Coomhola bridge and a right turn here follows the Coomhola river back down to the N71.

From Ballylickey it is a smooth road all the way into Bantry, passing various shops and a garden centre before entering the town along a narrow street that leads to the large town square.

GLENGARRIFF TO TRAFRASK BRIDGE AND BACK
A round trip of 16 miles/26 km
Take the Castletownbere road from Glengarriff with splendid mountain scenery to the right, Sugarloaf mountain ahead, and small lakes appearing on the left after 2.4 miles/4 km. Shortly after this the vista of Bantry Bay opens up and the road passes a turning on the left for Seal harbour. After 4 miles/6.5 km from Glengarriff the road begins to climb and after another 1 mile/1.6 km look for an unmarked turning on the right. It is 0.3 miles/0.7 km after a disused national school also on the right side.

Follow the minor road as it twists and turns through rocky land surrounded by patches of bog and gorse. There is little chance of encountering any traffic on this road apart from local farmers whose dwellings are passed on the way. After 3 miles/5 km this loop road comes to an end at a T-junction at Trafrask bridge. Turn left here for the return journey to Glengarriff along the main road.

CASTLETOWNBERE TO THE WEST AND BACK
A round trip of 12 miles/20 km

This is a short and very comfortable cycle that is easily extended to Allihies or the cable point for Dursey Island.

At the Allihies end of Castletownbere take the right turning that points to a stone circle and then to Dudley Cycles. It is a narrow but tarred road and after passing the stone circle open moorland opens up around you. After 2.7 miles/4.4 km there is a sign to a ring fort on the right side of the road. The Beara Way periodically joins this road and the walk signs will be seen along the route. About 1 mile/1.6 km after the ring fort the ruins of old dwellings are passed before the loop road rejoins the main R575 road. Turn left here to cycle back to Castletownbere.

CASTLETOWNBERE TO DURSEY ISLAND
A round trip of 27 miles/44 km

The first leg of this tour ends at the point where the cable car leaves for Dursey Island. Bikes are not normally allowed on the cable car.

Leave Castletownbere heading west along the R575, passing the turning on the left for Dunboy Castle and the Puxley Mansion. The road climbs to 600 feet before dropping down to a junction, 9 miles/14 km from Castletownbere, where the road divides for Allihies and Dursey. Take the road to the left for Dursey, stopping perhaps to visit the signposted wedge tomb at the side of the road. From here it is 5 miles/8 km to the cable car point. Retrace the route back to Castletownbere.

An alternative, but longer, route back to Castletownbere would involve cycling back to the junction where the wedge tomb is and, instead of turning right, going left for a superb approach to the village of Allihies. From here the road could be followed north around the peninsula towards Eyeries before turning right, signposted for Castletownbere by way of a small mountain pass. If this alternative was taken the whole return length of the tour would be doubled.

FROM AND TO CASTLETOWNBERE VIA LAURAGH AND THE HEALY PASS
A return trip of 52 miles/85 km

This tour's distance is not as demanding as it might seem because most of the route from Lauragh to Adrigole is downhill on the Healy Pass. Very little cycling is needed here, just a steady hand on a very reliable set of brakes.

Head north out of Castletownbere on the R571 and at the top of the pass, near Eyeries, turn right for Ardgroom. It is only about 4 miles/ 6 km from Eyeries to Ardgroom but if cycling down to Eyeries village itself be sure to get back on to the main road. Otherwise you'll end up on a coastal route that adds another ten miles to the journey. If time allows, though, this coastal route is very attractive and little traffic is encountered along its many bends and turns.

From Ardgroom stay on the main road to Lauragh where, just after the turning on the left for Derreen Gardens, the road turns right for the spectacular Healy Pass. After a short way uphill the road begins to descend in a series of vertiginous horseshoe bends all the way to Adrigole. At Adrigole turn right for the relaxing cycle back to Castletownbere.

DAYTIME ACTIVITIES AND SPORTS

BEACH GUIDE

The Beara has two comfortably sandy beaches which are never crowded. The rest of the shoreline is mostly shingly or rocky.

Ballydonegan at Allihies

When approaching the village of Allihies from Castletownbere the beach is unmissable. It has toilets close by and there is a small coffee shop. Wheelchair access is possible but would be easier if some bright spark hadn't stuck a bollard right in the middle of a pathway which motorbikes can get round easily but which defeat a wheelchair. The strand is supposed to have been caused by the outwashings of the coper mines but this is debateable, considering that the copper mines stopped years ago and the beach is still there looking very natural and very permanent.

How to get there The beach is at the south end of the village, easily seen if coming into Allihies from the main road from Castletownbere.

Garnish Strand

There are toilets and wheelchair access is possible. No other facilities but the fine white sand is very attractive.

How to get there. Follow the road from Allihies to the cable car point and turn right on to the road to Garnish Point. This brings you to the beach, known locally as the White Strand.

There are also several tiny sandy strands on Bere Island.

FISHING

Game Fishing

There is plenty of game fishing on the peninsula in the many tiny loughs and rivers. Sea trout, salmon and brown trout are available. Starting from Glengarriff and moving west and then back along the north side of the peninsula the recognised fishing spots are as follows:

The *Glengarriff River* which enters the sea at Glengarriff. It gets a run of grilse and sea trout. The open season on salmon runs from 17 March to 30 September; the best fishing begins about late June. Permission to fish from Mr Bernard Harrington, The Maple Leaf, Glengarriff, telephone 027–63021. Two Loughs, *Lower* and *Upper Loughs Avaul* are both situated along the main road to Castletownbere at 2 miles/3 km and 2.5 miles/4 km respectively. The lower lough is a clear water mountain lough, 8.5 acres with excellent shoreline angling. Large brown trout have been caught and the lough is stocked with rainbow trout. The best catches have been with worms and a float. There are also eel and rudd. The upper lough is 10 acres with many good angling sites around its shores. Same stocks as the lower lough. Fly fishing is best from a boat. Permits from Mr Bernard Harrington — see above. He can tell you about boats.

The *Caha mountain loughs* are pretty inaccessible but hold brown trout. There are about twenty loughs in all, scattered among the mountains. A quick look at a map will show that a few have turf roads going up to them while others require a serious hike. The *Adrigole River* is less difficult to get to, running into the sea at Adrigole harbour. It gets a run of grilse and sea trout in June. Open season for salmon is 17 March to 30 September and for sea trout is 17 March to 12 October. Permission from Mr John O'Hare, Main Street, Kenmare.

Glen Lough is a tiny lough, 2 miles/3.2 km north-east of Adrigole. A road, green towards the end, goes up to it from east of Adrigole, signposted for Mass Mountain. It is drained by the Adrigole river and gets some sea trout and salmon as well as brown trout. Enquiries to Mr John O'Hare — see above.

Near Allihies, on the Beara peninsula in West Cork

On the north side of the peninsula is *Glenbeg Lough*, just west of Ardgroom. Look for a road going south which goes along the lake shore. Small brown trout. Permission from Michael Harrington, Churchgate, Castletownbere, telephone 027–70011. Also accessible from the north coast road is *Lough Fadda* (not to be confused with the Lough Fadda near Sneem). Look for a north turning about 0.5 mile/1 km west of the turning for Glenbeg. Brown trout here too. Permission from Michael Harrington — see above. *Derryvegal Lake* is on the same road as Lough Fadda, has the wildest location imaginable and holds brown trout and is stocked with rainbow trout. It is only fifteen acres but has good shallow places along its shores about 60% of which are fishable. Permits from Michael Harrington — see above and a boat is available from Joe O'Sullivan, The Bungalow, Ardgroom.

Glanmore Lough is set in a valley south of Lauragh. Look for a road going south from the main road a few hundred yards west of the Healy Pass. The lough and the river which drains it get a run of salmon and grilse in spring and June respectively. Sea trout in August. Permission and information about the boat from Craigie's Hotel, Castletownbere, telephone 027–70379.

The *Cloonee* system consists of four loughs and the connecting river system south west of Kenmare. The whole system is accessible from north-east of Tuosist. Brown trout, sea trout in late July and occasional grilse. For the two Clonee lakes permission should be sought from Mrs Mary O'Shea at Lake House, Cloonee. For the two higher loughs, Uragh and Inchiquin, permission is from Mr John O'Hare, Main Street, Kenmare or the Estate Office, The Square, Kenmare. On Inchiquin most of the fishing is by boat. The estate office will have details.

Coarse Fishing
There is no coarse fishing on the peninsula.

Sea Fishing and Shore Fishing
Shore fishing is plentiful all around the coastline. You should ask locally about good places. Castletownbere has two fishing tackle shops, *O'Sullivan's* and *Moriarty's,* both in Main Street. The recognised spots are as follows:
Zetland pier about 3 miles/4.8 km west of Glengarriff, a mile west of the Loughs Avaul.
Shot Head is fairly inaccessible but recommended. It is another four miles beyond the two loughs. Look for a road junction where a road goes north just after an old national school and a community alert sign. A second road goes south almost immediately after. This takes you down to a pier from where you can hike your way to Shot Head. Beyond Adrigole several minor roads lead down to the sea and all are good spots for fishing. They are *Bank Harbour, Coarrid Point,* and *D.O.D pier.* At this last spot bottom fishing can produce thornback ray and dogfish. Mullet are possible using a float.
Castletownbere harbour is another good spot for shore fishing while further west at *Fair Head* there are good places for wrasse, pollock and mackerel. *Matthew's Rocks* is another good spot. Take the road west from Castletownbere and at the Y-junction take the left fork for Dursey and look for a lane going off to the shore. *Dursey Sound, Dursey Rocks* and *Ballydonegan Strand* provide some good spots. Wrasse, pollock and mackerel can be taken from the rocks while the beach provides bass and flatfish. Dogfish can be caught from the pier.

For deep sea fishing there is one approved boat, the *River Queen,* which can be hired from Michael O'Sullivan, Kenmare Holiday Cottages, Tuosist, Kenmare, telephone 066–26323. There are also a number of people operating out of Castletownbere. Enquiries could be made from the fishing tackle shops there.

AQUA SPORTS

Rooster Tail Ski Sports. Kilmakilloge Harbour, telephone 064–84282. Tube rides, kneeboarding, waterskiing. Lessons in all these activities at £8 per session. Wetsuits for all ages, special training equipment. Open every day from May to October, from 10 a.m. to 9 p.m.
The Wheel Inn. On the main road about 2 miles/3 km east of Castletownbere. Well signposted. Telephone 027–70090. Jet skis water skiing, kneeboarding, speedboat rides. 6–9 p.m. Tuesday, Wednesday, Thursday.
Argonauts. Canoes and curraghs for hire. £4 per session at Tralahan, Castletownbere. Sundays only 12 noon–6 p.m.

GOLF

Castletownbere Golf Club. 18 holes, telephone 027–70167.
Glengarriff Golf Club. 1.3 miles/2 km east of Glengarriff on the road to Bantry. 9 holes, telephone 027–63150.

HORSE RIDING

Dunboy Riding Stables. Dunboy Castle, telephone 027–70044. Trekking around Dunboy Castle and lessons.
Allihies Riding Centre. Lessons and trekking, telephone 027–70340.

SWIMMING

Sea bathing is possible from the two sandy beaches listed above. The Blue Pool at Glengarriff has a diving board and steps and is safe for children. Freshwater swimming is possible in the river at the Pouleen picnic site in Glengarriff Woods.

OTHER ACTIVITIES

Beara Sheepdogs. On the main road, 2.5 miles/4 km east of Castletownbere, telephone 027–70287. Working sheepdog demonstrations on a sheep farm. Border collies have appeared on television and won competitions. Demonstrations at 11 a.m., 2 p.m., 3.30 p.m. Closed Sundays. Admission £2 (children £1).

BOAT TRIPS

Neallie O'Sullivan. Telephone 027–73072. Boat trips from Ballydonegan Strand around the local area in a twenty-foot boat. Fishing is possible from the boat.

WALKS AND TOURS

Guided evening walks from *Bonnie Brae's Hostel* at Allihies, telephone 027–60132. Wednesday and Friday. Two-hour walks.
A person called Dessie does guided mountain walks from Allihies, telephone 027–73146.

EVENING ACTIVITIES

Evening activities in the Beara peninsula are pretty well restricted to the pubs and pub music. You should check in shop windows, especially in Castletownbere, for forthcoming events. The following pubs may have music on, especially at weekends.

Glengarriff
The *Blue Loo* and the *Singing Lounge* have music regularly in season.

Castletownbere
El Bar del Marinero in the Square may not have music but if there is a trawler fleet in town there will be lots of atmosphere because this is where the fishermen tend to congregate.
Lynch's in Main Street is another good pub with modern furniture but an old-fashioned style.
The Wheel Inn is not everybody's cup of tea with its cowhide furniture and noisy disco but it can boast a genuine holiday atmosphere and a good evening's entertainment with well-known ballad singers from time to time.
There are several other bars in town so you might like to try a pub crawl looking for the one that suits you best.

Ardgroom
The Holly Bar. Music most nights in summer and at weekends off season.

Eyeries
Causkey's Bar. Traditional and old time music every Sunday night all year. Bar food.

WHERE TO STAY

HOTELS

The following hotels are categorised here according to cost. A price of over £45 per person sharing is categorised under **high**, between £35 and £45 **moderate,** between £25 and £35 **budget** and £15–25 **economy.** Of course there are much cheaper places to stay but these would be B&Bs and guesthouses or hostels.

Castletownbere

Craigie's Cametringane House, Castletownbere, telephone 027–70379, fax 027–70506. TV, gardens, games room, tennis. Open all year. AE, DE, VB. Two Star. Rating: budget.

Glengarriff

Eccles Hotel, Glengarriff, telephone 027–63003, fax 027–63319. Faded Victorian elegance with disco. TV, gardens, games room, price reductions for children. Open all year. AM, AE, DE, VB. Two Star. Rating: budget.

Mountain View Hotel, Glengarriff, telephone 027–63103, fax 027–63034. TV, gardens, dog friendly, child reductions. Open all year. AM, AE, DE, VB. One Star. Rating: economy.

Casey's, Glengarriff telephone/fax 027–63010. AE, DE, VB. One Star. Rating: budget.

BED AND BREAKFAST

In the other sections B&Bs have not been listed because they are so easy to find, but they are a little rarer on Beara so details of some B&B accommodation follows. Prices are fairly standard.

Glen Ocean House, Glenera, Garnish, Allihies, telephone 027–73019.
Realt-na-Mara, Castletownbere, telephone 027–70101. Open all year, en suite rooms.
Mrs Ellen Gowan, Rodeen, Castletownbere, telephone 027–70158. En suite rooms, open all year.
Mrs Shanahan, Lugano House, Castletownbere, telephone 027–70116.
Mrs Harrington, Castletown House, Bank Place, Castletownbere, telephone 027–70252. One en suite room.
Mrs Murphy, Bay View House, West End, Castletownbere, telephone 027–70099.
Mrs Coghlan-Mason, Cussane House, Eyeries, telephone 027–74178. Open April to September, One en suite room.
Mrs O'Sullivan, Shamrock, Strand Road, Eyeries, telephone 027–74058. Open March to October.

SELF–CATERING ACCOMMODATION

There are no self-catering holiday complexes on the Beara Peninsula but there are some individual houses. They are listed below. The tourist office in Cork does a booking service if you ring them and tell them what you are looking for and where. Make the booking early since self-catering places fill up fast. They are particularly good value in early summer and spring before the season really gets under way.

Castletownbere Contact Sean O'Sullivan, Teer-na-Hillane, Castletownbere, telephone 027–70108. Two cottages, three bedrooms, all mod cons.
Bere Island Contact Dermot O'Sullivan, Harbour View, telephone 027–75011. Four-bedroomed house, all mod cons. Boat for hire.
Eyeries Contact Mrs O'Driscoll, Kilcatherine, telephone 027–74143. Three-bedroomed house. All mod cons.
Glengarriff Contact Mrs Eleanor O'Regan, Cashelfan, Durrus, telephone 027–61175, who has several houses at Glengarriff to hire, including one eleven-bedroomed mansion.

HOSTELS

Hostels usually offer dormitory accommodation for about £5 per bed per night. They often have family rooms and double rooms. All have kitchens and many have laundry rooms, free transport to the nearest point of departure and lots of practical advice on what to see and do. The one listed below is the only one registered with Bord Failte.

Bonnie Braes Hostel, Allihies, telephone 027–73107. Mountain bikes for hire at this town house in the village.

CARAVAN AND CAMPING SITES

Dowling's Caravan and Camping Park, Glengarrifff, telephone 027–63140. 1.2 miles/2 km west of Glengarriff on the road to Castletownbere. Shop on site, children's playground, launderette, TV room, electricity.
O'Shea's Caravan and Camping Site, Glengarriff, telephone 027–63140. Opposite Dowling's on the road to Castletownbere. Smaller site, with TV room, playroom and playground, tennis courts.

WHERE TO EAT

Restaurants are scarce on the Beara although you need not worry about going hungry. The restaurants are rated economy, budget, moderate and high.

Castletownbere

The Old Cottage Restaurant, telephone 027–70430. East of the town. Challenging menu of seafood, lamb and steaks. Well cooked vegetables, good wine list. Fresh flowers and pretty crockery. Reservations recommended. Open 12.30 to 2 p.m. and 6 to 9 p.m. Dinner only in off season. AM, VB. Rating: high.
Stephanie's, New restaurant decorated in simple but elegant style, stone floor. Seafood dishes. For reservations telephone 027–70639. Rating: high.
Jack Patrick's. Unpretentious diner doing burgers, chops etc. Children's menu. Vegetarian salad. Rating: economy.
Old Bank Seafood Restaurant. Small menu of locally caught seafood. Vegetarian dishes on request. Open 6 p.m. to 10.30 p.m. AM, AE, DE, VB. Closed November to February. Rating: moderate.
Old Bank Coffee Shop. Under the same management as the Old Bank Seafood Restaurant, this small coffee shop is next door opening onto the pavement and seats outside. Cakes and sandwiches.
Niki's. Restaurant in an old pharmacy which retains the old chemist's drawers, still labelled so that you can try to work out what the abbreviations mean while you're waiting for your food. Breakfast served from 10 a.m. to 12. Open 10 a.m. to 3 p.m., 7 p.m. to 9.30 p.m. Seafood. Interesting specials like swordfish or silver bream. Telephone 027–70625. AM, AE, DE, VB. Rating: moderate.
The Berehaven Inn. Restaurant and barfood. Evening meals from 6.30 to 9.30 p.m. and Sunday lunch. AM, VB. Rating: moderate.
Cronin's Hideaway. Café type food and takeaways, evenings only. Sunday lunch. Rating: economy.
Murphy's Restaurant. Diner type food but lots of it and good quality. Open 9 a.m. to 9 p.m. Monday to Saturday. Closes earlier out of season. Customers are welcome to bring their own wine. Children's menu, breakfast. Rating: economy.

Allihies

Cluin. At the copper mines end of town. Light lunches made from local produce, dinners seafood or lamb and a vegetarian choice. Great views of the copper mines. Late night pizzas. Open all day till late from June to September. Bring your own wine. Rating: budget.

Atlantic Seafood Restaurant. Fresh seafood served in a whitewashed town house in the village. Rating: moderate
O'Neill's Pub. Bar food, cold plates, sandwiches tea and coffee served all day.
The Lighthouse Bar. Bar food. Teas and sandwiches.
The Oak Bar. Homemade soup, sandwiches and snacks.
Bonnie Braes Hostel. Vegetarian meals.
Windy Point House. Close to the Dursey Island cable car. Snacks and drinks available, outdoor tables looking over the sea.

Eyeries
O'Neill's Bar. Pub food: burgers, sausage and chips, sandwiches.
Causkey's Bar. Pub food served all day.

Ardgroom
The Holly Bar. Bar food in an interesting location: a holly tree growing in the middle of the bar. Soup and sandwiches.

Glengarriff
The Eccles Hotel. A set lunch and dinner and good economical bar food which runs from open sandwiches to mixed grills and specials. The restaurant is only open for dinner and Sunday lunch. Vast dining room built in 1860. Nice views out of the windows but avoid Saturdays if there is a wedding party on. Telephone 027–63003. AM, AE, DE, VB. Rating: moderate.
Blue Pool House Hotel. Bar food and restaurant. Limited but interesting menu, daily specials. Rating: moderate.
The Spinning Wheel. Café type restaurant above gift shop.
Perrin Bar. Functional café with large menu, lunch specials. Rating: economy.

SHOPPING FOR GIFTS AND SOUVENIRS

Glengarriff
O'Shea's. Woollens, souvenir items and gifts.
The Spinning Wheel. Tourist paraphernalia.
Maureen's Handcrafts. Another teatowel and jumper type shop.
The Black Cat. Interesting walking sticks made from local wood and animal horns.

Look out for a person selling quite pretty pottery on the wall in the middle of the village.

Castletownbere
The Shell, Main Street. Jumpers and ceramics, candles, books, cards. 10 a.m. to 6 p.m. Monday to Saturday.

Adrigole
Rockfield Pottery. Some nice pots and a coffee shop. About halfway between Glengarriff and Adrigole.

Allihies
Allihies Folklore Group. Small coffee shop by the beach, selling pewter pendants, knitted items and jewellery all made in Allihies. Also some interesting clocks made by Cormac Boydell.
The Great Barrington Pottery. Just outside of the village on the coast road going north. Very pretty but expensive pieces of pottery made by Richard Bennet. Shop is open most afternoons and some morning but times are flexible.
Neallie O'Sullivan's Craft Shop. In the main street of village. Crafts and paintings by the owner.
Cormac Boydell. Coomeen, outside Allihies on the road to Eyeries. Ceramic artist. Open July and August, Monday to Friday, 12 noon to 6 p.m.
Allihies Globe Artichoke Co-operative. Pick your own artichokes. Bring a knife. Beyond Allihies on the coast road to Eyeries and signposted from the main road.

Eyeries

Dixons Original Knitwear. Open seven days a week for pottery, glass, silver, knitwear, jewellery and antiques such as tools and lamps.
Milleens Cheese. Cheeses can be bought direct from the dairy but phone first, telephone 027–74079.

CHILDREN'S ACTIVITIES

- Visit the Blue Pool amenity area and swimming place in Glengarriff.
- Swimming and clambering around the rocks on the shingle beach at Seal Harbour, signposted 3.4 miles/5.6 km west of Glengarriff on the left side of the road to Castletownbere, or at Zetland Pier which is 1.5 miles/2.4 km further on.
- A day at the beach at Ballydonegan Strand
- Climb Sugarloaf mountain but take your parents with you.
- Learn to canoe, water ski or go horseriding (see above).
- Visit Dereen Gardens and imagine you are in the jungle.
- Go fishing.
- Take a ride in a jaunting car from Allihies Riding Centre.
- Have a cable car ride to Dursey island.
- Visit Lehanemore Community Centre at Allihies and have a game of ball alley.
- Take a boat trip from Ballydonegan Strand.
- Take your parents up to the copper mines and, keeping away from the unfenced mine entrances, look for some interesting stones.
- Hire a bike and go for a cycle.
- Take a boat to Garnish Island and look for seals from the boat.

RAINY DAY ACTIVITIES

- Have a game of pool. There are bars with pool tables in Glengarriff (The Singing Lounge), Allihies (John Terry's) and east of Castletownbere (The Wheel Inn).
- Sit in the bar at the Eccles Hotel in Glengariff and soak up the atmosphere.
- Put on wet gear and go for a walk.
- If it is a Saturday evening visit the Buddhist centre between Castletownbere and Allihies, situated by the Garranes hostel that is signposted from the main road, and meditate.

ECOTOUR

This tour begins at Bantry, from where the last ecotour ended.

GEOLOGICAL INTRODUCTION

The Beara peninsula, like those to the north and the south of it, was formed by massive earth movements 300 million years ago. The effects on Ireland went far beyond the south-west of the country but the result of the convulsions can be seen most dramatically in the ridges thrown up along an east-west axis and making the mountain ranges of West Cork and Kerry. A kind of layer cake was made with hard red sandstone as the bottom layer and limestone and coal deposits on the top. These last two, being porous and easily eroded, disappeared over the millennia, remaining only in lowland places where they were sheltered from the elements. So the whole region, including the Beara, is a patchwork of limestone patches in the lowlands — Kenmare and the bays of Tralee and Bantry — and bare red sandstone on the mountains above. In Killarney this patchwork reaches its most interesting state with the limestone and sandstone existing side by side around Muckross Lake and Lough Leane.

Just to complicate matters there are areas of volcanic rock at the ends of some of the peninsulas — and the Beara is one of them — dating back to a time before the big shake-up when there were active volcanoes in the region. The present bays represent the drowned valleys of the mountain ranges and the offshore islands such as Dursey are the continuation of the lines of hills. Then, some 15,000 years ago, ice sheets descended on the area, smoothing the tops of the mountains and covering the lowlands with the debris they chipped off the mountains. They also created a very characteristic piece of Irish geography, the many coombs that cover the mountainsides. These are hollowed out bowls left by the glaciers. Their frequency in Ireland is evidenced by the fact that the geographical term coomb comes from the gaelic word *cúm*. In some places the mountain tops stood above the ice sheets in configurations called nunataks and these can be seen in the Caha range.

If Beara lacks the size and variety of the other peninsulas it manages to encapsulate in a small and easily accessible space many of the major events of Irish geological history.

A view of the Caha Mountains

Link Bantry to Glengarriff. 10 miles/17 km.

From Bantry the road to Glengarriff passes at first by the side of some houses which resemble the suburbs of a small English town, except that B&B signs are ubiquitous. They share the front gardens with exotic plants like the palm trees that grow so well in this climate, and the even more exotic garden gnomes and bambis that litter the front lawns.

Also along this first stretch of road, before reaching Ballylickey, there are grand old nineteenth-century houses tucked away on the right side that are now hotels and restaurants. After following the road around to the left at Ballylickey, where the right turn leads to Gougane Barra and Macroom, it is easy to miss the shell of Reenadesert House. The ruins sit crumbling away on the right side of the road behind some trees, covered in moss and with part of the roof still on. The house was built in the early seventeenth century by O'Sullivans, descendants of the protagonists of the Dunboy siege and the long march to the north that followed it. The house shows characteristic features of the times in which it was built: thick walls, tiny windows, and protruding corbels which could be used in defence. As late as the seventeenth century people of any prosperity in Beara still built houses that could be defended from an armed attack.

Stop at a car park area with stone picnic tables, on the left of the road 7 miles/11 km from Bantry.

From this point Whiddy Island comes into view and the now defunct oil storage tanks can be clearly seen. Bantry Bay is one of the deepest bays in the world and was used to bring in huge tankers which deposited their cargoes of oil on Whiddy. The project was developed by Gulf Oil and during the period of its successful operation it brought a great deal of wealth to Bantry. On occasion even some local farmers were known to complete their milking extra early in the morning so that they could then do a day's extra work on the island. The south shore of Bantry Bay has always been an inhospitable place but while Gulf Oil was paying wages a number of bungalows were built along there by the people drawn to the area for work. Then in 1979 there was an accident when a ship caught fire and fifty-one men were killed in the ensuing explosion. This was the end of Gulf Oil's operations and the prosperity soon fell away. The tanks are used now as an emergency fuel store.

Link from the car park to Glengarriff.

As the road carries on towards Glengarriff even the domestic scenery becomes wilder, with gardens now laid out around outcrops of rock turned into rockeries by their owners. The cultivated plants have moved out of their enclosures and into the wild — buddleia fills the hedgerows and bright orange montbretia sits on the banks. Fuchsia is commonplace. Ragwort, poisonous to cattle and a controllable plant, survives here at the roadside where nobody bothers pulling it up.

Sugarloaf mountain with its distinctive cone shape can be clearly seen in the distance. On the right, as the road continues, a huge wall of blue and grey rock has been exposed by a road widening scheme and it looks almost as if panels of alternating colours have been laid there. More examples of strange flora which has made itself at home in this climate can be seen — New Zealand flax which is widespread around these coasts and gunnera from South America looking like giant prickly rhubarb. Gunnera enjoys the wet climate and mild winters and grows well in the damp soil of the area.

Drive through the village of Glengarriff and at the far side take the right turn for Kenmare at the Y-junction. A short way along this road look for a sign pointing the way into Glengarriff Woods on the left.

Stop at the car park in Glegarriff Woods.

Unlike the other lowland areas in West Cork and Kerry, Glengarriff Woods is in an area of old red sandstone and the soil here is a mixture of acid brown earth, shallow peat and blanket bog. This is the most southerly point where the strange group of plants called the Lusitanian flora survives. Easily visible in the woods are St Patrick's cabbage, *Arbutus Unedo* which is better known as the strawberry tree, Irish spurge and kidney saxifrage. The spurge is highly noticeable in early summer when its bright green bushy leaves and awful yellow flower heads stand out. The valley is sheltered by the Caha mountains to the north while the effect of the Gulf Stream keeps temperatures above freezing in winter.

As late as the 1700s large tracts of the peninsula were covered in woodlands, chiefly oak forests which hid eagles and wolves. The woods were cut down to fuel smelting plants for the copper and iron ore that was found here. The ores made the fortunes of the landlord families with which they built their grand houses.

Glengarriff Woods has one of the few tracts of oak forest left. Few trees are the aboriginal species but are sessile oak planted by the White family in the early nineteenth century.

Walk from the car park back towards the iron bridge over the river, signposted for Lady Bantry's Lookout. Follow these signs.

Over the river you find yourself in oak woods, with the trees forming a sheltering canopy over the plants and helping to keep the already moist atmosphere even damper. The effects of this can be seen in the multitude of mosses and ferns which grow everywhere, even on the branches of the trees where they are living as epiphytes, not feeding from the branch that they sit on but using it as an anchorage and taking the nutrients that they need from the air. In this way an already crowded environment is extended. In spring before the oak grows its new leaves the forest floor is smothered in flowering woodland plants, all of which have adapted to do most of their reproduction while they can gain some access to the light. Bluebells, celandines, wood anemones, St Patrick's cabbage and several other similar saxifrage plants will all be here and flowering at this time. Later in the summer honeysuckle somehow manages to find enough light to grow under the trees, as does ivy, and the lower layers of the wood are filled with holly trees.

The holly is an evergreen plant and so makes use of the oak's season of bare branches to make its food. On the forest floor will be oak seedlings most of which will never make it to any size but their presence tells of the healthiness of this part of the wood. Follow the path up to the lookout point where Lady Bantry must have spent much time admiring all that she surveyed. From here the whole valley can be seen laid out with an obvious demarcation between the older oak woods and the newer conifers. In May it is easy to see the extent of the infestation by the rhododendron which stands out in great purple swathes throughout the forest, taking over rocky ledges as well as forming a dense under layer.

The forest supports a huge amount of wildlife; it is thought that oaks alone support 400 different plants and animals. Trees in the forest include birch and rowan — often planted at the outskirts of the conifer plantations to soften the ugliness of them — the strawberry tree, willow and alder in the damper spots. There are a few yew trees and Scots pines which were once indigenous plants but now are all introduced. Beech has also been planted in small numbers. The fauna is less obvious but just as numerous. There are seven species of bats in the woods that feed on the many insects the wood supports. Larger and shyer mammals are stoats, red squirrels and otters, foxes and badgers. Their prey are the smaller animals of the woodlands such as rabbits and bank voles. Jays are common and quite tame while the dipper is less easy to spot. These birds spend most of their time on stones in the streams looking for caddisfly larvae or other small creatures. When they see one they dip down into the water, hence their name. Wood pigeons are abundant and provide the evening meal for the peregrine falcon or long-eared owl. Ireland's largest grasshopper also lives here in the bog areas behind the conifer plantations and of course the Kerry slug has a home here too.

Link Glengarriff to Castletownbere.

Leave the woods and return to the Y-junction where a right turn leads onto the road to Castletownbere.

The road sets off into the Beara peninsula in the way it means to carry on, winding around rocks and past loughs while the bungalows get scarcer and the gardens rockier and wilder. Purple loosestrife grows here in great clumps in July and August and huge pink umbellifers grow beside them. Sugarloaf mountain has now come round to the right side of the road and dominates the landscape to the north. At 2.4 miles/4 km out of Glengarriff the two loughs Avaul open up on the left and there are more views of Whiddy Island. The first farmhouses seen in a long time appear below the road.

The land between the road and the sea was inhabited for a long period by a group of people called the Ranties. They are mentioned in a seventeenth-century description of the church in Ireland. They were apparently a small people, wore distinctive clothes and spoke a form of Irish that no-one else understood. They were said to follow some of the doctrines of Judaism, eating roast lamb before sunrise on Easter Day, and the head and other parts as well. On Good Friday they were said to make lamb pies and bring them to the priest who sprinkled them with holy water. The Ranties died out or had intermarried by the nineteenth century.

The road goes through the narrow lowlands between the Caha Mountains and Bantry Bay. The peaks of the Caha Mountains must have stood up above the levels of the ice sheets during the last ice age and have the characteristic flat topped shape of nunataks. Single boulders litter the landscape, dropped millennia ago by retreating ice sheets. As the road passes Adrigole the land becomes damp looking with the fields full of meadowsweet in the summer and irises in spring. The hedgerows are a mixture of once cultivated plants, such as the montbretia which was always planted on the bank opposite a cottage's front gate, bamboo, which almost certainly had its origins in a day trip to Garnish, and buddleia, an introduced plant which has spread all over the peninsula. It attracts many butterflies.

The commonest form of field division in the peninsula is the earth bank, built up with rocks cleared from the fields with the turned sods of centuries past piled up over them. Many field divisions are ancient but a prolonged spell of hedge planting began in Ireland after the Enclosure Acts of the seventeenth century. These embankments were rarely high enough to keep animals out or in and so cuttings of small trees would be put in beside them. Hawthorn was the most popular plant, growing quickly, being very hardy and having sharp thorns that kept the grazing animals away. Another well used plant was blackthorn, again with sharp thorns. As the generations passed birds came to rest on the developing hedges and dropped seed which germinated. It is possible to estimate the age of a hedgerow from the variety of plants growing in it; the older the hedgerow the more species will be there. A typical West Cork hedgerow will contain a top layer of plants such as those already described, plus elder or honeysuckle which uses the other plants as support, and brambles which are the food supply for the green hairstreak butterfly.

Elm, ash, gorse and especially willow have also become part of the new environment. Indeed, looking carefully at some of the more modern stake fences of the area it will be seen that the stakes are alive. They were cut from willow trees and hammered into the ground where their propensity for forming new roots allowed them to begin the process of hedgerow building again. Wild cherry and crab apple can also be found in the hedges. Besides the honeysuckle, other climbing plants make use of the banks and hedges such as ivy and travellers joy and particularly in this area the dog rose is widespread. Fuchsia was extensively planted in the nineteenth century since it roots easily from cuttings. It is pretty but a wider range of species is a better prospect for the wildlife that depends on the hedges. The annual attacks by cutting machines do a lot of damage to the lower levels of the hedgerow but without them the trees would grow up and no longer carry out their function.

At the lower levels of a hedgerow any number of plants can be spotted. In early summer pignut, locally known as matrimony, grows and wherever it can find a space sorrel is also found. As recently as the early twentieth century the hedgerow would have been a source of food for the children of the area and many older people around here can identify the edible plants. The common sheep's sorrel was eaten by children, as were the berries of the hawthorn despite their mild narcotic effect. Even the common stinging nettles were boiled and drunk.

In spring primroses, violets — the food plant of the relatively rare dark green fritillary butterfly — daffodils, ladies smock — the food plant of the orange tip butterfly — and celandines will thrive in the understorey of the hedgerow. In summer meadowsweet, purple loosestrife, nettles — the food plant of the peacock and small tortoiseshell butterflies — scabious, and knapweed grow. Bunches of purple flowering tufted vetch also enjoy the protection of the hedge.

In turn small mammals survive in the hedgerow using it for food, shelter and as a system of protected roadways along which they can travel. Field mice are easily spotted and in some areas unfrequented by cars baby rabbits will peer out of their burrows in wonder as you pass by. Ireland's only lizard can easily be spotted on quiet sunny afternoons basking in the sun on a projecting rock. Badgers use the banks for their sets but are nocturnal animals. In the early morning there will be seen squashed creatures on the road, trapped by the headlights of cars during the night: rabbits most commonly, the odd hedgehog or badger, an inexperienced young fox and the occasional domestic cat. All will have tried to make a dash from the shelter of the hedge to the fields on the other side.

At the higher levels of the food chain foxes hunt in the hedgerows as do stoats and barn owls. Birds too find food in the hedgerow in the form of insects and fruit. Yellowhammers are commonly seen as well as wrens, robins and seed-eating species such as the chaffinch and greenfinch.

There are lots of places along the road, especially close to houses, where the hedgerow can be examined more closely. The machines which tear great chunks out of them in early summer do much initial damage and perhaps threaten some of the low-lying species which flower late in the year but they also help keep the hedgerows in place. The tendency over the years has been to remove the hedges because they get in the way of the large pieces of agricultural machinery that cut the grass and bale it.

Stop at Dinish island just before entering Castletownbere.

It is possible to drive onto this small island and round the circular road. Dinish, which must once have been a green and living island, is now a depressing sight with derelict-looking factories and processing plants. The road surrounds a piece of unused land in the middle of the island. It is interesting to notice the flora of this area. This ground must have been disturbed quite recently since it is at the stage of secondary regrowth. Grasses, shrubs and small saplings are beginning to take over the area. If this place is left for a longer period of time, say a hundred years, the saplings will have grown up, birds will have brought new saplings into the area and a deciduous forest will be in place, probably made up of sycamore which seeds itself very effectively and can prevent other plants from succeeding, and other indigenous species such as willow and ash.

Castletownbere has been the centre for several changes in the local ecosystem over the years. It once supported a lucrative fishing industry when pilchards swam in these waters, which must have been warmer then. The pilchards disappeared and later mackerel shoals came. These too either found the climate changing or were over-fished; either way they are now less numerous in the offshore waters. Whitefish are plentiful and the town has a fish processing factory. It is possible to tell when the mackerel are close to land because wherever they go the gannets can be seen diving into the water after them. Local fishermen used this as sign to get their boats out.

Emigration has always been a factor in this area and farms that once supported twelve or fifteen children in one family now have only a few children, and most of them will go off to a city or abroad in search of work. The farms are small with much of the land uncultivable, even after drainage and artificial fertilisers.

Link Castletownbere to Allihies. 10 miles/16 km.

The road continues on past the ruins of Dunboy Castle. Plantations of conifers appear to the left of the road while the landscape becomes wilder, all hedgerows and green fields left behind. The signpost to the

Garranes hostel, where there is a Buddhist meditation centre, gives the almost eerie surroundings just that touch of serenity that makes this area so worthwhile. In the richer patches of soil the plant life is dominated in midsummer by hundreds of umbellifers and hedge woundwort, making pretty designs of purple, pink and white.

At Allihies there is an interesting series of field barriers. Entering the village someone has erected a truly hideous prefabricated concrete wall on which someone has scrawled 'this wall is atrocious'. Next to it is an older prefabricated concrete wall which still is not attractive but has settled into its environment and now supports lichens, some climbers and some small plants which use its shelter to avoid being cut down. Next to that again is a much older wall made from natural stones, most probably collected from the local area, and supporting a large variety of plant and animal life — from the tiny clinging ferns to ground ivy and any number of insects living within its crevices.

Drive through the village and at the top end go to the right at the fork in the road. Continue along this road for a short distance, passing another road on the right that returns to the village, and look for a scruffy dump area on the left of the road. This is the entrance and car park for the old copper mines.

Stop at the car park beneath the old mine buildings.

Towering ominously above the village are the remains of the copper mines. Some of this area is part of the chain of volcanic rock found at the ends of these peninsulas and the copper was no doubt formed as part of that volcanic activity. The ore was brought down to the road in a tracked carriage and carried away by boat to Swansea. A walk up to the mines will reveal the open mine shafts. Much of the scree lying about around contains interesting minerals taken out of the mountain itself long ago. Crystals of quartz glow in the sunlight as you walk up the track. Considering just how much work went on around here (see page 64) the area is little damaged by the old workings.

Link Allihies to Lauragh.

The road north from Allihies continues around the coastline of the tip of the peninsula. The mountains towering to the east are the Slieve Miskish range, their highest point being Knockgour at 1,610 ft. Many of the houses are abandoned or taken over by ceramic artists or painters. The road carries on through almost frighteningly empty terrain with sheer rock walls towering above the road and, on fine days, some of the best scenery to be enjoyed anywhere in Ireland.

Beyond Eyeries a wide fertile plain opens up, the hedgerows and wild flowers return and the scenically minded driver might want to take a detour here, turning west just after Eyeries to follow a narrow loop road that goes around the coastline opening up vistas of the convoluted island shore and rocks.

Follow the road around to Ardgroom Bay. Vast tracts of mussel nets can be seen in the shelter of the bay. Mussel farming has become big business in West Cork and Bantry's main festival is a mussel fair. A string of rafts and buoys are put out into the waters where tiny mussels, floating about in the sea looking for somewhere to anchor, find the ropes hanging down from the floats and obligingly attach themselves. The bay is warm and shallow and provides enough food for the hundreds of mussels that cling to the ropes and within two years a rope is ready to be harvested. The mussels bring high prices in Cork and beyond and require little or no maintenance. They have a low impact on the ecosystem of the bay and are preferable to the mussels on the shore, many of which are growing in poisonous algae blooms caused by excess nitrates washed down from the fields.

Continue along the road until at Lauragh a sign on the left points the way into Dereen Gardens.

Stop at Dereen Gardens, Lauragh.

Dereen Gardens, planted by descendants of William Petty (see page 65), were originally aboriginal oak woods. By the early nineteenth century the gardens were fairly bare and the fifth earl of Lansdowne began the planting. It was common at that time to create amusing gardens full of rockeries, winding their way to interesting views by way of rare and unusual plants. As many other landowners came to realise, this part of Ireland was far better at supporting rare plants than the gardens of their English peers. The situation of Dereen in particular was very suitable, sheltered in the farthest point of Kilakilloge Harbour with the protection of the Caha Mountains around the other three sides. The fifth earl actually spent a lot of his time at Dereen, in between being Governor-General of Canada and Viceroy of India. Much of his time was spent working on the gardens which very quickly became completely overrun with the plants which naturalised quickly and grew even more quickly in the soft climate.

Walking around the footpaths now, tall rhododendrons overhang the path and are almost as tall as the trees. They densely shade the understorey which is consequently bare of other plants. They are evergreen and leave no chance for any of the natural understorey plants of Irish forests to grow. Similarly, great groves of bamboo fill the space they occupy leaving no room for indigenous plants. The gardens survive by judicious clearing of the rhododendron and bamboo. The most spectacular plants are the New Zealand tree ferns which grow equally luxuriantly high in the mountains of places like Malaysia. They seed themselves quite naturally and have formed huge groves growing to sizeable plants within a few years.

Interesting trees which have burgeoned here are the Thuya Plicata, or western red cedar, which are trees from a completely different forest

The town of Kenmare in Co. Kerry

structure to native Irish woods. They grow to 140 feet and form the top canopy of thick rainforests. Here they have grown to their proper height and their means of support can be seen at the base of the trunks in the form of buttress roots.

Link Dereen Gardens to Kenmare.

Leave the gardens and continue eastwards to Kenmare.

The road goes on through pleasant scenery past the Cloonee lough system where a detour might be taken up the narrow road past the system of loughs to the final coomb, Inchquin Lough. The sides of the mountains here are rich grounds for botanists being home to many of the rarer Kerry plants like butterwort, Irish spurge, some rare saxifrages and the arbutus. The oakwoods overlooking Inchquin are genuine aboriginal oak forests. Further along the main road the area around Dinish island (not to be confused with the one outside Castletownbere) was once the home of a flourishing oyster trade. The remains of thousands of oyster shells can be seen by the landing stage to the island.

IVERAGH

Undoubtedly one of the most visited and scenic areas in Ireland — home to the famous 111 miles/179 kilometre Ring of Kerry and that unendangered species, the tour bus — the Iveragh peninsula also contains some wonderfully empty beaches, rare plants, historical sites of major and minor importance, and most activities the sports fanatic could ask for. After spending a few days discovering this area it is easy to feel sorry for the people in the green hats carrying plastic shillelaghs climbing in and out of their tour buses. They see so little and in such unpleasant circumstances. On one of the area's soft misty days it must be a lot like commuting to work.

If there is only time for the drive around the Ring of Kerry — and it does provide its share of scenic moments — then in the high season it is better to travel anticlockwise, starting in Killorglin and travelling through Glenbeigh and back through Sneem to Kenmare. This is the opposite direction to the tour buses and at least will ensure that you are not stuck behind one for hours. If at all possible, though, try to find time to take a detour off the main circuit and discover some of the beauty that lies waiting to be enjoyed.

ESSENTIAL INFORMATION

BANKS

Cahersiveen
AIB, Main Street, telephone 066–72022.
Bank of Ireland, Church Street, telephone 066–72122.
For opening hours see under bureaux de change.

Glenbeigh
There is no permanent bank in Glenbeigh but a mobile bank visits on Thursday mornings. Times have a habit of being flexible so enquire at the Post Office.

Kenmare

The *AIB* bank, telephone 064–41010, is on the corner of Main Street and Henry Street. Hours are Monday to Friday 10 a.m. to 3 p.m., closed for lunch 12.30 to 1.30 p.m. Late openings Wednesday till 5 p.m. Similar hours for the *Bank of Ireland*, telephone 064–41255.

Killorglin

AIB, telephone 066–61134, and *Bank of Ireland*, telephone 066–61147, have branches in Main Street. Both have cashpoints. Banking hours are 10.30 a.m. to 12.30 p.m., 1.30 p.m. to 3.00 p.m., late opening Wednesday.

Sneem

The *AIB* bank is open on Thursdays from 1.30 pm. to 3.30 p.m. The *Bank of Ireland* is open Tuesday from 10.30 a.m. to 12.30 p.m..

Valentia Island

The *AIB* bank (you've got to see it to believe it) is open from 10.15 a.m. to 11.30 a.m. Wednesdays. Don't be late! It is at Knightstown opposite the pier.

BICYCLE HIRE

Cahersiveen

Casey's Bicycles, New Street, telephone 066–72474. Daily and weekly rates.

Kenmare

Finnegan's, Henry Street, telephone 064–41083. There is also a biking club that organises tours during June and July. Bikes can be hired by non-members. Telephone 064–41333 for details.

Killorglin

O'Shea's Cycle Centre, Lower Bridge Street, telephone 066–61919. Helmets and panniers also for hire.

Sneem

Burn's Bike Hire. Telephone 064–45140. Open 7 days. Daily and weekly rates.

Valentia Island

Currans Supermarket, Chapeltown, has bikes for hire, telephone 066–76297.

BUREAUX DE CHANGE

Caherdaniel

The *Wave Crest Caravan and Camping Site*.

Cahersiveen

AIB Main Street, telephone 066–72022. Open Tuesday to Friday 10 a.m. to 3.00 p.m. Closed for lunch 12.30–1.30 p.m. Monday late opening 10 a.m. to 5 p.m. Lunch hour 12.30–1.30 p.m.
Bank of Ireland, Church Street, telephone 066–72122. Hours as above.

Glenbeigh

Peter O'Sullivan's, opposite Towers Hotel.

Kenmare

The official bureau de change is in Main Street. Its opening hours are 9 a.m. to 6 p.m. Monday to Saturday including bank holidays. There is also a bureau de change in *The Spindle and Treadle* in Main Street.

Killorglin

Irish Permanent Building Society, Main Street, telephone 066–61195. Office hours.
Bank of Ireland, Main Street, telephone 066–61147. Usual banking hours.

Sneem

There is a bureau de change operating in the south square from June to October, open 10 a.m. to 5 p.m. Monday to Saturday.

Waterville
The tourist office on the sea front has a bureau de change and there is another at *Waterville Craft Market* on the road to Caherdaniel.

CAR HIRE/REPAIRS/24-HOUR PETROL
Cahersiveen
Jack McCarthy Garage, telephone 066–72573. Repairs.
Kerry Murphy Car Hire, telephone 066–72421.
Kenmare
Randles Brothers Car Rental, Shelbourne Street, telephone 064–41355.
Waterville
John O'Shea's Garage, telephone 066–74300. Repairs and towing.

CHURCH SERVICES
Caherdaniel
St Crohane's Church, Saturday Vigil 9 p.m. July and August. Sunday Mass 9.30 a.m.
Cahersiveen
O'Connell Memorial Church, Saturday Vigil 8 p.m. Sunday Mass 8 a.m., 9.30 a.m., 12 noon.
Glenbeigh
Catholic St James. Saturday Vigil 8 p.m., Sunday Mass 9 a.m., 11.30 a.m. The Church Of Ireland is on the corner of the road to Cahiersiveen and has services at 10 a.m. on Sundays during July and August.
Glencar
St Stephen's Church, Saturday Vigil 6.30 p.m., Sunday Mass 10 a.m.
Kenmare
Holy Cross Church, Sunday Mass 8 a.m., 10 a.m., 12 noon.
Church of Ireland, 10 a.m.
Killorglin
St James Catholic Church Saturdays: 7.30 p.m. winter, 8.00 p.m. summer. Sundays: 8 a.m., 10 a.m., 12 noon.
St James Church of Ireland Sundays 11.30 a.m.
Sneem
Church of Ireland, service at 10 a.m. on Sundays.
Catholic St Michael has Saturday Vigil at 8 p.m. and Sunday Mass at 11.30 a.m.
Valentia Island
Knightstown/Chapeltown Saturday Vigil 8 p.m. Knightstown Sunday Mass 9 a.m. Chapeltown Sunday Mass 11 a.m.
Waterville
St Finan's Church Saturday Vigil 8 p.m.; Sunday Mass 9 a.m., 11 a.m.
Church Of Ireland. Services vary. Please check the noticeboard on the Church porch.

GARDAÍ (POLICE)
Cahersiveen
Fair Green, telephone 066–72111.
Glenbeigh
Telephone 066–68202.
Kenmare
Telephone 064–41177.

Killorglin
Junction of Main Street and Upper Bridge Street, telephone 066–61113.

Sneem
Telephone 064–45101.

Valentia Island
Telephone 066–76102.

Waterville
Telephone 066–77601.

LAUNDERETTES

Kenmare
The Laundry Basket, Market Street.

Killorglin
Laune Launderette, Upper Bridge Street.
Starlite, Langford Street.
Day Care Centre, St Finan's Bay, The Glen, telephone 066–79276.

PHARMACIES

Cahersiveen
O'Connor, Medical Hall, 066–72309.

Kenmare
Thomas Brosnan, 19 Henry Street, telephone 064–41318.

Killorglin
Mulvihill's, Main Street, 9 a.m.–5.30 p.m.

Sneem
Cyril Burke, South Square, telephone 064–45159.

Waterville
K. O'Connell, Main Street, telephone 066–74141.

POST OFFICES

Most post offices and sub-post offices keep the same hours: 9 a.m. to 5 p.m. with an hour from 1 to 2 p.m. for lunch. Saturdays are a half day. Only the slight variations from these standard hours are noted below.

Caherdaniel
Main Street in Freddie's Food shop and off-licence.

Cahersiveen
Church Street, telephone 066–72287. Open 9.30 a.m. to 5.30 p.m. Monday to Friday. Closed for lunch 1 to 2 p.m. Saturday 9.30 to 1 p.m.

Glenbeigh
Opposite Towers Hotel, telephone 066–68201. Hours as above.

Kenmare
Henry Street, telephone 064–41490

Killorglin
Iveragh Road, telephone 066–61101, Monday-Friday 9.00 a.m. to 5.30 p.m. Closed for lunch 1 to 2 p.m. Saturdays 9.00 a.m. to 1 p.m.

Waterville
Telephone 066–74100.

TAXIS

Cahersiveen
McCarthy's Taxi Service, telephone 066–72249.
Keatings Taxi and Minibus, telephone 066–72074.

Kenmare
Finnegan's Limousine Service, telephone 064–41083.

Valentia Island
Kennedy's Taxis, telephone 066–76183.

TOURIST OFFICES

Cahersiveen
The Old Oratory, New Street, telephone 066–72043.

Kenmare
Next door to the new heritage centre at the town square. Open Monday to Saturday 9.30 a.m. to 7 p.m. all through the summer.

Killorglin
Market Street, open 10 a.m. to 6 p.m., closed for lunch 1 to 2 p.m. 2 to 6 p.m. Saturday.

Sneem
The Homestead Gift Shop in New Street provides information for tourists seven days a week. It has copies of a useful guide to walks in the area. Telephone 064–45179.

Waterville
The tourist office is located on the seafront in front of the Butler Arms Hotel. It has a bureau de change and public toilets.

TRAVEL AGENTS

Kenmare
Torc Travel, Main Street, Telephone 064–41354.

Killorglin
Torc Travel, Lower Bridge Street, telephone 066–61044.

FESTIVALS AND SPECIAL EVENTS

June
Kenmare has a Walking Festival during the first week of June. Contact the tourist office for details.

Cibeal festival, Kenmare, is an arts festival which brings musicians, visual artists, street entertainers and singers to town. It has been in existence since 1980 and has developed a considerable reputation.

August
Puck Fair Second weekend in August, Killorglin. If you are around, don't miss it. Each year, a male wild goat is captured from the surrounding hills, tidied up, decorated and brought into town where the poor creature is hoisted up on a platform on top of a pole for the duration of the festivities. No pubs have been known to close and experts can remain inebriated for the entire duration of the festival. Accommodation can be a problem during this weekend so if you intend to go you should book well in advance.

Sneem Welcome Home Festival End of the month.

Kenmare Fruits de Mer A culinary festival which brings chefs to town.

Regattas are a regular feature of the peninsula. Kells holds one in July, Cahersiveen in July, Valentia in August, Killorglin in August, Portmagee in September. These dates can change from year to year.

WHAT TO SEE

KENMARE HERITAGE CENTRE
The Centre is in the town square and adjoined to a new tourist office. The history of the town is covered as well as notable local people such as the Nun of Kenmare and Sir William Petty. Admission is £2 (children and students £1.50, family £5).

KENMARE STONE CIRCLE AND OLD CEMETERY
This ancient stone circle is made up of fifteen stones. It is signposted from the square and is only a few minutes walk.

The old cemetery is reached from the Glengarriff road, near the Sheen Falls Lodge hotel. It contains the ruins of the Church of St Fenian dating back to before the arrival of the Vikings in the ninth century. In the cemetery there is also a small stone dedicated to the more than 5,000 people in the area who died during the Famine years.

SNEEM SCULPTURE PARK
Sneem is a quaint little picture postcard place with a sculpture park in the middle of the village. The Cearbhall Ó Dálaigh monument commemorates the life of one of Ireland's former presidents who retired to Sneem. It is an abstract pyramid structure. The erection of this in 1983 was followed by the arrival of a metal tree, donated by President Herzog of Israel in memory of Ó Dálaigh. Then the people of China contributed a white marble panda, again due to the efforts of Ó Dálaigh in promoting international understanding. In the grounds of Sneem church is a statue of the risen Christ presented by a Singaporean sculptor, Joe McNally, and in a garden beside St Michael's Church is a sculpture called 'The Way the Fairies went' by James Scanlan.

SNEEM MUSEUM
The museum, containing exhibits of local interest, is located in the old courthouse in Main Street. The curator, Tim Reilly, can provide lots of interesting background to the exhibits. The museum is open from 10 a.m. to 5.30 p.m. seven days a week in the summer. It closes for lunch from 1 to 2 p.m. Admission is 50p.

STAIGUE FORT

If this were in England it would figure on postage stamps and be a national monument; here, it stands in the middle of somebody's farm with an honesty box beside it. The fort is around 2,000 years old with an eighteen-foot high circular wall, in places thirteen-feet thick. It is thought to have been built as a means of defence for an entire village but some aspects of it suggest it might have been a nobleman's house. Built into the wall is an elaborate stairway. The fort is well camouflaged by its position so that while it has views of the sea, any invader coming from that direction cannot see it.

Parts of the fort were reconstructed in the last century but do not detract from an appreciation of the astonishing architectural achievement on show here. It was built without mortar and the workmanship of the dry-stone walls is exceptional. Equally astonishing is the draughtsmanship that so successfully created the circular design. It is unclear whether the structure was completed in sections, or whether two semi-circular halves were later joined up, or whether it is one complete piece of work. Many skilled hands went into its construction but it is equally clear that one highly talented architect masterminded the whole process. The fact that it still stands today in such remarkable condition is the highest testimony to its builders.

The absence of any obvious buildings inside the walls has been taken as evidence that it was used by the nobility; the argument being that peasants used stone while the rich had sophisticated wooden dwellings. But the interior has never been excavated so there may be stone foundations under the ground. There are no references to the fort in any literature, so a certain amount of mystery surrounds the place.

How to get there The fort is signposted off the Ring of Kerry road near Castlecove. In summer be prepared for traffic jams on the single track farm road.

DERRYNANE HOUSE AND PARK, CAHERDANIEL

The word Derrynane is the anglicisation of the original Irish name which meant oakwood of St Fionan who was thought to have established the monastery, the remains of which still stand on nearby Abbey Island. The estate, now maintained by the National Parks and Monuments Service, was once the home of Daniel O'Connell, a major figure in Irish history.

The house itself was built in 1702 by Captain John O'Connell. The O'Connells were hereditary constables of Ballycarbery Castle during the Middle Ages, not a prominent position but important enough to get into recorded history. In the seventeenth century they became embroiled in the wars against Cromwell and were forced to destroy the castle, whose ruins are still to be seen near Cahersiveen. The family were forced to move to Tarmons near Waterford although they kept their Kerry connections and a little of their land. In the next generation, John O'Connell fought at Limerick with the forces of James II against those of William of Orange.

Despite the penal laws which prevented Catholics from owning land the O'Connells quietly accumulated grazing land and herds of cattle in Kerry until they settled at Derrynane in 1702 and began building a house. John's son, Donal, married Maire ní Dhuibh, one of the O'Donoghues, and they had many children including Morgan, the father of Daniel. Daniel himself was the adopted heir to the estate at Derrynane. His uncle, the eldest son of Donal and Maire ní Dhuibh O'Connell, known affectionately as Hunting Cap, had no sons. Another of Daniel's uncles became a general in the French army.

The branch of the family that settled at Derrynane became wealthy, using sympathetic Protestants to buy up land for them and smuggling goods from France and Spain. The 1702 house was a substantial farmhouse rather than a mansion, having three stories and a walled courtyard. Extensions were built during Hunting Cap's time and these remain today although the original building has been demolished.

Daniel himself spent his early life at Derrynane, before going away to school first to Cobh, near Cork, and then to France. Finishing his education he went to first to England to study law and later to Dublin to finish his studies. He inherited the house in 1825, and altered it considerably, adding a south wing with two big rooms looking out to sea, and a library.

O'Connell mobilised the mass of Irish Catholics as no political figure had ever done before. In the 1820s he led a nationwide campaign of mass agitation in support of Catholic Emancipation. This meant the removal of the remaining major disabilities against Catholics, of which the most important was the prohibition on Catholics becoming Members of Parliament. In 1829 he secured the passage of the Catholic Emancipation Act and he himself became the first Irish Catholic to sit in the British House of Commons.

O'Connell is, in a sense, the father of modern Irish nationalism. He developed its organisational structures; he became the first great mass agitator in modern Ireland; and with Emancipation he delivered the first big success. He was a nationalist but not a separatist: he envisaged Ireland as a self-governing unit within the United Kingdom. Thus he also campaigned for the Repeal of the Act of Union.

In this, he was less successful, although once more he began a tradition which was built on by later leaders. He died in 1847, worn out by a lifetime of struggle and agitation, just as Ireland was in the throes of the Great Famine.

After O'Connell's time his family continued to live in Derrynane until

1958 but long before that the house had begun to decay and when it was taken over by the Commissioner for Public Works in 1964 it was largely a ruin, with the older part of the building unrepairable. What is seen today are largely the parts that O'Connell himself built with the older middle section demolished and turned into a courtyard.

Inside, the house has been converted to a memorial to O'Connell. Some of the original furniture put there by him is still in place and many of the knick-knacks were owned by him. The house is full of portraits, the most outlandish being an allegorical painting of the hero as Hercules breaking the chains of slavery. The library which he built now holds lots of items presented to him in his lifetime and documents charting the history of his career. Here you can also see his rosary beads, his writing desk and his duelling pistols.

The 300-acre grounds are now part of the Derrynane National Park and contain some pretty, well-maintained gardens full of delicate plants that survive in this sheltered spot. To the south of the house is an excellent beach and sand dunes. A nature trail has been laid out around the grounds.

Abbey Island is part of the park and can be accessed from the beach. There is a footpath around the island, along high cliffs with excellent views of the Skelligs and the coastline. The ruins of the abbey are tenth century and its graveyard holds the remains of several of Daniel's ancestors.

How to get there Derrynane is a turning off the main Ring of Kerry road at Caherdaniel. It is signposted from the road.

CAHERSIVEEN HERITAGE CENTRE
The centre is housed in what was once a barracks of the Royal Irish Constabulary built after the Fenian rising of 1867 and burned down during the civil war of 1922 by anti-treaty forces. Admission is £3 (children under 12 and students £2, family £6).

THE SKELLIGS
'I tell you the thing does not belong to any world that you and I have lived and worked in: it is part of our dream world.'
Bernard Shaw, 1910

A boat trip to the Skellig Islands is one of the highlights of Ireland and the validity of Shaw's comment is readily apparent after seeing these islands and putting foot on Skellig Michael, the largest of the two. The 217 metre (712 feet) high jagged rock of Skellig Michael looks like the last place on earth that anyone would try to land on, let alone establish a community. And yet early Christian monks maintained their life here from the seventh century until the twelfth or thirteenth. They were influenced by the Egyptian Coptic Church founded by St Anthony in the deserts of Egypt and Libya and the emphasis on solitude led them to this remote, most westerly corner of Europe.

In 1582 Pope Gregory XII decreed a ten-day change in the calendar. Because of its precarious situation in English-ruled Ireland and because perhaps of its remoteness the community on Skellig Michael did not conform to the new calendar and so the legend of the Skellig Lists began, lasting well into the twentieth century. Marriage was banned during the period of Lent and it was a tradition for folk to be married by the priest on the night of Shrove Tuesday, just before Lent. Many people in Ireland today tell stories of their grandparents marrying in this fashion. After Lent those who were still eligible but unmarried became legitimate objects of fun. The Skellig Lists were drawn up of people who could still escape the stigma of being unmarried by running off to Skellig Michael where Shrove Tuesday had not yet occurred. The Lists were comic verses describing the bachelors and spinsters and pairing them off, usually in an unkind way, for their journey to the Skelligs. After the introduction of the Gregorian calendar, therefore, Skellig became a popular spot for weddings in the early days of Lent. In time these annual pilgrimages became an excuse for jollification and crates of alcohol were hauled over to facilitate the merrymaking. There is even a record of the police being called to the island.

The Monastery

The monastic buildings are perched on a saddle in the rock, some 150 metres (500 feet) above sea level. The two boat-shaped oratories and six beehive cells vary in size, the largest cell having a floor space of 4.5 by 3.6 metres (15 feet by 12), but they're all astounding. The projecting stones on the outside have more than one possible explanation; steps to reach the top and release chimney stones or maybe holding places for sods of turfs that covered the exterior. There are interior rows of stone in some of the cells.The guides who live on the rock during the summer and meet you at the top of the steps will provide a possible explanation for these as well.

Very little is known about the life of the monastery although ancient annals record a Viking raid in 812 and again in 823 and 833. Monks were killed and taken away but the community recovered and carried on.

There are also the remains of a medieval chapel made of stones and mortar with a timbered and slated roof. This church indicates that at some stage the original monks were replaced by Augustinians, a mission whose ideas were more about parish work than contemplation. Under their influence the Skelligs became a place for penitential journeys rather than a seat of learning and meditation. The monastery on the island was closed down and the main body of monks moved to Ballinskelligs.

How to get there From Ballinskelligs Joe Roddy, telephone 066-74268, does trips out to Skellig Michael in either a fast launch which does the journey in about half an hour or a slower one which takes about an hour. His boats go at 10 a.m. and 3.30 p.m. Fares are around £15 per head. Children and student fares are negotiable. There are several other operators with similar rates operating from Portmagee and Valentia. Try Sean Feehan, telephone 066-79182 or J.B. Walsh, telephone 066-79147. From Portmagee, Brendan O'Keefe can be contacted in The Fisherman's Bar, telephone 066-77103, or try Murphy's, telephone 066-77156. Casey's boats go from Portmagee around 11 a.m., telephone 066-77125, and can be booked in Cahersiveen, telephone 066-77125. From Valentia Lavelle's, telephone 066-76144, takes passengers out or The Royal Pier Hostel can arrange trips.

Bird Life

The boat trip, and around the steps leading to the monastery, provides an exceptional opportunity to view seabirds at close quarters. From the boat look out for the diminutive storm petrel, a black bird that darts around over the water like a swallow, and the large fulmar with a wingspan of 107 cm (42 inches). Kittiwakes, seagulls with a black tip to the wings, are easy to see and hear around the covered walkway just after stepping off the boat. They spend the winter at sea but thousands come to Skellig Michael to breed between March and August.

On the rock itself the delightful puffins are all around and their multicoloured beaks and waddling steps make them unmistakeable. The puffin lays one egg in May at the end of a burrow and the parent bird will be seen guarding its nest, with as much dignity as appearances allow.

The boat trip should take you past the Little Skellig where some 20,000 pairs of gannet breed. Check beforehand if the boat will pause for an opportunity to see the basking seals which are a common sight. The Visitor Centre at The Skellig Experience has a good display on the birdlife and it's worth going there before your trip.

The Skellig Experience

Situated on Valentia Island, this is an interpretative centre with detailed accounts of the lives of the monks and the story of the lighthouse that was established on Skelligs in 1826. Three lighthouse keepers were on duty at any one time, relieved by helicopter from Castletownbere, until the machinery was automated in 1986.

There is a café and well displayed information about the wildlife of the islands. The centre has its own boat that goes around the Skelligs and while there is a running commentary the boat doesn't land. Ideally, the centre should be visited for its informative displays before taking a boat out to Skellig Michael. Admission to the exhibition is £3 (children £1.50, students £2.70, family with up to four children under 12 £7).

How to get there Crossing from Portmagee to Valentia, the Skellig Experience is on the left side of the bridge.

THE SKELLIG RING, AROUND BALLINSKELLIGS
This is a picturesque drive lasting about an hour around Ballinskelligs and St Finan's Bay, including a small Gaeltacht area. It is fairly well signposted from both Waterville and Portmagee and on a fine day is well worth the trip. From the pier in Glen you can watch fishermen at work or take a (long) walk or bumpy drive out to Bolus Head. At St Finan's bay there is a wild scenic beach and at Ballinskelligs the remains of a thirteenth-century Augustinian monastery. The tourist office at Killorglin or Killarney or Waterville will have free copies of a map outlining the route and pointing out the sites of historical interest.

How to get there The Skellig Ring is signposted from just outside Waterville on the road to Glenbeigh.

VALENTIA ISLAND
Valentia is easily missed out on a whirlwind trip around the Iveragh peninsula but for many people it is one of the gems of the area. It has a long, well-recorded history and reeks splendidly of a lost Victorian past where various Knights of Kerry ruled beneficently over the peasantry.

It is well worth a stay on the island to really wander around and get the feel of the place. The island is reached via a land bridge built, after much aggravation, between 1967 and 1971. Such was the ill feeling built up over the delays of decades in building the bridge that Kerry County Council — who financed the project — were not invited to the opening ceremony and held their own ceremony two months later.

Anyone who listens to the BBC weather forecasts will be familiar with the name of Valentia, the island being the site of an important meteorological station (now moved to Cahersiveen). It was also chosen as the site for the first transatlantic cable station and plans were made to make it the foremost port in Europe with people from all over Europe travelling there by train to make the shortest possible transatlantic sea crossing. A railway was built at huge expense to the island but somehow the major port did not emerge and the advent of ocean liners and then air flight ended the dream. The railway closed in 1957, after functioning for less than sixty years.

But picture the scene in 1857 when the first transatlantic cable was being laid. Valentia was in the forefront of scientific discovery — the Silicon Valley and Cape Canaveral of Victorian Britain. The cable was

Cahergall stone fort near Cahirsiveen on the Ring of Kerry

brought ashore at Ballycarbery Strand amidst great publicity. A whole fleet of ships went slowly out to sea lowering cables as they did so. Then, 280 miles out, the cable snapped and the attempt was abandoned. The next year a second attempt was successful, with an American ship setting out from Halifax laying its own cable and preparing to meet a British ship half way. This attempt succeeded. The cable station set up listening and transmitting devices and later Queen Victoria sent a cable message to the President of the United States. Eventually, after several more cable layings and breaks, a cable station was established transmitting Morse code at the rate of seventeen words per minute. The men who operated the cable transmitters were a well-paid elite on the island and almost to a man were not Irish. By the end of World War I there were 200 men employed on Valentia, enjoying the equivalent kind of expatriate lifestyle that Westerners expect when they take up employment today in the Middle East. A few local boys wormed their way into jobs in the station and joined the elite society with their own tennis courts, neat gardens, and even a cricket pitch. During the nationalist struggle for independence the cable station became a significant military target. Not surprisingly, the cable station men were loyal to Britain but one cable message did slip out to the USA with news of the 1916 Easter Rising.

Valentia's days as a cable station were short lived. Ironically, it engineered its own demise, being the site of experiments for a new type of cable powerful enough not to need relay stations. The station closed in 1965 and today the wind blows across the crumbling asphalt of the old tennis courts and the empty houses gradually crumble away.

Part of the cable company's daily service was a weather report and this prompted in 1867 the building of a weather observatory. It functioned on Valentia for almost twenty years before being moved to Cahersiveen.

How to get there There is the road bridge over to the island from Portmagee. For hitchhikers and pedestrians coming from Glenbeigh it would be quicker to use the ferry from Reenard which takes about fifteen minutes and goes across about ten times a day.

Valentia Slate Quarry, Valentia Island

Another awe-inspiring Victorian effort that focused on Valentia was the slate quarry began in 1816 at the instigation of the Knight of Kerry. After eleven years he handed it over to the Irish Mining Company which extended it and then gave up. The Knight took over again until he was able to interest an English company in the project in 1839. The Knight, whose reputation as a landlord was not a good one, invested a considerable fortune in the quarry and without his interest it would have foundered. As it was it supported up to 400 men and women even during the Famine years. But by 1877 it came under competition from cheaper Welsh slate and finally closed in 1884. It was reopened temporarily in 1900 as a relief effort for the poor but closed again after a massive rock fall.

In the heyday of the quarry there were three main flagstone beds providing huge sheets of slate 14 feet long which were carried out of the mine and cut to size on site by a steam powered saw, the remains of which can still be seen at the mouth of the quarry. One of the beds produced much smaller pieces which were cut up for roof slates. Many of the buildings which were first built at the quarry are now buried under the huge heap of spoil which built up.

When cut, the slate was taken down into Knightstown to be worked into whatever shape was needed. Besides roof tiles the slate was carved into headstones, garden furniture, and used as the base for billiard tables. The roofs of many prominent London buildings are covered with Valentia slate. Some even went to Bahia in South America for use on the San Salvador Railway.

How to get there Approaching Knightstown turn left at the T-junction, signposted for the quarry. From there keep following the signs for the quarry.

Valentia Museum, Valentia Island

The stories of Valentia Island, including much oral history, have been faithfully collected and can be seen in the old National School building at Knightstown. It is an excellent little museum with one schoolroom intact, another dedicated to local craft industries and the third giving the history of the cable station and observatory.

How to get there The museum is on the right side of the road just outside Knightstown on the road to the quarry.

Beginish and Church Islands, off Valentia Island
From Valentia it is possible to get boats out to Church and Beginish islands where there are pleasant beaches and archaeological sites. On Beginish are the remains of a medieval fishing community. Iron smelting remains have also been found, as have shell middens. A house which has been excavated was found to be eleventh century and other remains suggest the presence of Vikings on the island.

On Church island are the remains of an eighth-century oratory and wooden houses.

How to get there Enquire at the Royal Pier hostel about boats out to the islands, or at Portmagee.

CAITIN BEATEAR'S, KELLS
A pub and restaurant with a tiny heritage centre beside it built in the style of a crannog, a fourth-century Celtic dwelling house. On display are old pieces of farm machinery, musical instruments and lots of newspaper cuttings recording famous events of the area. Particularly interesting are the reports of the Fenian Uprising in 12 February 1867 when a crowd of men marched from Cahersiveen on to Kells, attacked the coastguard station and then went on to Glenbeigh, Glencar and Caragh Lake plundering as they went. They rested in Tomies Wood outside Killarney and returned to Cahersiveen the next day.

How to get there Caitin Beatear's is on the main Ring of Kerry road at Kells, south-west of Glenbeigh.

KERRY BOG VILLAGE MUSEUM, GLENBEIGH
This is a series of replica houses of the various types of people who lived in a local village. Each cottage reflects the work and lifestyle of the person who would have lived in it. There is a turf cutter's house, with a turf roof and flagstone floor. The blacksmith's house includes his forge with only two tiny windows so that he could see the metal getting red hot. The stableman's house incorporated the cow shed which helped heat the main house while the thatcher, as a tradesman, had a much better quality home with a second storey and good quality furniture. A good afternoon's visit with lots of authentic items and a well laid out vegetable garden. Admission is £2 (children £1, students £1.50, family £6).

How to get there The museum is beside the Red Fox pub outside Glenbeigh. Telephone 066-69184.

KILLORGLIN'S PUCK FAIR

Killorglin is a pretty working town which manages to mix catering to the summer tourist trade with a more workaday atmosphere. The town has its moment of fame each year in the second week of August when Puck Fair takes place. This happy event owes its origins to the god Lug, an opponent of the nasty one-eyed sun god whom most of the heroes of Irish mythology spent their time fighting. This Lug was particularly popular in Kerry and it is thought that he has given his name to such places as Dunloe (Dun Loich). Lug's day was celebrated on 1 August but when calendar changes were made in the eighteenth century the day was put back to the 12th. Puck Fair was celebrated in the name of Lug and was a harvest festival. In the old days festivities would have included sacrificing a bull, eating bilberries, taking a sacred head up to a nearby hill and burying it, a play of Lug destroying the god of want — Crom Dubh — and three days of festivities presided over by the god Lug himself or at least the actor playing his part. Over time this healthy pagan festival was Christianised, with St Patrick taking the place of Lug and converting Crom Dubh rather than burying his head. In modern, more secular Killorglin the whole three days have been ritualised down to a concentrated drinking session, officially sanctioned with extended closing hours, lots of music and racing thrown in. Nowadays a feral goat is brought down from the mountains to represent Lug and watches over the proceedings from a platform which is specially positioned on the top of a pole. Killorglin is very crowded on the three days of the festival and it is by no means only tourists who fill the pubs. This seems to be a genuine piece of pagan Ireland surviving into the late twentieth century.

WALK THE KERRY WAY

One excellent way of really getting to grips with the Iveragh peninsula is to walk the Kerry Way or at least part of it. If you plan to do the walk the tourist board has its own map guide for £2 which divides the entire Way into twelve sections, but far more useful is the new 1:50,000 Ordnance Survey map No. 78, entitled *The Reeks*. The Way is clearly marked and there are some general notes on the different sections. Two books cover the whole walk in quite good detail mapping it out in daily stretches: *Irish Long Distance Walks* by Michael Fewer and *Walk Guide: Southwest of Ireland* by Seán Ó Súilleabháin, both published by Gill & Macmillan.

If you don't have time for the whole 135 miles/215 km Kerry Way — which takes at least a week — the following three-day section is a more manageable proposition. It cuts out the very beginning of the walk, from Killarney to the Torc Waterfall, and makes the first day's walking less demanding.

Killarney to Black Valley. Day 1

The walk should start early in the morning from the Torc Waterfall car park by the side of the main road from Killarney to Kenmare. If you leave a car there for the three days of your walk it will be quite safe but the car park fills up with tour buses so park it carefully.

This first day covers a distance of 13 miles/21 km and should take about $6\frac{1}{2}$ hours to walk. Follow the signs up to the waterfall, stopping to admire the views on the way up. The path crosses the waterfall by means of a stone bridge and joins a green road. Turn left on to it and a few yards later ignore the walking sign that takes you off to the right. Stay on the green road, keeping the river below you on your left. This is the old Kenmare road which travels across very squashy bog to meet a surfaced road with a sign pointing to the left for Kenmare and right for the Black Valley. Follow the Black Valley sign and you eventually meet the main Killarney to Kenmare road by the side of an old church.

Turn left on to the road and walk for a few yards where a Way sign points you across the road and into a wood. They are typical oak woods, crowded with lichens and mosses, honeysuckle, oak and holly. A clear path takes you along the river to Lord Brandon's Cottage where tour groups coming from the Gap of Dunloe join the boat rides back to Killarney. Here you can rest for a while. The Way carries on along a little used road to the Black Valley Youth Hostel, telephone 064-34712. If you are going to stay here in summer you should book ahead because it gets very full. You need membership cards or you can join at the hostel. It is closed until the dot of five when lots of tired hungry people pour in. There are B&B places at each side of it.

Black Valley to Glencar. Day 2

The next day's walk, 12 miles/20 km, is one of the very best parts of the Kerry Way. It should take you about 7 hours. The walk begins when you turn left out of the hostel and head past the green road leading to the Gap of Dunloe and towards a road marked by a cul de sac sign. You are travelling west and soon leave the surfaced road behind and begin to cut across the Black Valley itself. At first the Way goes through a planted conifer wood and then passes through pasture land. It is easy to get lost here since the Way signs are tiny stakes about a foot high and are easily missed. Keep heading west at a steady distance from the river down below you. Eventually you come out on to a green road following the curve of the mountain to your right. If you hit a tarred road instead turn right and the green road will begin after a few yards. The green road goes through a deserted farm yard and starts to head up a pass through the mountains. The way is marked more clearly here by cairns.

Over the top of the pass you enter another valley and move down quite quickly through another farmyard with car door gateways to the old Lack Road which was once used as a means of getting to Killorglin. Your next point to look for is the surfaced road which you turn left on to and follow for several hundred yards until another Way sign points you up over the rest of the Lack Road. Descending the other side of the mountain you come to Lough Acoose and then the surfaced road again. Turn left and find your way to the Climber's Inn, telephone 066-60101, which is dilapidated but very well placed for the next day's walk. There is also a B&B in the area which will pick you up from the inn, telephone 066-60162.

Glencar to Glenbeigh. Day 3
The next day's journey is the shortest of all, some of it along roads. The distance is 11 miles/17.5 km and the walking time is 5 hours. From the inn go down the green road directly opposite and turn right into the surfaced road. A few hundred yards further on at the road junction cross the road and look for the next Way sign which takes you over the river and along its banks for a while and then into plantations. Walking through you can really appreciate how little manages to survive in these woods besides the trees. The Way signs are all clearly marked along here and take you in and out of the forests and along surfaced road for short periods. At one stage, near Blackstone Bridge, there is small shop. At a Y-junction further on, the Way starts to head uphill on the last stretch of the day's walk into Glenbeigh.

At the top of the hill there are two routes into Glenbeigh. To take the shorter route look for a fading walking sign and turn to the left through a gate. This leads through the Windy Gap at the top of which Glenbeigh and the Dingle peninsula come into view. The views are glorious and the colours of heather and gorse magnificent. It's an easy walk down the other side along a quiet road into the town.

The other route involves staying on the green road and offers magnificent views of Caragh Lake. The route ends along surfaced road again and down into the village of Glenbeigh.

CYCLE TOURS

CAHERSIVEEN TO KILLARNEY VIA BALLAGHASHEEN
40 miles/64 km

Leave Cahersiveen on the main road to Kells and Glenbeigh and after two miles turn right on the road to Lissatinnig Bridge, a journey of about 11 miles/17 km. At the bridge junction turn to the left for the spectacular route through the Ballaghasheen Pass, rising to about 1,000 feet after passing though the Derreenageeha woods. The next junction is at Bealalaw Bridge where the Kerry Way is encountered. Turn to the left here on the main road, which shortly bends to the right for Glencar. Do not turn to the right at the bridge. It is 7.5 miles/12 km from Lissatinnig Bridge to Glencar and the Climbers' Inn pub/shop/post office/hostel.

From Glencar follow the road that goes past Lake Acoose, ignoring the left turn signposted for Glenbeigh 12 miles/19 km to the north-west. After 3.5 miles/6 km from Glencar there is a left turn signposted for Killorglin 5.5 miles to the north. Ignore this and keep to the right, signposted for Killarney and Beaufort. After 0.6 miles/1 km bear right for the road to the Gap of Dunloe and Killarney.

FROM AND TO CAHERSIVEEN VIA GLENBEIGH
A return journey of 48 miles/57 km

Follow the Cahersiveen to Killarney route above as far as the Climber's Inn at Glencar. With the Climber's Inn on your left continue along the road to Lake Acoose and Killarney for 1.1 miles/1.8 km until a turning is reached on the left signposted to Glenbeigh, 12 miles. Go along this road for 1.5 miles/3.5 km to a T-junction and turn left to Blackstone's Bridge 1 mile/1.6 km away.

From Blackstone's Bridge the road makes its scenic way to the north, following the shore of Caragh Lake before turning to the west and meeting the N70. Turn left for Glenbeigh and the return to Cahersiveen along the main Ring of Kerry road.

FROM AND TO KENMARE VIA SNEEM
A return journey of 38.5 miles/61 km

Leave Kenmare on the main road to Killarney. After 6 miles/9.6 km of moderate climbing Moll's Gap is reached. Turn left at the junction immediately past the café and head down for 7 miles/11.2 km to Gearha Bridge. From the bridge the road begins an ascent for 2.5 miles/4 km before descending to Sneem. The total length from Moll's Gap to Sneem is 15 miles/24 km. From Sneem take the main road via Blackwater Bridge and return to Kenmare.

FROM AND TO WATERVILLE VIA THE BALLINSKELLIG RING
A return trip of around 50 miles/80 km
Leave Waterville on the main Ring of Kerry road for Cahersiveen and, after 3 miles/5 km, take the left turn (R567) signposted the Skellig Ring. After 1.8 miles/2.8 km from the beginning of the Skellig Ring road there is an unmarked road going down to a lovely inlet of Ballinskellig Bay. It makes for an interesting little detour just to appreciate the privacy and wildness of the spot.

Back on the main road carry on for 2 miles/3.2 km until a T-junction is reached. The right turn goes to Cahersiveen, 6.5 miles/13 km away. Turn left instead, passing the Sigerson Arms pub and reaching a small junction where four roads meet. The left turn here goes onto the sandy expanse of Ballinskellig Bay beach with an old ruin on a spit of land that can be reached on foot. Going straight ahead at the junction leads down to a pier from where a boat trip to the Skelligs departs. Turn right, instead, at the junction and pass the An Óige hostel on the right side of the road.

Keep on the road for the Glen, a small village from where the road twists and turns its way to Portmagee. Follow the signs for the Skellig Ring.

From Portmagee a trip can be made across the bridge to Valentia island or the R565 can be followed to the east where it joins up with the Ring of Kerry road. At this junction with the main road, a right turn returns to Waterville.

Daytime Activities and Sports

BEACH GUIDE

There are many sandy safe beaches along the peninsula. These are listed in an anti-clockwise direction starting at Killorglin and going west to Portmagee and then south and east to Kenmare.

Dooks

This is a long stretch of sandy beach backed by the sand dunes of the Dooks Golf Course.
How to get there From Killorglin take the road to Cromane. At the T-junction before Cromane village take the left turn and after about a mile the beach is signposted.

Rossbeigh Strand and White Strand

Both are accessible from the car park at Rossbeigh near the Red Fox Pub. Long stretches of white sand stretching out to Rossbeigh Point. Safe for swimming. Wheelchair access good. Pub and restaurants close by.

Kells Bay

This is a smallish blue flag beach with good facilities and tea shops nearby. Wheelchair access might be difficult. Lifeguard on duty in the summer. Could get crowded.
How to get there From Glenbeigh take the main road to Cahersiveen. About 1.6

miles/2.5 km past Caitin Beatear's Pub (unmissable) take a right turn, signposted to Kells bay.

Valentia Island
The best sandy beach is at Glanlean, signposted from Knightstown.
How to get there Follow the road out to the quarry and take a right fork signposted Glanlean. The beach is about half a mile down a cul-de-sac. No facilities, wheelchair access difficult.

St Finan's Bay
This is a beautiful but dangerous beach. It has magnificent views and excellent surf but swimming is dangerous. Above the beach are picnic tables and parking space but access is difficult for wheelchairs. No facilities.
How to get there From Portmagee follow the signs indicating the Skellig Ring. St Finan's Bay is signposted. 5 miles/8.5 kilometres out of Portmagee take a right turn signposted Ballinskelligs. 0.3 miles/0.5 km further on is the beach.

Ballinskelligs
An excellent, long, crescent-shaped sandy beach, quite sheltered with dunes behind for picnics. Toilets are close by (just along the road and signposted); walks out to a ruined abbey.
How to get there From Waterville travelling west towards Cahersiveen leave the main road 3 miles/5 km outside town at a left turn signposted for the Skellig Ring. About 3.5 miles/6 km further on is a T-junction. Again, take the left turn signposted for the Skellig Ring. The beach is a left turn 2.5 miles/4 km past a foodstore/inn called the Sigerson's Arms.

Reenroe Strand
Further along towards Waterville is another stretch of sand, quite as safe and sandy as Ballinskelligs beach. Keep away from the Inny estuary area though. No facilities and difficult for wheelchairs.
How to get there On the Skellig Ring road to Waterville 3 miles/5.3 km from Ballinskelligs, at a crossroads with a blue sign for Iveragh Ceramics, a road goes down towards the sea. From Waterville leave the Ring of Kerry road 3 miles/5 km out of town at the Skellig Ring sign and 2.6 miles/4.4 km further on look for the blue Iveragh Ceramics sign. Further on towards Waterville is another unmarked potholed track down to the sea but this is much closer to the estuary. Good for bird spotting though.

Waterville Beach
Directly beside the village of Waterville, it is safe for swimming and has public toilets and access to shops/restaurants. Another beach area is close by the Waterville golf course.

Derrynane
In the grounds of the Derrynane National Park are two excellent beaches although there are dangerous currents marked at the beach in front of the house. The furthest beach, close by Abbey Island, is more sheltered and safer for swimming.
Toilets are in Derrynane House. Wheelchair access. Both beaches have car parks.
How to get there To get to the beaches follow the signs for Derrynane House from the Ring of Kerry road at Waterville or at Caherdaniel.

Silver Strand
Clearly visible from the Ring of Kerry road at Caherdaniel, this beach is well sheltered and safe for swimming. Good wheelchair access and facilities close by at O'Carroll's Beach Bar.
How to get there At Caherdaniel look for the signposted road going off to the beach.

White Strand
Safe, sheltered and good for swimming. No facilities but good wheelchair access.
How to get there A mile out of Castlecove village on the road to Sneem. Not much parking space.

FISHING

Fresh Water Fishing

The Iveragh peninsula is a fisherman's paradise. There are several major river systems offering salmon and sea trout, and many lakes with native brown trout and stocked rainbow trout.

Starting from Kenmare and working westwards and then back to Killorglin, they are:

The Roughty River. Sea trout and brown trout from 15 March to 12 October, salmon from 15 March to 30 September. The river flows through various parcels of land and permission should be sought from the landowners. There are no well-established fishing spots except at Kilgarvan where permits can be bought from John O'Hare, fishing tackle shop, Main Street, Kenmare.

The Finnihy River. This is north-west of Kenmare and produces grilse, sea trout and brown trout. Permits from the Estate Office, Kenmare, telephone 064–41341.

Barfinnihy Lake. 6 miles/10 km north-west of Kenmare, on the Sneem-Killarney road. 35 acres and close to the road. The whole shoreline is accessible and good for fishing. Try worms using a float or artificial flies or a small spinner. This is regularly stocked with rainbow trout by the Fisheries Board and has native wild brown trout. Information and permits from O'Hare's fishing tackle shop, Kenmare.

Blackwater River. 7 miles/11.9 km west of Kenmare on the Ring of Kerry. Salmon, grilse and sea trout. Ask at the Estate Office, Kenmare.

Lough Fadda. 15 June – 31 August. 11 miles/15 km south-west of Kenmare, 3 miles/ 5 km from Sneem. 14-acre lake conveniently beside the road. At the eastern end is a good area for fly fishing using artificial flies or a spinner but the northern steep banks make angling difficult. It is stocked with rainbow trout and there are some rudd and eels. Boats and permits from Mrs O'Sullivan, Direenamackion, Tahilla, or from Mrs N. Hussey, Sneem.

Sneem River. A spate river. Grilse and sea trout in July and August. Apply to Mr Henry Cooper, Sneem.

The Waterville system. This is a system of ten lakes which drain onto one another and then via the Waterville River to the sea. The small stretch of river from Lake Currane to the sea is a private fishery which occasionally allows fishing. It gets spring salmon and grilse. Permission should be sought from Waterville House, telephone 066–74244.

Lough Currane. Fishing here is free and public access is via the Bog, the Bridge and Water Lily bay. It is noted for very large sea trout, which begin arriving in April peaking in mid-June. It also gets spring salmon which can be fished from 17 January. Grilse peak in June. Many people hire boats in Waterville. Try Mr Michael Sullivan, The Lobster Bar, Waterville.

Cummeragh River. This feeds Lough Currane. It occasionally gets spring salmon and is good for sea trout and grilse. Fishing is private. Contact Waterville House. The loughs above the Cummeragh River have small brown trout, and sea trout and salmon late in the season, especially September and October. Ask at Waterville House.

Inny River. North-west of Waterville, not the best fishing, usually only good in spate conditions. Fishing rights are owned by many different landowners. Enquire at the Butler Arms Hotel, Waterville.

The Behy River system. Loughs Coomncronia, Coomaglaslaw, and Coomasaharn feed the river Behy which runs down into Rossbeigh. Coomasaharn has a special kind of salmon — Steel blue char. The lower reaches of the river are good for salmon and sea trout. Enquire at the hotels in Glenbeigh.

The Caragh River system. This is a system of six small loughs which drain into Caragh Lake and from there via the River Caragh into Dingle Bay. Loughs Cloon, and Reagh at the extremes of the system have brown trout and some salmon. The Caragh River between here and Caragh Lake is well known for its fishing, especially around Glencar. Ask at the Glencar Hotel, telephone 066–60102.

Lough Nakirka, 6 miles/9.5 km south-west of Killorglin, a 20-acre mountain lake. Good access to 90 percent of the shore on a surfaced road. Brown trout, rainbow trout, eel and rudd.

Sea Fishing

There are many good spots for shore angling around the peninsula. Starting from Kenmare, *Blackwater Harbour*, where the river Blackwater meets the sea, is good for bottom fishing and spinning for pollack, conger, ray, and sea trout. Around Sneem, *Gleesk, Oysterbed Pier, Tahilla Cove* and *Rossmore Island* provide good spots for wrasse, pollock, dogfish, conger, mackerel and sea trout. Around Waterville good spots for shore fishing are the beach below the car park, where flounder, plaice, dogfish and bass can be caught; at *Hog's Head Point* fishing off the rocks into deep water provides pollack, dab, conger, wrasse, codling and mackerel; at *Inny Strand* surf fishing at the river mouth and beach fishing for flatfish and bass. In the Skellig ring area surf fishing is possible at *St Finan's Bay* for flounder, dab and bass. On Valentia Island *Valentia Harbour* is a good spot, *Culloo* has rocks where pollock, wrasse and mackerel can be caught while the harbour at *Glanleam* is good for bottom fishing for ray and conger and float fishing for mullet. The bridge from *Portmagee* on to the island can provide good spots for dogfish and small pollock. Along the north shore of the peninsula shore fishing is best at *Glenbeigh* where spinning for sea trout is possible at *Rossbeigh Creek*, and surf fishing at the beach. At *Cromane Point* bass can be caught by spinning on the early flood, while at the eastern side of the point there is bottom fishing for flounder.

Deep Sea Fishing

There are any number of boats for hire from Valentia, Waterville, Kells Bay, Portmagee, Killorglin, Sneem, Caherdaniel. Fishing is carried out at a depth of 30 to 50 fathoms and can include blue shark. Approved boats for hire from Paudie O'Shea of Stone House, Sneem, telephone 064–45188; Aidan McAuliffe of Locktar Cua, Waterville, telephone 066–74519; Dan McCrohan of Knightstown, Valentia, telephone 066–76142; Sean O'Shea of Bunavalla, Caherdaniel, telephone 066–75129; Michael O'Sullivan at the Lobster Bar, Waterville, telephone 066–74255; Michael Lynch, Sea View, Kells Bay, telephone 066–77610.

Derrynane House, home of Daniel O'Connell, Co. Kerry

AQUA SPORTS

The Kenmare River can be windsurfed. The stretch between the pier and the islands near Dromquinna is recommended for tacking and gybing.

Derrynane Sea Sports, Bunvalla, Caherdaniel, telephone 066–75266, is based at Derrynane Harbour and has sailboards, rescue boats, wetsuits, etc and offers instruction using a simulator and on site. They will do four- and six-hour courses or arrange residential courses.

At *Caragh Lake* boats can be hired from *Aldersgrove House,* telephone 066–69275. Water Ski-ing on the lake is possible plus hire of equipment and lessons, telephone 066–69200.

Cappanlea Outdoor Education Centre, telephone 066–69244, offers windsurfing and canoeing courses.

At *Valentia* are two Diving Centres. *Des Lavelle's,* telephone 066–76124, at Knightstown does holiday packages including accommodation, boat, air compressors and weights or will do non-residential weekly/daily or part-daily packages from April to October. The *Valentia Hyperbaric Centre,* telephone 066–76225 has two boats, a decompression chamber and professional divers to accompany expeditions. It also offers B&B packages plus daily rates.

Skellig Aquatics Centre, Caherdaniel, telephone 066–75277, offers diving expeditions accompanied by experienced divers and marine biologist. Compressors, hire cylinders and weights and self-catering accommodation. Daily and weekly rates. Experienced divers only.

Waterskiing is arranged by *The Great Southern Hotel,* Parknasilla, telephone 064–45122, from May to September. Advance booking essential. Skis and wetsuits provided.

Waterville Leisure Hostel. This centre at Waterville is a water sports centre. Telephone 066–74644.

DRAGHUNTING

This may be a new sport to the visitor to Ireland. It consists of a bait being pulled over a course and hounds released to follow it. The first one to the bait is the winner. At least it's better than foxhunting! There are local draghunts every Sunday at various locations. John Sugrue at the Beentee Hotel, Cahersiveen knows all about the year's fixtures.

GOLF

There are eight golf courses in Co. Kerry, four of them on this peninsula. Green fees vary but range between £15 and £35 per day. If you are keen to play you should book well in advance.

The Kenmare Golf Club. Clubs and caddy cars available for hire (telephone 064–41291)

Dooks Golf Club, Glenbeigh, telephone 066–68205.

Waterville Golf Club, Waterville. Championship course. Telephone 066–4102. Liam Higgins has a golf clinic there and there is a pro shop.

Killorglin Country Club, telephone 066–61106.

HORSE RIDING

Hazlefort Farm. Ballymalis, Beaufort, telephone 066–44298. Next to Beaufort Castle. Pony trekking, pony and trap trips, around castle.

The Dromquinna Stables, telephone 066–41043. Situated 3 miles/4.7 km outside of Kenmare on the Sneem road. Horses and ponies for hire and tuition is available.

Glenbeigh Riding Stables. Telephone 066–68143. Open April–October. Offers trekking and hacking.

Brendan O'Donoghue. Cahersiveen, telephone 066–72703, trekking and trap rides.

ORIENTEERING

The Hostel, Caherdaniel, telephone 066–75277, fax 066–75277, organises courses in hill walking, campcraft, abseiling, rock climbing, survival training, navigation and orienteering.

WALKING TOURS AND HOLIDAYS

There are several organisations which will arrange guided walks of the hills of the peninsula concentrating on wildlife, historical sites.

Walk-a-Way Holidays, Lower Bridge Street, Killorglin, telephone 066–61940, arranges trips.

Kerry Country Rambles (see Killarney section). The Kerry Way crosses the peninsula and is an excellent week's walk.

Kenmare Leisure Ltd, telephone 064–41044. Guided walking tours around Kenmare and guided walks and climbs in McGillycuddy's Reeks, the Caha Mountains and the Dunkerrons. They also hold an annual walking festival on the June bank holiday weekend.

EVENING ACTIVITIES

As in other chapters this will be more or less a list of good pubs to visit with live music or good atmosphere.

Caherdaniel

The Blind Piper. Games room and traditional music most nights.

Tom's Beach Bar. The only beach bar in Ireland and has music most nights.

Cahersiveen

There are fifty-two bars and pubs in Cahersiveen, many of them offering live music in the evenings in the summer.

The *Shebeen* and the *Town House* have tourist oriented music lounges.

The *Skellig Rock Bar* has music every night.

Tom's Tavern has music and dancing from Thursday to Sunday nights.

The Harp sometimes has discos.

The Anchor doesn't have music but has a good atmosphere.

Glenbeigh

Towers Hotel. Singalongs in the dining room for diners and various musical events nightly in the bar.

The Olde Glenbeigh Hotel. Music and dancing in the bar.

The Red Fox Inn. Music from Wednesday to Sunday in the summer.

The Ross Inn. This place often has bands performing but you should check shop windows for news of any event.

Caitin Beatear's. Outside of Glenbeigh is just along the road to Kenmare at Kells, is very tour bus oriented and has traditional dancing and music sessions every night.

Kenmare

Music is a very spontaneous busines in Kenmare and it's worth having a good look around to see what is on.

The Lansdowne Arms. Music every night except Sunday.

Crowley's, Brennan's, The Atlantic Bar. All have music sessions quite regularly, as well as old time and set dancing.

Killorglin

Oisin Cinema, The Square. Current movies every night except Thursday.

The Old Forge, Main Street. Traditional ballad singers, Thursday to Sunday.

The Kingdom Bar, Main Street, traditional music nightly. Pub food.

The Castle Bar, Main Street, Live music and dancing at weekends.

Bianconi's, Lower Bridge Street. Has a piano player every evening.

Sneem

Sneem is very definitely geared to the tour bus trade and although a very pretty little village, don't expect terribly authentic entertainment.

Cantharella Hotel has traditional ballad sessions as does *Sneem House, Dan Murphy's* and the *Blue Bull.*

Valentia Island

Live music is to be had at *The Royal Pier Hostel* and *Boston's Bar* (Fridays and Sundays).

The Ring Lynne. Music on Mondays and Wednesdays.

The Bridge Bar, Portmagee (on the other side of the bridge) has music on Friday and Sunday all year also Tuesday and Wednesday from June to September, and free set dancing lessons every Tuesday night.

Waterville

The *Villa Maria* and *The Fisherman's* are olde worlde style bars, while *The Lobster, The Bay View,* and *The Jolly Swagman,* have ballad singing sessions. Discos may be enjoyed at *The Bay View* and *The Strand. The Lobster* also has a pool table.

The Inny Tavern has traditional music and set dancing every Friday and Sunday night from July to September. The pub is at Killeenleigh on the road to the Ballaghisheen Pass.

WHERE TO STAY

HOTELS

The following hotels are categorised here according to cost, again using the descending scale of high, moderate, budget, and ecenomy.

Caherdaniel

Derrynane Hotel, telephone 066–75136, fax 066–75160. Large modern hotel with outdoor pool, games room, TV lounge. Babysitting, children's playroom. Closed November to February. AE, AM, DE, VB. Three star. Rating: budget.

Scarriff Inn, telephone 066–75132. Guest house with a restaurant and bar, a games room, garden, and offers children's meals. AM, VB. Closed November to February. One star. Rating: economy.

Cahersiveen

Ringside Rest, Valentia Road, telephone 066–72543. Wheelchair friendly. AM, AE, DE, VB. One star. Rating: economy.

Glenbeigh

Falcon Inn Hotel, telephone 066–68215, fax 066-68411. Children's meals, a garden, some en suite rooms, games room. AM, VB. One star. Rating: economy.

Glenbeigh Hotel, telephone 066–68333. 150-year-old inn with garden, children's meals, babysitting service. AM, VB. One star. Rating: economy.

Towers Hotel, telephone 066–68212, fax 066–68260. Gardens, TV, children's meals, AM, AE, DE, VB. Three star. Rating: budget.

Kenmare

The Park, telephone 064–41200, fax 064–41402. Very classy hotel. TV, gardens, lifts, games room, children's meals. AM, AE, DE, VB. Five star. Rating: high.

Sheen Falls Lodge, telephone 064–41600, fax 064–41386. TV, tennis, gardens, lots of class. AM, AE, DE, VB. Five Star. Rating: high.

Riversdale, telephone 064–41299, fax 064–41075. Close to the Sheen Falls Lodge, gardens, TV, gardens games room, tennis, children's meals. AM, AE, DE, VB. Three star. Rating: budget.

Lansdowne Arms Hotel, telephone 064–41368, fax 064–41114. TV and video in rooms, tea making facilities, and lots of history. AM, AE, VB. Open all year. Two star. Rating: budget.

Kenmare Bay Hotel, telephone 064–41300, fax 064–41541, geared to families, with a babysitting service, gardens, and child meals. AM, AE, DE, VB. Closed January to March. Three star. Rating: budget.

Dromquinna Manor Hotel, telephone 064–41657, fax 064–41791. TV, gardens tennis, lifts. Another very exclusive hotel in a nineteenth-century mansion with vast grounds, its own stables, a large sea frontage and a treehouse! AM, AE, DE, VB. Three star. Rating: moderate to high.

The Wander Inn, telephone 064–41038. One star. Rating: economy.

Killorglin

Ard Na Sidhe, Caragh Lake, telephone 066–69105, fax 066–69282. Victorian mansion beside Caragh Lake. Lots of antiques, good as base for golf enthusiast. Gardens, fishing, boating. AM, AE, DE, VB. Closed October to April. Four Star. Rating: high.

Caragh Lodge, Caragh Lake, telephone 066–69115, fax 066–69316. Victorian fishing lodge, 7.5 acres of rare and subtropical plants, swimming, fishing in lake, tennis, sauna. AM, VB. Closed October to Easter. Four star guesthouse. Rating: moderate.

Bianconi, Annadale Road, telephone 066–61146, fax 066–61950. Children's meals, TV lounge, gardens, babysitting arranged. AM, AE, DE, VB. Three star guesthouse. Rating: economy.

Sneem

Great Southern Hotel, Parknasilla, telephone 064–45122, fax 064–45323. Megaposh hotel in nineteenth-century mansion. 121 hectares of semitropical gardens. TV, indoor heated saltwater pool, sauna, games room, tennis, horses, private 9 hole golf course — the list is endless. AM, AE, DE, VB. Closed January to Easter. Four star. Rating: high.

Cantharella Country Inn. At the Kenmare end of town, telephone 064–4517 has en suite rooms, satellite TV in rooms and does evening meals. AM, AE. One star. Rating: economy.

Waterville

Club Med, Upmarket leisure hotel, telephone 066–74133, fax 066–74483. Set at the side of Lough Currane east of the town. All sorts of facilities. Club Med is more a holiday centre than just a hotel. Most people spend whole holidays in the hotel and arrange package deals. AM, AE, DE, VB. Four star. Rating: high.

Butler Arms Hotel, telephone 066–74144, fax 066–774520. Family run hotel with long list of famous guests including Charlie Chaplin and Virginia Woolf. Free salmon fishing for guests, babysitting, children's meals, TV lounge, tennis, snooker, gardens. Reductions in green fees. AM, AE, DE, VB. Three star. Rating: high.

Smuggler's Inn, telephone 066–774330, fax 066–74422. Small family-run guesthouse on sandy beach, playground, children's meals, gardens. AM, AE, DE, VB. Two star. Rating: economy.

Villa Maria Hotel, telephone 066–74248, fax 066–74635. TV, Pub/ disco/ hotel. AM, AE, DE, VB. One star. Rating: economy.

Strand Hotel, telephone 066–74436, fax 066–74635. Children's meals. AM, VB. One star. Rating: economy.

SELF-CATERING

There are lots of individual self-catering places throughout the peninsula. The tourist board has a system which will book any one of their listed places for you. Self-catering places are very popular and should be booked as far in advance as possible.

The following is a list of the holiday villages or groups of bungalows in the area.

Caragh Village Holiday Centre, telephone 066–69200. Three-star, three-bedroomed cottages, all mod cons, near Caragh Lake. Caragh Village Holiday Homes, Caragh Lake.

Derrynane Garden Village. four-star cottages, four-bedroomed, near to Caherdaniel, close to sandy beach, fully serviced, all mod cons. Trident Holiday Homes, Unit 2 Sandymount Village Centre, Dublin 4, telephone 01–683543, fax 01–606466.

Rossbeigh Beach Holiday Cottages. Two-star. Overlooking beach, all mod cons, three bedrooms. The Cahill family, Rossbeigh Beach Holiday Cottages, Rossbeigh beach, Glenbeigh, telephone 066–68236, fax 021–27350.

Dunkerron Holiday Cottages. two-star three-bedroomed, all mod cons, close to water's edge, 2.5 miles/4 km from Kenmare. Trident Holiday Homes (for address and phone/fax see above)

Kenmare River Holiday Cottages. Three-star. One- to five-bedroomed cottages, all mod cons, on waterfront. Bridie O'Sullivan, Kenmare River Holiday Cottages, 45 Ard na Lee, Oakpark, Tralee, telephone 066–26323, fax 066–23422.

HOSTELS

Hostels offer dormitory accommodation plus cooking facilities at the lowest cost, probably including camping. Most places charge around £5–£6 per night. Many other services such as private rooms, the use of bicycles, packed lunches, evening meals. They are great places to exchange information with other independent travellers if you don't mind the lack of privacy.

Caherdaniel
Carrigbeg Hostel, telephone 066–75229, is 1 mile/1.7 km outside Caherdaniel on the road to Waterville. Open all year, dormitory accommodation, meals available and laundry.

Village Hostel, telephone 066–75277. Open all year, showers extra, low season discount, laundry.

Cahersiveen
Sive Hostel, at east end of town, telephone 066–72717. Common room with TV, laundry facilities, private rooms. Open all year, showers extra.

Kenmare
The *IHO Fáilte Hostel* is situated in town at the corner of Shelbourne Street and Henry Street. On the road to Glengarriff, 4.3 miles/7 km from Kenmare, the *Bonane Hostel* (telephone 064–41098) has 20 beds. It is situated immediately behind the Catholic church on the main road.

Failte Hostel, telephone 064–41083. Private rooms and dormitory accommodation, free showers, open all year, bike hire, pick-up from nearest town or village.

Killorglin
Laune Valley Farm Hostel, telephone 066–61488, open all year, meals available, off-season discount, laundry, wheelchair friendly, satellite TV. 1.3 miles/2 km out of town on the road to Tralee.

Valentia
Ring Lynne, Chapeltown, telephone 066–76103. Open all year, dormitory and double sharing accommodation, showers extra, low-season discount, family rooms. Laundry, camping, free pick-up, wheelchair friendly. TV, music, darts.

Royal and Pier Hostel, Knightstown, telephone 066–76144. Open all year, showers extra, laundry. Faded luxury of old Victorian hotel, TV, pool table, darts, restaurant, organised activities.

An Óige, Knightstown, telephone 066–76141. Converted coastguardmen's cottages, family rooms available. An Óige membership card needed. Accessible all day.

Waterville
Waterville Leisure Hostel. Open from March to end September, telephone 066–74644, showers extra, meals available, family rooms, laundry, bike hire, wheelchair friendly.

CAMPING AND CARAVAN SITES

Caherdaniel
Wave Crest Caravan and Camping Park, telephone 066–75188. TV room, shop, playground, dog friendly. Four-star.

Cahersiveen
Mannix Point Caravan and Camping Park, telephone 066–72806. Free showers, sitting room, tourist information, situated on Kerry Way. Two-star.

Glenbeigh
Falvey's Caravan Park, telephone 066–68238. Pitches for caravans and tents, sited mobile homes for hire, close to forest and beach. Two-star.
Glenross Caravan and Camping Park, telephone 066–68451. Open May–September. Washing machines, playground, dog friendly. Three-star.

Kells
Kells Bay Caravan and Camping Park, telephone 066–77647. Open from March–September. Shop, playground, dog friendly. One-star.

Kenmare
Ring of Kerry Caravan and Camping Site, telephone 064–41366. Washing machines, shop, playroom, TV room. Four-star.

Killorglin
West's Camping Site. 2 km from bridge on road to Killarney. Telephone 066–61240. Washing facilities, TV room, shop, playroom, playground. Three-star.

Waterville
Waterville Caravan and Camping Park, telephone 066–74191. 1 km from sea, small swimming pool, shop, playground, playroom, TV lounge, dog friendly, washing machines. Open from March to September. Four-star.

WHERE TO EAT

As before, the ratings descend in the following order, based roughly on cost: high, moderate, budget, economy.

Caherdaniel
The Courthouse Café. Main Street, snacks and light meals. Rating: economy.
Loaves and Fishes. Open from 6 to 9.30 p.m. Limited but high-quality menu, recommended by all sorts of magazines. No children. AM, VB. Closed from end September to Easter. Vegetarian dishes on request. Rating: high.
The Blind Piper. This pub has a restaurant and also does bar food. Rating: budget to moderate.
Scarriff Inn. Seafood and steak restaurant. Great views but watch out for the coach parties. Children's menu. AM, VB. Rating: budget
O'Carroll's Cove Beach Bar. Self-service food and a la carte seafood restaurant. Rating: budget.

Cahersiveen
Grudles. Good value economy food. Rating: economy.
The Old Schoolhouse. Telephone 066–72426. Exclusive and expensive seafood restaurant but with excellent reputation. AM, AE, DE, VB. Rating: high.
O'Driscoll's Town House, Newmarket Street. Serves good food of the steak and pizza variety at reasonable prices. Rating: budget.
Ringside Rest, telephone 066–72543. Mass food for coach parties. AM, VB. Rating: budget.
The Red Rose. Opposite O'Connell Memorial Church, wine bar, coffee bar, takeouts from 6 to 10 p.m. Rating: budget.
Kevy's Fast Food. Main Street, Burgers etc. Rating: economy.
The *Beentee Hotel* and the *Daniel O'Connell Hotel* both serve evening meals, both budget prices.
The *Central Bar, The Shebeen, Tom's Tavern* and the *Fertha Bar* both do pub food as

does the *Sceilig Rock Bar.*

Glenbeigh

Towers Hotel, telephone 066–68212. Large menu, seafood specialities with piano and singalong. AM, AE, DE, VB. Rating: high.

The Olde Glenbeigh Hotel. Has an interesting dining room full of antiques and a relaxing atmosphere. Large menu and wine list. Seafood a speciality. Open 7 days. Rating high. It also does bar food daily. AM, VB. Rating: moderate.

The Falcon Inn. Modest menu. AM, VB. Rating: moderate.

The Glendale. Children's meals. Rating: economy.

Bini's. Open till 10 p.m. Children's meals. Rating: economy.

The Red Fox Inn. Restaurant and bar food. Pub lunches 12 to 3 p.m.

Ross Inn. Pub food and full meals.

Caitin Beatear's. Kells. Open for food all day — very much geared to passing traffic, especially buses. Music in morning and evening. Rating: budget.

Kenmare

Kenmare is very much a vital part of the Ring of Kerry circuit and more than half of the establishments in town are geared to the tourist market. Restaurants abound, particularly at lunch time and there is a menu and price to suit every pocket. For some of its more exclusive restaurants, Kenmare really needs a new category in the price range, very high.

The Park, telephone 064–41200 and *Sheen Falls Lodge*, telephone 064–41600 have French-style restaurants. Both are in the very high price range even for lunches. AM, AE, DE, VB. Both close from January to Easter.

Long Lake, telephone 064–45100. Eleven miles out of town on the road to Sneem. Reservations are necessary and the five-course evening meal is expensive but excellent. AM, AE, DE, VB. Rating: high.

The Lansdowne Arms, William Street. Has a restaurant with traditional steak/soups and sandwiches type menu. AM, AE, VB. Rating: moderate.

The Lime Tree, telephone 064–41225. An old stone building which has been renovated and serves French-style cuisine. It is open from 6.30 p.m. to 9.30 p.m., closed on Sundays and from November to April. AM, VB. Rating: moderate.

Darcy's Restaurant. Situated in the Old Bank House, Main Street. First-class inventive menu, especially the starters. AM, VB. Rating: high.

The Coachman Inn, Henry Street. Has a good lunch menu of salads, sandwiches and hot dishes for economy prices while its dinner menu is also well priced. Rating: moderate.

Le Brasserie, Henry Street. Offers good choices including vegetarian and child priced meals and is unpretentious inside.

The Swiss Bell, opposite the Kenmore Bay Hotel on the road to Sneem. Offers fine dining at corresponding prices. Rating: high.

An Leath Pingin, Main Street. Open from 6 p.m. and does Italian style food, mostly pizza and pasta dishes at good prices. Rating: budget.

The Horseshoe, Main Street. Pub cum restaurant, comfortable looking inside with some nice starters, open from 6–10 p.m. It also does bar snacks.

Brennan's, Main Street. Another pub doing meals which are listed on blackboard outside and change daily. Rating: moderate.

The Atlantic. Bar which does a daily lunch special. Rating: moderate.

Micky Ned's, Main Street. Coffee shop in Henry Street doing sandwiches and salads with vegetarian choices from 9 a.m. to 5.30 p.m. Rating: economy.

Clifford's Bakery and Coffee Shop. Does a similar range — soups, pizza, sandwiches. Rating: economy.

Foley's, Henry Street. Pub food all day and a reasonable restaurant. Rating: moderate.

The Purple Heather Bistro, Henry Street. Open Monday to Saturday, 11 a.m. to 7 p.m. Small and does snacks, soup and paté rather than meals. Rating: budget.

Kenmare aslo has several takeaway burger joints.

Killorglin

Bunkers. Takeaway and restaurant. Budget food. Steaks, grills, fish and pasta, vegetarian salad. Open 7 days, dinner specials.

Nick's, Lower Bridge Street, telephone 066–61219. Seafood and steaks. Open from 6 p.m. Bar food during day. AE, VB. Rating: moderate.

Bianconi, Lower Bridge Street, telephone 066–61146. Bar food till 9.30, set dinner in restaurant from 6.30 p.m., possibilities for vegetarians. Pizza bar closes with the pub. AM, AE, DE, VB. Rating: moderate.

Caragh Lodge, Caragh Lake, telephone 066–69115. Dinner from 7.30 – 8.30 p.m., reservations necessary, lots of ambience, lake views, fireside drinks. Make a night of it. Easter–mid October. AM, AE, DE, VB. Rating: high.

The Fishery, telephone 066–61670. Open 7 days, 'Irish' night on Sundays. Dinner and cabaret. Lunches 12.30–2 p.m. May to end August. AM, AE, DE, VB. Rating: high.

The Goat Inn, Langford Street, telephone 066–61621. Large menu, tourist set dinner, few vegetarian choices, lunch menu and bar food. Rating: budget.

Starlite Diner. The Square, cafeteria atmosphere and food. Rating: economy.

Egan's Restaurant. The Square. Similar style and food.

Sneem

Cantharella Hotel. Reasonable prices for standard meals. Telephone 064–45187. AM, AE. Rating: budget.

Blue Bull. Bar food including Irish Stew, chicken curry, sandwiches and soup. Rating: budget. It also has a regular restaurant with an extensive menu. Telephone 064–45382. AM, AE, DE, VB. Rating: moderate to high.

Riverain. Has a tourist evening menu as well as an a la carte. AM, AE, VB. Rating: moderate to high.

Pygmalion. The restaurant at the Great Southern Hotel has a huge reputation to match its prices. AM, AE, DE, VB. Rating: high.

There is also the *Village Kitchen, Riverside Coffee Shop* and *The Green House* doing Irish Stew and sandwiches.

Valentia Island

The Islander. Café at western end of Knightstown. Café style food with some nice items such as garlic mussels. No vegetarian choices except salad. Rating: budget.

Gallery Kitchen. Restaurant, wine bar, sculpture gallery. AE, VB. Rating: budget.

The Ring Lynne. This is a hostel but does food for non-residents. Meals served till 10 p.m. Rating: budget.

Tailor Casey's. Restaurant attached to the Boston Bar. Daily specials. Pub food all day. Rating: economy.

The Royal Pier Hostel. This hostel has a restaurant which serves evening meals at budget prices. Rating: budget.

Harbour Pantry. Restaurant and wine bar. Rating: budget.

Curran's supermarket at Churchtown has a tiny burger bar which opens at odd hours doing sandwiches and burgers. Rating: economy.

The Bridge Bar and *The Fisherman's Bar* at Portmagee also do pub food. The Fisherman's Bar has a restaurant serving fresh catch of the day — oysters, mussels, lobster. Open from 7 to 9 p.m. Rating: budget.

Waterville

Sheilin Seafood Restaurant, telephone 066–74231. Bistro-ish. Good value tourist menu. AM, AE, DE, VB. Open from 12.30 to 10.30 p.m. Rating: high.

Smugglers' Inn Restaurant, Cliff Road, telephone 066–774330. On the beach near to Waterville Golf Club. Seafood and meat, vegetarian choices, open from 12.30 to 10 p.m. Closed from November to February. AM, AE, DE, VB. Rating: high.

The Huntsman. West of Waterville, has both a restaurant and a café style menu and does fairly good value lunches and expensive but good quality evening meals. Caters to large coach parties as well as smaller groups. AM, DE, VB. Rating: tourist menu, moderate; restaurant, high.

Lobster Bar. Noticeable by virtue of the gigantic lobster clinging to the outside wall, does mostly fish dishes with steak and bolognaise. Meals range from economy dishes such as chicken and chips to expensive lobster, scallops etc. AM, DE, VB. Rating: budget to high.

Fisherman's Bar and Restaurant. Butler Arms Hotel. Seafood, meat dishes. Bar food lunches. AM, AE, DE, VB. Rating: moderate.

The Inny Tavern. Outside Waterville on the road to Ballaghisheen Pass. Bar snacks all day. Rating: economy.

The Jolly Swagman is another pub, half a kilometre west of town, doing pub food. Rating: budget.

The *Villa Maria Hotel* does bar food as does the *Bay View Hotel.* Rating: economy to budget.

SHOPPING FOR GIFTS AND SOUVENIRS

Caherdaniel
Staigue Fort Pottery, Castle Cove. Local pottery and other items.

Cahersiveen
Human Clay. Pottery and gallery which sells hand-made pots and landscape paintings by Pauline Bewick. Open 7 days, 10 a.m. to 6 p.m.

The Studio, 1 New Street. Crafts from around the world and paintings by John Baskeyfield.

Art, by Regine Bartsch, New Street. Tapestries.

Elma Shine, picture gallery, 3 New Street. Original paintings and framing.

Scelig Crystal is located at Unit 7, Cahersiveen Industrial Estate and is open from 9 a.m. to 5 p.m. all year. Craft workshops can be visited and there is a mail order service.

The Old Oratory is on West Main Street and opens until 7 p.m. in the summer. An old church has been converted to an art gallery and craft shop. Ceramics, batik, glass and designer knitware.

Thatch Craft Cottage is at Strandsend and opens from 10 a.m. to 6 p.m. including Sunday. Knitware, pottery, crystal, books and tapes, souvenirs.

Fuschia Cottage Pottery is 4 miles/7 km from Cahersiveen on the main road to Waterville. Hand-made figures and animals, sculptures and paintings and jewellery. The tourist office also has a small craft shop.

Kells
The Thatch Craft Cottage sells crafts and has a coffee shop and crazy golf.

Pat's Craft Shop, situated on the main road, is a family-run store with craft items and gifts.

Kenmare
Quill's Woollen Market is a large shop that stocks a combination of quality garments, gifts and souvenirs.

Nostalgia in Henry Street sells lace, patchwork and other reminders of bygone days. Open from 10.30 a.m. to 5 p.m.

The *Kenmare Bookshop* in Shelbourne Street has an extensive list of books about Ireland and of local interest as well as children's books and novels. *Curlew Craft Shop* in Main Street sells an interesting collection of foreign and local crafts while *De Barra* next door is a jewellers with some pretty silver jewellery including Celtic designs. Close by, *The Craft Shop* sells stained glass and pottery all of Irish manufacture.

The Spindle and Treadle in Main Street is a weavers' workshop selling materials for weaving and the products of the loom.

In Henry Street *Stone Circle Crafts* has some nice pieces of pottery and locally made candles while further along *Kenmare Pottery and Iverni Art Gallery* sells crafts and original paintings.

Cleo's, Shelbourne Street, sells outstanding clothes in linen, tweed and other fabrics, all cut to traditional patterns and styles.

Killorglin
O'Boyle Jewellers, The Square, Claddagh jewellery, Celtic designed necklets and earrings.
Crowley's Irish Lace Shop, Market Street, Irish lace tableware and bedlinen.
Sheeog Craft Shop, Langford Street, Irish crafts and art gallery.

Sneem
There is a branch of *Quill's Woollen Mills* in Sneem selling the same things as the branches in Killarney and Kenmare, mostly woollens and green things with Ireland written on.
Brushwood Studios is a craft shop selling Irish arts and crafts and original paintings, batik and sculptures. It is open from 9 a.m. to 9 p.m.
The Homestead Gift Shop, New Street, sells inexpensive small gifts.

Waterville
Waterville Craft Market, 0.7 miles/1 km out of town on the road to Caherdaniel. Arts and crafts, books, art gallery.
Iveragh Ceramics, Fermoyle, Ballinskelligs, telephone 066–79276. Handmade stoneware pottery.

CHILDREN'S ACTIVITIES

- *Cappanlea Outdoor Education Centre.* Oulagh West, Caragh Lake, telephone 066–69244. Day or week courses in mountaineering, canoeing, orienteering, windsurfing, sailing etc.
- An afternoon's *pony trekking*; see horse riding above.
- *Killorglin Sports and Leisure Centre,* telephone 066–61755, offers courses and activities for children aged seven to fifteen.
- *The Kerry Bog Village.* See page 101.
- Check out the cinemas particularly if it is a school holiday.
- Build sandcastles on the beach and watch the sea wash them away.
- Visit the heritage centre at Valentia and see what an old Irish national school looked like.
- Have a game of pool in the Pier Hotel in Valentia or the Lobster Bar in Waterville.
- Watch the big screen TV at the Lobster Bar in Waterville.

RAINY DAY ACTIVITIES

- Do a tour of the heritage centres: they are Kenmare heritage centre, beside the tourist office in Kenmare; Sneem museum; Cahersiveen; The Skellig experience at Valentia; the old national school at Knightstown, Valentia; Caitin Beatear's at Kells; and the Bog Village at Glenbeigh.
- Ignore the rain and go for a walk.
- Try the cinema at Killorglin.
- Spend the day wandering through gift shops looking for holiday gifts.
- Find a good pub.
- Visit the Blind Piper at Caherdaniel which has a games room.

ECOTOUR

KENMARE TO THE GAP OF DUNLOE VIA DERRYNANE, VALENTIA ISLAND, WATERVILLE, THE BALLAGHASHEEN PASS AND GLENCAR

This tour begins at Kenmare and follows the main Ring of Kerry route until Waterville. From here the ecotour visits Valentia Island and then returns to Waterville from where it heads inland through the middle of the peninsula. The remainder of the Ring of Kerry circuit, from Waterville to Killarney via Kells and Glenbeigh, is worth sacrificing for the unsurpassed scenery afforded by the Ballaghbeama Pass and the road that follows the shore of Caragh Lake to Glenbeigh.

An aerial view of Skellig Island, Co. Kerry

The Iveragh peninsula has always been an agricultural area with little or no other industry besides tourism. Chief among the types of farming carried out here has always been cattle rearing while the few crops grown are — or rather were, for they are becoming more and more marginalised — potatoes, fodder beet and oats. The onset of artificial fertiliser has helped to raise the importance of growing grass since there is no longer any need to supplement the cattle's diet of grass with other foods. At the same time, the effect of EU agricultural policy, as it affects Kerry and West Cork, has been to focus farmers' attention on the production of milk to the exclusion of everything else.

Partly as a result of this, very few non-native plant species have been able to establish themselves here. Whereas in other parts of Ireland introduced crops have had an effect on the local flora here there is little regularly cultivated land and so foreign species get little opportunity to find a niche. There are some dramatic exceptions to this general rule in the gardens cultivated at Derrynane, around Parknasilla and on Valentia Island but basically the flora of the area is poor but indigenous.

The tour starts at Kenmare, a town created for planters in 1670 and planned by the first Marquis of Lansdowne in 1775 with a pair of wide roads crossing at right angles. The basic plan is still obvious today with the old market square now housing a new heritage centre and tourist office, while the green planned two hundred years ago still provides a playspace for children. The town sits in an area of limestone laid down in the carboniferous era when all of Ireland lay beneath a shallow sea and shelled creatures died and sank to the sea floor. The limestone makes this valley a very fertile area and gives Kenmare a distinctive flora. Now given over to grass, fields in this area twenty years ago held crops of swedes, mangels and potatoes.

Link Kenmare to the River Blackwater, along the N70, 7 miles/11 km.

Travel north-west out of Kenmare on the road to Killarney and almost immediately out of town turn left for Sneem. The environment here is one of fertile low limestone hills. Some of the fields are dedicated to sheep farming with low grey stone walls and mature trees at the perimeter. The hedgerows at the sides of the road have a diversity of plant life; whitethorn and blackthorn are indigenous species but the sycamore which is also present is an invasive plant and can wipe out other species if left unchecked.

About 7 miles/11 km out of Kenmare the road twists sharply as it crosses the Blackwater river at its meeting with the sea.

Stop at the roadside near the bridge wherever it is convenient to park, 7 miles/11 km from Kenmare.

Below the bridge the river falls through a deep gorge into a deep and narrow inlet of the sea. Looking up the river you can see that it has flowed through a rib of rock but before this the river has formed a wide and open valley as a brief drive up the road signposted to Glencar will show. The woods around you and back towards Kenmare are Dromore Wood, once the ancestral home of the O'Mahony family whose castle, privately owned, still stands. The overhanging trees here at the bridge provide an interesting environment for plant life which enjoys shade, scanty soil and lots of dampness. Around the road in spring will be seen many primroses. Foxgloves show later and down under the bridge some quite rare ferns have developed unusual forms in order to survive. St Patrick's Cabbage is also here in an almost epiphytic state, growing on the moss covered oak trees.

Walk just beyond the bridge in the direction of Kenmare.

Beyond the bridge, in the direction of Kenmare, a gate leads to a forest road. Turning right off this road, on a path marked Cliff Walk, you find yourself on part of the Kerry Way on a walk of a few hundred metres following the shoreline. Across the Kenmare River you can see the glen which holds the Cloonee loughs and Glaninchiquin. Kenmare sits at the head of a ria, a river-carved valley deepened by glacier run-off water and submerged when sea levels rose. It is the longest and narrowest of the sea inlets of Kerry. The bed of the ria is shallow and V-shaped, offering good anchorage and calm waters to boats. The whole southern shore of the Iveragh peninsula is dotted with small safe anchorages now given over largely to water sports and pleasure trips where once small fishing boats put out in search of mackerel.

Link Blackwater river to coral beach. 17 miles/27 km.

Back on the road to Sneem, the land which up till now has been full of a diversity of plant life becomes bare. The road travels the very edge of the land through low twisted scrub of gorse and willow. Pools of water collect in the bare rock and only stunted forms of the indigenous trees survive. Across to the south are fine views of the Beara peninsula. The fuchsia, so common along the first few miles out of Kenmare, has disappeared.

Around 11 miles/18 km out of Kenmare the road passes through Tahilla, little more than a sub-post office and a church. Signs of habitation are the huge gunnera plant, a native of South America, which is becoming quite naturalised in some parts of the peninsula. Rhododendrons too make their presence felt; they are planted as windbreaks. Whereas in Killarney these plants are a threat to the native oak woods here they serve a useful purpose in providing shelter for other plants. Later, the road goes through pine plantations which have been planted at their outer edges with indigenous trees such as birch and willow.

The Parknasilla Hotel and adjacent gardens are 13 miles/2 km from Kenmare. The mild climate and sheltered position allow a variety of sub-tropical plants, such as tree ferns, gunnera in profusion, arbutus and many varieties of rhododendron to grow here. The gardens are open to the public and there is a pleasant walk along the shore.

Sneem is the next place of any importance. Here the river is an important spot for salmon fishing especially when it is in spate. After Sneem the landscape opens out a little as the hills get higher; the range of mountains begun in Killarney extend west and south to the sea. The road passes through more pine tree plantations set in rough damp marshy land. Among the plantations of Sitka spruce are larch trees, the only deciduous pine tree and one which allows a much greater diversity of life to live beneath its shade. In spring the larch plantations stand out as bright green patches on the hillsides. Smaller and newer plantations are growing up beside the older ones. There is little other sign of any other kind of agriculture.

A few miles after Sneem, the hills give way to a flat unfertile looking valley with much evidence of turf cutting. Five miles/8 km out of Sneem take a left turning signposted 'Coral Beach Bed and Breakfast'. Looking back across the valley tiny spots of green fertile land stand out in the dull green of boglands. In this peninsula most farms are still fairly tiny, consisting of ten or more acres of cultivable land surrounded by rough pasture. Only one-quarter of the total land is farmed even with the addition of artificial fertiliser. The population now is less than forty people to the square mile, less than half what it was in the late nineteenth century.

After 2 miles/3.5 km bear right where a green road goes off to the left. Another half km reveals Gleesk pier, a tiny sheltered spot with small sailboats moored.

Stop at the car park at Gleesk pier.

Park at the pier and walk eastwards back along the edge of the sea towards Sneem. Damp-loving plants grow here, especially the yellow iris, blooming in June. They can be identified even before they flower by the sharply pointed flat spikes, a little like domestic gladioli stems. Their yellow flower is like a large garden iris. Earlier in the year the cuckoo flower — the only food plant of the larvae of the orange tip butterfly — is widespread. The cuckoo flower stands high up out of the grass with distictive lavender-pink flowers in a spike at the top. From March to May celandines also blossom here. Closer to the sea, thrift dominates the bare rocky places.

About 100 metres past the pier a broken wire fence is easily crossed and the tiny coral beach, one of only two in the whole of Ireland, is revealed. Living corals can only survive in the warm waters of the tropics and in shallow water where light can penetrate. The fossil corals here date back to times when the seas around Ireland were much warmer. They are characteristically horn shaped and probably became extinct around 245 million years ago. There are other patches of coral like this in the region — and at one time an industry was formed dredging Bantry Bay collecting the coral for fertiliser — but a beach of coral like this is a rare phemonenon. The basic material of the coral is limestone.

Link Gleesk pier to Derrynane House. 9 miles/15km.

Return to the main Ring of Kerry road. The road continues along the lowland area for a time. To the north-west are the hills of Esknaloughogue and Eagles Hill, while the road is sandwiched between these hills and the sea. About 8 miles/13 km from Sneem the vista of White Strand beach opens up for a few seconds. Past the tiny village of Castlecove and the tourist infrastructure built up around Staigue Fort, Silver Strand opens up below. Here the impact of tourism on the region is glaringly obvious: holiday villages, caravan sites, shops and bars catering to the passing trade all litter the sea front.

Continuing along the Ring of Kerry road into Caherdaniel take a left turn signposted for Derrynane, the one-time home of O'Connell and now a National Park.

Stop in the car park in front of Derrynane House.

In front of Derrynane House is another of the sub-tropical gardens which flourish so well in West Cork and Kerry. Around the gates to the house are gunnera, New Zealand flax and tree ferns. Closer to the house a gap in the sheltering trees opens up and the effect of the winds from the sea can be seen in the stunted and damaged plants at the front of the house.

A walk around these gardens, particularly in spring, shows a profusion of plant life. St Patrick's Cabbage flourishes in the shade of the access road while other saxifrages are abundant. Under the trees are bluebells, celandines, St John's Wort, hedgerow cranesbill, herb robert, periwinkles, ragged robin, hart's tongue fern and pennywort.

Walk from the front of the entrance gates to the house to the left along the pathway going to the beach.

Follow the path as far as the sea. Here is an extensive system of dunes, a few thousand years old, where it is possible to see each of the stages of dune development and also what happens if the fragile dune system is damaged. At the edge of the beach are huge stones held together with nets. This area has in the immediate past been so eroded, not least by visitors to Derrynane House, that the covering flora which held the dunes together disappeared, leaving an exposed piece of sand. High winds began to breach the whole dune system threatening to bring the sea far into the established grassy areas. The wall serves to hold back the sea while the plant life regenerates. Small fences trap the sand, encouraging new growth. Marram grass, the basic skeleton which holds dunes together, was also planted.

Walk along the back of the beach in a south-easterly direction, towards the salt marshes. An upright post with the marker 7 on it should be noticeable as you walk. This marker shows the first stage of dune development. The plants growing here are sea sandwort and sand couchgrass. They can both tolerate occasional drenching in salt water. The fleshy leaves of the sea sandwort, which is a yellowish green with greenish white leaves, and the low nature of the plant help protect it from the winds. The plant traps sand and helps build up tiny dunes. As the sand covers the plants they put up new shoots and so a structure which holds the sand in place is built up.

At this point turn in across the dunes a little way. The vegetation changes and marram grass dominates with sea holly, rock cress and sea pea providing great attractions to butterflies. Further back, shrubs are able gain a safe hold on the sand. Burnet rose appears with creamy pink flowers from May to July. This is a rare plant in southern England but flourishes here. Dwarf willow also has a foothold. Further inland than this, the soil is now stable and the typical flora are fresh water marsh plants, celandines, cuckoo flower, yellow flags, marsh bedstraw. The land behind this, close to the wildlife sanctuary car park, shows signs of cultivation, the ridges of disused lazy beds showing through the grass. This area would have only been worth cultivating during those times when cultivable land was scarce, before the Famine and perhaps after the taking of the census of 1891. One of the best kept secrets of this area is the whereabouts of the Kerry Lily which grows on the heath behind the dunes and around the island. The lily has grasslike leaves and a stem holding up a bunch of white bell-shaped flowers with purple veins which flower in May. Unless it is flowering it would look very much like grass. If you accidentally stumble upon one, please bear in mind that any damage it receives could well be fatal to the whole species. Another rarity which is said to flourish here is the Irish Ladies Tresses in among the dunes themselves. Among the birds to spot in the dunes are skylarks and meadow pipits. The dunes are covered also in the shells of snails, distinctively ringed and easy for predators to spot.

Link Derrynane to Lough Currane. 10 miles/16 km.

Return to the main Ring of Kerry road. Continue westwards towards Waterville. The road passes through the lower slopes of Cahernageeha Mountain and through the Coomakesta Pass, one of the highlights of the tour bus route. The Skelligs appear to the west. At the outskirts of Waterville look for a Club Med sign to the right and turn up the road to Lough Currane. About 2.5 miles/4 km past the hotel the Lough comes into view. The road continues on for about another 2 miles/3.2 km and then peters out into green road where you will see a Kerry way marker.

Stop at the Kerry Way marker.

The lake is surrounded by early Christian remains and old butter and turf roads that signify a very different lifestyle to that represented by the Club Med development. Turf and butter were two of the few means of additional income that the cabin-dwelling Irish peasants had in the nineteenth century. They meant the difference between having enough money for the rent and food for the hungry month of May and going out begging on the streets. The turf road enabled a donkey and panniers to get to the turf which would have been cut and dried ready for sale. Butter roads were the old routes to the nearest town where the butter could be sold.

The lake is rich in freshwater fish. Salmon find their way here through the Waterville river, a private fishery. The life story of the Currane system salmon begins in about November when adult salmon have found their way to a safe place high up beyond this lake in the Cummeragh river or even higher in Loughs Currane, Iskanamactery, Derriana, or Cappal. The salmon pair off and find a place to build a nest in the river bed. The eggs are fertilised as they fall into the nest of reeds and are covered over with gravel. The fast flowing water supplies oxygen to the eggs, sometimes as many as 4,500 in any one laying. Around January tiny hatchlings appear carrying a large yolk sac which supplies their food for the next two months. By March the fry have found their way to the surface of the water and are feeding on crustaceans and the larvae of insects. For two years or more the fry live in one patch of stream, protecting it against other salmon fry because food is scarce. Many fry fail at this stage. Unable to find a territory of their own they slip away downstream and are eaten. When the fry, now called a parr, reaches about 20 centimetres it is ready to change its habitat. In the spring they change colour from brown to silver, swim downstream and go off to sea for a year or so.

Somehow, a year later, the salmon manage to find the exact stream they came out of and begin the long and very dangerous journey back to their mating grounds. The salmon must wait until the rivers are in spate before they can attempt the journey so there can be long periods while the salmon wait in the mouth of the Waterville river. This is a risky time for the salmon that swim in shoals just below the surface. Then drift nets are put out to catch them. The nets are highly regulated by law and cannot be longer than 730 metres.

Those salmon that get past the drift nets are then at risk in the mouth of the river from draft nets. These are held by one person on the shore while others row out to the river mouth and turn a semicircle, hopefully trapping the salmon inside the net as they turn back to the shore. If the salmon escape both these means of netting they are then at risk from the angler, although he or she is much less of a threat to the salmon than the commercial means of collecting them.

By this time the surviving salmon have undergone another change; unable to readapt to a freshwater environment they have stored up enough food to last them for the whole period of their journey upstream. Their scales darken again to reddish brown and the females begin to produce eggs. The salmon begin to arrive in the rivers in December and do not mate until the following November. During all that time they do not eat. The males often die after mating but many females survive and return to the sea.

The salmon's lifestyle may seem arduous but it is an efficient one. Fish such as cod must produce millions of eggs each time if they are to survive the predators of the sea. But because they choose to lay their eggs in waters which can support very little other life, the salmon fry are relatively safe from predators. Even so, of the 4,500 eggs laid only about twenty-five will survive to make the journey back up river.

On an island in the centre of Lough Currane is the ruin of a twelfth-century church and beehive huts. The lake was once known as Lough Luigh after the wife of Lug, the sun god. The town of Waterville itself, though, is very modern: it was established in the eighteenth century. Around the lake is wild glacier-carved country: bare sandstone rock, a few native birch and holly trees, while the mountains to the east, Coomcallee and Knocknagantee, reach heights of 2,000 feet/600 metres. The ice sheets cut many small coombs into the sides of the valleys and many small unvisited loughs lie to the east of this area.

Link Waterville to Ballinskelligs, Portmagee or Valentia for boat to Skellig Michael. See page 97 for details of the various ways of reaching the Skelligs.

Stop Skellig Michael.

Quite apart from the island's historical significance (see pages 95-6) Skellig Michael has a fascinating ecology and a visit here is worthwhile for the birdlife alone.

But first there is the amazing boat trip out to the islands to enjoy, spotting storm petrels skimming over the water looking much like swallows, kittiwakes looking much like seagulls with a black tip to their wings and the much larger fulmar. The boat should pass the Little Skellig on its way and it is there that you will be able to spot the thousands of nesting gannets. They are large white seabirds easily recognised by their habit of suddenly diving into the sea with their wings folded.

The island's isolation has ensured that very few plant species have reached it and the weather conditions that prevail make sure that only very wind- and salt-tolerant plants survive. Only thirty-nine plant species have been recorded, thrift being the dominant one. It covers the island although on the southern slopes it has died leaving dead clumps for nesting puffins to burrow under. They are becoming covered over with rock sea spurrey. Sea campion also survives alongside the thrift throughout the rock. Close to the gull colonies and probably brought to the island by them are scentless mayweed and common sorrel. The fulmar colonies seem to attract scurvy grass and orache, an ugly grey-green little plant with grey-green flower heads. It is related to and looks like the common garden weed fat hen. All of these are creeping or low-lying plants which can tolerate salt water. Within the shelter of the monastery buildings other plants have found a niche to survive. Scarlet pimpernel grows on the south-east slopes or in the lee of the monastery walls. It is sensitive to humidity, opening its petals only when humidity is low and there is no danger to it from sea water or rain.

Although there is little soil here the decay of the plants that have found niches creates a soil, while the guano left by seabirds is high in nutrients for those plants that can tolerate these conditions. The plants have few predators. The only mammals on the island are some rabbits which have inbred to the point where some are black, a few mice and reputedly a feral goat left here by lighthousemen.

Bird life here is teeming. Numbers of nesting rarities go into the thousands; 5,000 pairs of Manx shearwaters, 10,000 pairs of storm petrels, 6,000 pairs of puffins. All three of these birds nest in burrows hollowed out under the tussocks of thrift. The shearwaters are so unafraid of their human visitors that they burrow around the monastery walls. On the rocks nest fulmars, kittiwakes, razorbills, and guillemots in their thousands. There are much smaller colonies of gulls — 120 pairs of herring gulls, fifty pairs of black-backed gulls and less than ten pairs of greater black-backed gulls.

In comparison, few landbirds make their home here. Rock pipits, a few wheatears, one pair of choughs, and the peregrines.

But Skellig Michael is home for parts of the year to many migrant species. Waders, warblers, flycatchers, and redstarts all spend some time here as they move to warmer habitats in August to October. In winter, as food sources get scarce on the mainland, some thrushes, finches and buntings find their way here in search of food.

Link Skellig Michael to Valentia, varying according to whether the boat arrives back at Ballinskelligs, Portmagee or Valentia itself.

Valentia is an area of lowland hills separated from the mainland as the sea levels rose. It is an extension of the low hills that characterise the end of the peninsula. It has been inhabited at least since pre-Christian times and there is widespread evidence of medieval settlements here. The slate quarry on the island tells of a carboniferous past when sand and silt were laid down over the older sandstones. Human survival on this part of the peninsula was for a long time a precarious business despite its proximity to the shore. Provisions had to be brought on to the island and livestock carried away.

The island shows an interesting flora, chiefly due to the efforts of one of the Knights of Kerry who chose to establish the sub-tropical vegetation here. New Zealand flax and gunnera flourish well away from any planting by human hands as can be seen in the little field beside the An Óige hostel at Knightstown. Other efforts by the Knights of Kerry established a small weaving and dying industry here and the old national school at Knightstown, now a heritage centre, has records of the natural dyes used to colour the cloth or wool. Sorrel and chickweed were used to make green dye but only when the plants were in flower. The blossom of purple loosestrife made dark brown, while soot was used to make fox. New Zealand flax which can be found all round the island was used to make linen cloth. The thick spiny stems were steeped in water until they rotted and the long sinews of the leaves removed. These were combed out, carded, and spun. The mordant or fixer for the dye was human urine. Before a piece of cloth was dyed the supplier was not to eat cabbage or turnip beforehand! Other materials turned into cloth were blackberry and ragwort stems.

Link Valentia to Ballaghisheen Pass. 16 miles/26 km.

Return to Waterville on the Ring of Kerry Road. The rest of the Ring of Kerry road is very scenic but for the ecotour the interesting features lie inland in a path across the peninsula. At Waterville the road inland is very poorly signposted opposite the Butler Arms Hotel. The signposts indicate Loughs Currane and Derriana. The road heads inland across poorly drained boggy soils with little sign of farming. To the right are Loughs Currane, Deriana and the mountains of Knocknagantee. Much of the area here is given over to forestry. Natural vegetation consists of low willow and holly, a few remnants of the oak woods of the past and some planted deciduous trees around the edges of the pinewood. After 6 miles/10 km turn left at a blue grotto at a crossroads signposted to Cloonaghlin on the right and Cahersiveen to the left. The road crosses more conifer plantations and little else in the way of productive farming. This is the river valley of the River Inny. After 2 miles/3 km a crossroads is met where a right turn indicates the road to Glencar. Follow the sign to Glencar.

Sheep make an appearance as well as the occasional depressed-looking cow. Turf cutting is obvious here. Further on high hedgerows of holly and willow indicate slightly more fertile land. The road is now closely following the course of the Inny. After another 3 miles/5 km, at a T-junction, the route turns right to Ballaghisheen. This is not so much a village as a narrow mountain pass between the two peaks of Knocknagapple and Knocknacusha. The road is marked as unsafe for heavy traffic. It is built over bogland and has no solid foundations. It passes between more pine forest planted again with deciduous trees at the outskirts.

The road begins to climb the steep gradient of the mountain. On a fine day there are amazing views of Carrauntoohil, the highest point in Ireland. This whole area is a series of ice carved U-shaped valleys whose sides are dotted with loughs held back by moraines, heaps of boulders and gravel thrown down by the sudden melting of a glacier. As the road moves over the crest of this pass it leaves behind the Inny valley and enters the Caragh valley created as a glacier moved slowly from east to west, grinding out what was already a river valley to flatten the base and roughen the mountain sides leaving piles of scree in its wake.

The road descends through hairpin bends following the course of a stream which will eventually join the Caragh river. Along its banks grow willow and huge rocks brought down in torrential floods lie in the stream bed. Occasional sheep leap from ledge to ledge of bare red sandstone rock.

Stop 16 miles/26 km from Waterville beside exposed turf cutting area.

At about 16 miles/26 km from Waterville the road turns across the stream it has been following and enters an area where much turf cutting is in evidence close by the road. Stop after the bridge and walk over to the exposed cross section of blanket bog. This type of bogland occupies about 500,000 hectares of Irish mountain and lowland. It is typical of areas which have a rainfall higher than 1,200 mm per year, or about 235 days per year of rain. Anyone who spends any amount of time in Kerry will understand why so much of its highland area consists of blanket bog. The bog is caused because the high rainfall washes the minerals in the soil down to the lower layers where materials such as iron form an 'iron pan' impermeable to water. The water collects on the surface of the soil and the plant life dies. Because of the acidity of the water caused by the nature of the rocks beneath, the plants do not rot and over hundreds of years form a layer of peat. Blanket bog can be anywhere between two and six metres deep and at the depths here probably took a period of about 4,000 years to develop. The bottom of the bog you are looking down into probably last saw the light of day 3,000 years ago.

It is well recorded how important these areas can be as archaeological sites. Often beneath the bog whole field systems lie intact alongside foundations and even whole walls of settlements. Butter put into the bog to cool thousands of years ago has been found intact. But it not just as archaeological sites that the bog is important. Ireland is the most westerly country in Europe and while most of its neighbours such as Holland — where they were once large bog areas — have removed the bog for fuel and for land reclamation, Ireland has still large areas. The kind of turf cutting seen here has gone on for hundreds of years and has done no harm to the bogs but the extensive mechanised cutting of the midlands has removed vast areas of bogland forever.

Although on a cursory glance, this seems to be an inhospitable wasteland in reality it is home to hundreds of creatures. The heather that covers the area is obvious but there are many other quite beautiful plants beside this which begin the lower level of a delicate food chain. Sphagnum moss is the single plant responsible for the bogs. It acts as a sponge soaking up water during rainfall and holding on to it during dry seasons, ensuring that the damp conditions creating the bog do not vary with the seasons. Well into this century sphagnum moss was used in medicine to soak up blood in deep wounds while its acidity helped to sterilise the wound.

In the nutrient-deprived acid environment plants have developed that can survive on what they can take from the air itself. Sundew plants, tiny, insectivorous and bright green, can be seen if you care to crouch down and peer at the soil. In May the glaring purple and bright green of butterwort, another insectivorous plant, are scattered around. Bog cotton is obvious from the waving tassels of cotton of June and July. Tiny yellow tormentil is everywhere while rushes and sedges dominate in the damp conditions. In August the beautiful yellowy-orange flowered bog asphodel carpets whole areas while several rare and protected plants can be spotted by the keen botanist. Bog orchid and marsh saxifrage, a relation of St Patrick's Cabbage, can be found in this type of habitat.

Looking across the surface of the bog different areas can be picked out. The drier spots are caused by the plants that grow there: cushion moss, silver haired moss and bog moss create dry hummocks. The darker looking holes between the hummocks are filled with what looks like frogspawn and is algae, microscopic creatures forming layers up to 10 centimetres thick. As this dries up in drought conditions it forms a scab on the surface of the bog keeping conditions beneath moist. In the open pools bog bean and pondweed grow and on the islands in the pools quite large plants, such as crowberry and juniper can survive. Plants attract plant-eating creatures and there is a multitude of creepy crawlies in the bog. Water scorpions, giant water beetles and water spiders inhabit the wetter areas while dragonflies, speckled wood, common blue orange tip and small tortoiseshell butterflies dance above it, the dragonfly searching the surface for water skaters and other floating larvae while the butterflies are attracted by the blossom. This is the only place you are likely to see the Large Heath butterfly which only inhabits bogs where the food plant of its larval stage, the beaked rush, is found. Frogs and lizards are happy in this environment while the Irish hare, foxes and even otters venture into the bog in search of food.

Killorglin, Co. Kerry

Birdlife too appears scarce at a first glance but the bog attracts golden plovers which nest on the wetter quaking areas in early summer. You are more likely to hear them than see them since they give a high pitched repetitive alarm call at the approach of humans. It is common also to spot kestrels or merlins high up scouring the area for prey and then hovering high above before they dart down for lunch. Ravens, choughs, wrens, dunnocks, willow warblers and chiffchaffs are inhabitants of the more wooded areas near the stream while reed bunting sit high on the reeds where they make their nests.

Just standing by the bog for a few minutes will hardly reveal this multitude of life but it is there and the most obvious must be the butterflies, midges and flowers of spring and summer.

Link Ballagasheen Pass to Lough Acoose via Glencar. 6 miles/10 km.

The road continues along the course of one of the tributaries of the Caragh river surrounded by more exposed bog. After heavy rain the water is brown from the debris of soil it has picked up along the way. This particular stream began up above the pass you have just come through and is acid, its route so far having been through the boglands. It feeds into the Caragh river and eventually into Caragh Lake, a famous salmon fishing lake. The river occasionally gets salmon and a few may find their way up this far to lay their eggs in the acid water. As the road descends the plant life becomes a little less bare looking with small low holly and willow trees, and sheep finding enough grass to forage. As the signs of human habitation return, planted species are common again — birch tress and rhododendron and of course montbretia.

At 3 miles/5 km beyond the last stop Bealalaw Bridge is reached where the road turns to the left and then to the right into Glencar where the Climbers' Inn pub/shop/post office/ hostel is reached. Do not turn left on the road to Killorglin but keep the Climbers' Inn on your left and follow the road to Lough Acoose. The land is now flat and fertile. To the east are MacGillycuddy's Reeks with the peak of Carrauntoohil at the highest point. Temperatures at the top of this mountain are generally ten degrees lower than in the valley below. Its slopes are covered in scree and there are sheer walls of rock with corrie lakes hanging below them. In heavy rain flash floods can occur in the rivers that descend from the mountain, causing considerable damage. North and east lies the limestone lowland which extends towards Castlemaine. In the seventeenth century large tracts of this land were bought up by Sir William Petty. Beside Caragh Lake are the remains of some of his entrepreneurial devastation. This area was once aboriginal oak forest until iron deposits were discovered at Blackstones to the north-west. Petty had a smelting plant built here and one by one the oaks disappeared to make charcoal.

Continuing along the road with Lough Acoose to the immediate right look for a turning to the right at the north-west end of the lough. Turn right here, past the houses, and drive down a little way until the track peters out.

Stop at the end of the track by Lough Acoose.

You are now about three miles from the summit of Carrauntoohil. Here you meet the Kerry Way which has just passed through the Black Valley and crossed the Lack Road, a path through MacGillycuddy's Reeks. This road was used within living memory to drive cattle to the Killorglin Fair. The journey would be begun at midnight in order to arrive there early in the morning. In the more distant past the road was a paved pathway travelled by horses carrying butter to Killorglin. Before the road starts to rise the plant life of the area is sparse due to leaching of the soil and constant fires that begin in the early spring before the sap rises and the plants begin to grow again. The only plants that are able to survive in these kinds of condition are those whose roots survive the burning such as bracken and heather. This area would once all have been oak woodlands but now only a few holly trees remain. A few fields open up, patches of cultivation among the bare bracken infested land.

Around the lough the flora is that typical of marshy acid soils. In particular bog orchid grows here, flowering in July and August. Both types of butterwort grow here, as well as the unusual blue-eyed grass, a plant more common in North America but fairly widespread in the damp grasslands of Kerry. Higher up the mountain alpine plants grow. These are starry saxifrage and St Patrick's Cabbage, saxifrage rosaecea, hirta and incurvifolia. All look fairly similar and resemble the London Pride of English gardens; bright green spoon-shaped leaves with spikes of starry pink flowers. These may be relics of the last ice age that somehow survived or their presence only on the west coast may have something to do with the way the species spreads. In this case they may have come through Ulster where they are also common, or from Scotland. They do not occur on the east side of Ireland although there are high mountain ranges there also.

The top of the mountain, besides being 10 degrees colder than below, is subject to high winds and so the type of vegetation at the very top consists of plants that can tolerate those conditions. It is also very acid peaty soil. If you were to climb to the top of Carrauntoohil you would find tormentil, a low-lying plant with tiny yellow star shape flowers, and heath bedstraw another prostrate perennial plant. Perennials have a greater chance of surviving the difficult conditions because they store food resources through the winter and do not have to start again each year from seed. Bilberry is another low-lying plant that prefers acid conditions and stores energy in its roots over winter. It can be recognised by its woody stem and pinkish green flowers in April to July. Its long flowering season gives it added survival value. Heather, thrift and wild thyme are also low-lying perennial plants that can survive in harsh conditions. These plants are all common at lower levels but share the ability to tolerate high winds and harsh conditions.

Link Lough Acoose to the Gap of Dunloe. 10 miles/16 km.

Return to the main road and turn right to continue towards Killarney. After 2.5 miles/4 km take the right turn signposted for Beaufort and Killarney. (Left goes up to Killorglin.) After another 0.7 miles/1 km bear right. The road runs into the valley of the River Laune which drains Lough Leane. The landscape fills up with holiday homes and green fields, with the foothills of MacGillycuddy's Reeks to the south.

Stop Turn right at the signposted turning to Kate Kearney's Cottage and park.

The cottage/pub/restaurant was home to Kate Kearney who served poteen in her bar. This is the famous Gap of Dunloe whose origins are not quite clear but are obviously the work of a glacier at some time. One theory suggests that a glacier once sat in the Black Valley at the south end of the gap and grew so large that it overgrew its valley and forced its way through to this end, making the river change direction as it did so. The Gap climbs for about two-thirds of its passage and the road follows the river through a string of paternoster lakes, each one scooped out by its own patch of ice forming a pattern like a string of rosary beads. There is no way out of the Gap once you are in it except by turning back or going on. Steep rock faces line the sides of the valley.

The road was built by the local landlord during the middle of the nineteenth century but it was a mountain track long before that. From Cnoc an Bhraca, the high point about halfway through the Gap on the west side, there begins the Reeks ridge that goes along the tops of the mountains all the way to Glencar. The walk is fairly stiff but takes no real mountaineering skill and until recently a party of several hundred people did the walk every June on the first Saturday of the month. The tradition was discontinued when the organisers began to notice that the delicate structure of the bog was being destroyed by so many feet. The bog contains large amounts of water and any pressure at all can cause serious erosion in it, leading to great slides of soil which leave the mountainside bare.

The trip through the Gap is very rewarding and can provide a wonderfully solitary journey outside of the summer months. It makes a superb cycle tour (see page 144).

The Gap has not always been deserted. Halfway along the pass by Auger Lake is the ruin of a Royal Irish Constabulary barracks which housed twenty-one men. Nearby is another ruin, that of Arbutus Cottage, where craftsmen once made engraved furniture.

KILLARNEY
INTRODUCTION

On the wrong day in July or August Killarney can seem a nightmare. Tour buses, backpackers, traffic jams, cars pulling over without warning to look at a view, crowded restaurants, stuffed leprechauns, loud 'traditional' music, and troupes of affluent tourists with a small fortune in photographic equipment slung round their necks. That's the bad news. The good news is that all of this is wonderfully easy to shake off and it's easy to find yourself — even in the middle of August — alone in some of the most beautiful and unspoilt countryside in Ireland. Out of season, and even in the summer months, Killarney has a lot to offer the discerning tourist, especially if one is willing to leave the beaten track and wander off into ancient oak woods, glowing moorland, pretty parks or the largest yew forest in Europe.

Even with the most popular sites it is easy to escape the crowds. A typical example of this is the Gap of Dunloe, one of the town's major tourist attractions. At Kate Kearney's Cottage, the beginning of the Gap of Dunloe, there are coaches and buses, ponies and traps, people trying to sell you rides, tour guides and so on. Walk a little way into the valley — beyond the point where most of the pony and trap rides turn back — and behold, you are alone in the middle of a valley carved by the overflow from a great glacier thousands upon thousands of years ago. No cars, the ponies and traps are few and far between, and the only other people will be like-minded folk enjoying nature in its raw state. On many days outside the holiday season it is possible to walk or cycle through the Gap of Dunloe without meeting a soul.

In Killarney you will also find yourself close by some of the best hotels, sports facilities, evening entertainment and day trips in Ireland. Killarney is a grand place to use as a base for exploring Kerry and its creature comforts help make it an ideal resting place after the relative rigours of the nearby peninsulas.

Killarney itself developed as a tourist spot and catering for visitors remains its chief industry today. The various landed gentry who came to live in this area made efforts to develop it, setting up copper and iron mines, smelting the iron using the area's plentiful supply of oakwoods, setting up craft schools for at least a few of the local peasants and encouraging the development of inns and taverns. At first it was the Bianconi cars (stage-coaches called after the Italian-born entrepreneur who first introduced them to Ireland) that brought in the wealthy tourists but the development of a railway link made the whole business of getting to Killarney that much easier and broadened its appeal.

The fact that so much of the area has been preserved and is now a National Park is due, by way of accident, to the landed gentry who preserved their oakwoods and their herds of deer for hunting.

Killarney's history goes back well beyond its development in the eighteenth and nineteenth centuries as a tourist spot. The area is rich in ogham stones and ancient castles whose ruins tell their own story of the many battles fought over this area. Some of the copper mines found on Ross Island go back to the Bronze Age, as the stone awls and hammers found among the debris of later workings testify. On the shores of Muckross Lake a souterrain has been found suggesting more Bronze Age activity and at Lissyvigeen, east of Killarney, is a stone circle.

In early Christian times Killarney was ruled over by a clan called the Eoghnacht Locha Lein, with Lough Leane at the centre of the kingdom. As the Normans invaded the north of Kerry the McCarthy clan, kings of south Munster, were driven back to this area and took it from the Eoghnacht Locha Lein. The Normans were particularly unsuccessful in their attempts to gain control over this area and for a time two clans divided the area up between them: the McCarthys ruling around Muckross and the area to the north while the O'Donoghues were based around Ross Castle and Killarney itself. It was O'Donoghue lands that were confiscated by Cromwell and given to Sir Valentine Brown, the ancestor of the earls of Kenmare. Another clan, the O'Sullivans, held land around Dunloe and their castle ruins can still be seen incorporated into the Hotel Castle Dunloe.

The McCarthys must have been a wilier bunch than the O'Donoghues because their land remained in the family even after Cromwell's time and it passed by inheritance to a family called the Herberts in the eighteenth century. These are the people responsible for building Muckross House and creating the estate.

Essential Information

BANKS
There is a large number of banks in town, all open during the regular banking hours: 10 a.m.–4 p.m. Late opening Wednesday until 5 p.m.

BICYCLE HIRE
O'Sullivan's, Pawn Office Lane, off High Street, telephone 064–31282.
The Laurels Pub, Old Market Lane, alongside the pub. Telephone 064–32578. Hire includes a map and panniers.
O'Neill's, Plunkett Street. Includes some children's bikes and free delivery to your accommodation. Telephone 064–31970.
Hostels. Many of the hostels have bike hire for their residents but, if available, will hire out to non-residents.

BUREAUX DE CHANGE
Killarney Travel. Junction of High Street, Main Street and New Street. Open 7 days during summer, 9 a.m.–10 p.m. Winter 6 days, 9 a.m.–6 p.m. The tourist office also has an exchange facility.

CAR HIRE/REPAIRS/24-HOUR PETROL
Hertz. Three Lakes Hotel, Kenmare Place, telephone 064–34126, fax 064–33217.
Killarney Autos (Avis), Park Road, telephone 064–31355.
Randles Brothers, Muckross Road, telephone 064–31237
Budget, telephone 064–34341

CHURCH SERVICES
Franciscan Friary: Sunday 8.30 a.m., 9.30 a.m., 10.30 a.m., 11.30 a.m. *Catholic Cathedral:* 11.00 a.m., 12.15 a.m.
Church of Ireland: Sunday 8 a.m., July and August. 10.30 a.m., April-September. 11 a.m., October to March.
Presbyterian Church: Sunday 11 a.m., June to September.

GARDAÍ (POLICE)
Telephone 064–31222.

LAUNDERETTES
The Four Seasons, Innisfallen Shopping Mall.
Gleeson's, Brewery Lane, College Square.

PHARMACIES
Shanahan's, 52 High Street, telephone 064–32630.
Sewell's Medical Hall, New Street, telephone 064–31027.
William's, New Street, telephone 064–34212.
Aherne, Farranfore, telephone 066–64722.

POST OFFICES
The Post Office is in New Street and its opening hours are the same as all Post Offices: 9 a.m. to 5.30 p.m. Closed for lunch 1–2 p.m. Saturday half day.

TAXIS
Dero's Tours and Taxis, 064–31251. 24-hour service.

Taxi Cabs and Ranks, College Square, 064–31331.
Corcoran's, telephone 064–43151

TOURIST OFFICE

The Old Town Hall, High Street. Open Monday to Friday, 9.15 a.m.–5.30 p.m.;
Saturday, 9.15 a.m. –1.00 p.m. Closed for lunch 1–2.15 p.m. each day.

TRAVEL AGENT

Killarney Travel, High Street, opposite the turning into New Street. Open Monday to
Friday, 9.15 a.m. to 5.30 p.m; Saturday, 10 a.m. to 2 p.m.

FESTIVALS

Killarney has a festival on St Patrick's Day (17 March) which involves a parade,
traditional singing and other events.

WHAT TO SEE

KILLARNEY

Killarney is a town with a history, much of it now lost in the
modernisation of the community but still visible if you care to look
closely enough. In 1588 the land confiscated from the Earl of Glencar
for his part in the Desmond rebellion was granted to Sir Valentine
Brown. His original 6,560 acres were added to by marriage and by
purchase. He lived at Ross Castle originally but moved to a new home
in 1721, in the area which was to become Killarney. By 1747 a place by
that name existed and consisted of the Browns' (now earls of Kenmare)
mansion, a few slate-roofed houses and a hundred or so thatched
cottages. By 1756 the tourist industry had begun and a new main road
was built along with a large inn to accommodate the travellers who
came to view the beautiful lakes. More inns followed and major roads
were begun, making the trip to the area easier in the days of horse-
drawn carriages.

Killarney was really put on the map in 1861 when Queen Victoria
put in an appearance. Massive work was done in the area preparing
places for all the people who would attend her and the tourists who
would come to see the queen. A whole cottage was even built in
Derrycunnihy Wood so that the queen could take tea in an idyllic
country cottage. Its ruins are still there.

A town walk

The name Killarney is thought to be a translation from the Irish Cill
Áirne, church of the sloes or blackthorns. The site of this church is
where the town walk begins, St Mary's Church, opposite the Tourist
Information Office in Main Street. The present building was constructed

139

in the nineteenth century but the site is much older and may have even been a pagan temple in Ireland's distant past. The interior of the church has some excellent Victorian stained glass including a version of Holman Hunt's 'The Light of the World'. The organ is also a masterpiece of its kind, built in 1889 in Huddersfield, and has decorated pipes. The Church has recently been restored with repairs to the roof and spire, and storm glazing on the windows. Outside the church the tourist office and town hall confront you. Behind the town hall building is a holy well which was for a long time a spot for local pilgrimages. Pilgrims walked around the well reciting prayers and then drank some of the water.

Walking towards the main road junction of the town, where High Street and Main Street meet, you come across what was in slower times the town's main market place. This is still called Market Cross although anyone setting up a stall here now might encounter some problems. Country people would have come here from miles around to sell butter, turf and whatever other items they could produce. Most farms subsisted on a potato garden and a small vegetable plot. Any extra produce that the farm provided, such as hens or eggs or milk, would have gone for sale in order to pay the rent on the cottage. Women would also have made small pieces of cloth for selling either from flax or wool, or made them into garments for sale and domestic use. In the eighteenth and nineteenth centuries women were able to supplement the meagre incomes of their families in this way. Many women must have stood at this very spot, calculating just how much they needed to sell in order to find the year's rent.

Turning left at the junction and heading down New Street, you pass the modern post office on your left built with the surplus bricks left over from the building of Lord Kenmare's mansion. There are several new developments going up in this area but beside the post office is Green Lane, a pretty little alleyway which must have been typical of the lanes and roads that made up Killarney in the days before motor vehicles. At the end of New Street are some old buildings situated around the cathedral, all with a long history.

At the very end of the street is West End House which was once the scene of one of Ireland's many schemes run by the wives of landed gentry which aimed to improve the conditions of the peasants. This particular place was a woodcarving school set up by Lady Kenmare in 1894 and one of its teachers was Anton Lang from Oberammergau, a member of one of the families there who enacted the Passion Plays. Much later it became a training college for domestic science teachers.

Opposite is the Presentation Convent, a fine stone building dating from 1803. The nuns had first established themselves here in 1793 with a complement of two. This was a typical arrangement of the time; many convents were established with a small amount of money in private houses and gradually grew in size as they attracted new recruits and gained the support of the local gentry. The nuns set up a school teaching literacy, needlework and spinning to local girls. They became highly successful, built the present building and expanded to other orders at Tralee, Milltown and Listowel. They set up a national school in Killarney and in 1878 a lace industry was established in the building with the encouragement of Lady Kenmare.

Between the cathedral and the convent is a pathway called Bishop's Path. A journey along it will bring you to an ogham stone brought here from the Dunloe area.

Back on Cathedral Place, the continuation of New Road, is St Mary's Cathedral and opposite that is Knockreer Estate, once the Kenmare estate. The grounds are now administered by the national parks service. There are many pleasant walks around the estate as far as the recently modernised Ross Castle and the lakesides.

Heading back to the main crossroads of High Street, New Street and Main Street, look down into some of the tiny laneways branching off from the road. These lanes were built by sub-landlords of Lord Kenmare who in the eighteenth century realised the potential of the place as a tourist spot and hoped to encourage the building of places which would accommodate the tourists.

Crossing the road to the laneway which forms the fourth cross of the crossroads you find yourself in Glebe Lane, once the portion of land owned by the local clergyman, at another time an army barracks. Following Glebe Lane reveals some of the old shopfronts which still remain, although many of them are now being given new fake Georgian facades to replace the old genuine ones they already possessed.

In College Street is the Franciscan friary. The Franciscan order originally came to the area in the 1440s and built Muckross Friary (usually but erroneously called Muckross Abbey), the ruins of which still stand in the grounds of Muckross House. The friary was first suppressed by Henry VIII in 1541 and after two restorations was finally closed by the Cromwellians in 1652. Some friars fled and went into hiding around Mangerton Mountain. There are many 'Mass rocks' in the area where they said mass for the local people. When a more tolerant climate returned, so did the friars and they set up a school for boys in College Street. The present church was built between 1864 and 1867. Fund raising on behalf of the friars included a bazaar attended by King Leopold II of Belgium and several French dukes. The interior of the church was designed by the younger Pugin, a son of the designer of the cathedral. It has fine oak panels and a stained glass window by Harry Clarke. The three altars are in an ornate Flemish style.

141

Outside the church on the opposite side of the road the statue *Speir Bean* marks the spot where public executions were carried out including that of Piaras Feiritéir, one of the four Kerry poets (see next section).

From College Street to East Avenue Road there is another small lane that evokes a part of Killarney's history. This is Brewery Lane where many small breweries operated about a hundred years ago. It was also in this lane — in one of the disused breweries — that the film *The Dawn* was made when a local cinema owner, Tom Cooper, and 250 local people got together to make a low budget film in the 1930s. The film, set in the War of Independence, was a considerable commercial success and there but for fortune an Irish film industry might have developed.

The tour of the town ends at the nearby railway station and the splendid Great Southern Hotel, which cost the grand sum of £50,000 to build in 1854. It was built and owned by the railway company and in the lobby there are some of the original posters advertising excursions to the hotel on the grand new railway. In the 1950s the famous playwright Brendan Behan stayed there and was asked how he liked it. He reminded the interviewer that he knew the hotel very well since, as an unknown decorator, he had helped his father paint it a few years earlier.

Monument to the Kerry Poets
Facing the Franciscan Friary near College Street.
The monument was put up in 1940 in memory of Piaras Feiritéir (c.1610-53), Seafradh Ó Donnchadha (1620-90), Aodhagán Ó Rathaille (1670-1726) and Eoghan Rua Ó Súilleabháin (1748-84). Feiritéir took part in battle against the Cromwellian forces in 1642-53 and was hanged as a consequence. The poetry of Ó Donnchadha is very down to earth, writing about his local scenery and memories of the past, and not so prescient as Ó Rathaille's verse. Ó Rathaille lamented and excoriated the destruction of Gaelic Ireland in savage, satirical and withering verses. Ó Súilleabháin has been compared to Robert Burns in his subject matter and popular style. A roistering, philandering charmer, he wrote the most beautiful Irish lyric poetry of the eighteenth century.

Saint Mary's Cathedral
Situated in Cathedral Place at the end of New Street.
Like many other cathedrals in Ireland this one isn't very old. It was designed by Pugin, the master of Gothic Revival, and built over a long period in the nineteenth century; the Famine brought contributions to the building fund and all work to an end. During those bad times the

partly finished shell of the building was used as a hospice for the dying. It was finally consecrated in 1855 although work was still unfinished. Another building spell got under way between 1908 and 1912 when the spire, all 285 feet of it, was put in place. Under the encouragement of Bishop Eamon Casey, the cathedral was restored between 1972 and 1973.

The cathedral is cruciform in style with a square tower topped by the spire. Interesting features are the Lady Chapel, kept in the original style with good carvings on the reredos and altar, and the beautiful stonework and stained glass of the nave.

How to get there Walk down New Street to Cathedral Place.

National Museum of Irish Transport

By the side of East Avenue Rd, in Scott's Garden, almost opposite the Killarney Park Hotel and the cinema.

Opened in 1987 the Transport Museum is a good afternoon's wander down memory lane. On display are a huge range of cars, cycles and fire engines collected over the last 40 years. Exhibits include a 1910 Wolseley which belonged to the Gore Booth family in Sligo and was driven by Countess Markievicz with W. B. Yeats as a passenger. A mockup of a 1930's car workshop and lots of old car magazines plus an unused 1844 Meteor Stanley tricycle found in a shop's unsold stock. Open from April to October, 10 a.m. to 8 p.m. daily July and August, 6 p.m. the rest of the year. Entry £2.50 adults, £1 children.

How to get there Walk from any part of town to Scott's Garden.

OUTSIDE KILLARNEY
Aghadoe and Parkonvear

About 2.5 miles/4 km from Killarney on the main road to Tralee, there are the ruins of a round tower (only 22 feet of it left) and a church. Nearby Aghadoe Hill (400 feet/120 metres) offers splendid views of the Killarney area.

An old monastery was said to have been founded here in the seventh century and a church is mentioned in the twelfth century. The western end of the existing ruins date from this period, as evidenced by the Romanesque doorway and decorations.

To the south-west of the church are the remains of a thirteenth-century castle; two storeys, a staircase and the remains of a fireplace. Nothing is known for certain about this ruin.

How to get there From Killarney take the road to Tralee. After 2.5 miles/4 km look for a signposted turning to the left.

Gap of Dunloe

6 miles/9.5 km west of Killarney.

During the holiday season this is best visited either early in the morning or late afternoon. The gap is about eight miles in length, a stiff walk but a good cycle. (See page 135.) Cars can drive through it but during the summer this would be a futile exercise due to the number of pony and traps using it. It would also be anti-social. There is some excellent scenery in this valley which is thought to have been carved by the meltwater of a huge glacier. The water built up behind these mountains and then burst through carrying debris in its wake and spreading it over the plain below.

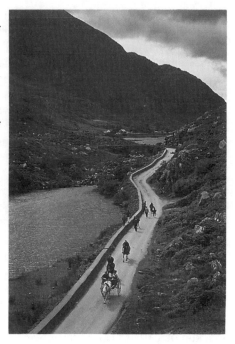

The Gap of Dunloe, Killarney, Co. Kerry

The standard Gap of Dunloe tour, available from every tour company in town and bookable on the spot outside Kate Kearney's Cottage, is to take a pony trap ride through the Gap, have lunch at Lord Brandon's Cottage and then board a boat for the journey back to town. This is a full day tour. Alternatively, at the entrance to the Gap, book a pony ride for a couple of miles into the Gap and back. Or just take a walk through the Gap for as long as you like. Be warned: the first mile or two is busy in July and August. A two hour jarvey ride costs £15 per head.

How to get there Take Port Road out of town, heading for Killorglin and the Ring of Kerry, and one km after the village of Fossa the Gap is signposted on the left. After 2.6 kilometres turn right at a T-junction and follow the signs to the Gap.

Ross Castle

The castle was built in the fifteenth century by the O'Donoghues who lost it after the Desmond rebellion at the end of the sixteenth century. A family called Browne were rewarded for their support for Cromwell with vast tracts of the countryside around what was to be Killarney, including the castle. They eventually became the earls of Kenmare, took over the fifteenth-century castle and added a seventeenth-century house. Later they moved into the Kenmare Estate and the castle became a military post until 1815.

Ross Castle was one of the last strongholds in the country to hold out against Cromwellian forces. Popular legend would have the defender, Lord Muskerry, bravely holding out against the English forces under Ludlow, firm in the belief that the castle could never be captured from land. Ludlow, however, had decided to attack from the water and had ships built in Kinsale and brought up to Killarney by land and river. The defenders, seeing an attack being mounted from the lake, immediately capitulated. The truth is that Muskerry had already decided to surrender, knowing that by 1652 there was no chance of defeating the Cromwellians, and the appearance of the boats provided as good an excuse as any.

For a long time it fell into disrepair but has now undergone major repairs and is open to the public.

How to get there At the beginning of the road to Kenmare turn left opposite the Esso garage. At the end of the road is a car park and you can continue on foot from there.

Ross Island
Land running to the left of Ross Castle.

To the left of the castle is Ross Island, actually not an island at all but a peninsula jutting out into the lake. It is covered in woodland and walks have been laid out around it to the copper mines and various beauty spots and viewpoints. From the castle and Ross Island can be seen Inisfallen Island.

The disused copper mines remind one that Lough Leane was once busy with boats laden with copper and cobalt (there were also mines on the southern shore of the lough near Muckross House). The boats could sail down the River Laune to Killorglin and the sea.

How to get there Signposted walks begin near Ross Castle.

Inisfallen Island
A monastery was situated here from the seventh century to the seventeenth, founded by St Finian the Leper. Still standing on the island are the ruins of a twelfth-century oratory with a fine Romanesque doorway. Legend has it that Brian Boru, defeater of the Vikings, was educated on the island in the late tenth century. His tutor, Maelsuthan Ua Cerbaill, was probably the first scribe to begin what later became known as the Annals of Innisfallen. This chronicle of ancient Irish life was compiled by various hands over a 300-year period. It is the oldest of the great Irish annals. The volume is now in the Bodleian Library, Oxford. Perhaps the Irish government and the Greek government could

get together to form some kind of pressure group: give back the Elgin Marbles and the Annals of Inisfallen.

How to get there Rowing boats can be hired from alongside Ross Castle. Boats are £3 an hour or £12 for the day.

Muckross Estate

The lands now known as the Muckross Estate were consolidated by the McCarthy clan, whose leader was known as McCarthy Mór. Their castle lies in ruins outside the National Park area but these lands were dominated by this clan from the time of the Norman invasion to the eighteenth century, despite various attempts at confiscation. They passed to a family called Herbert in 1770. The Herberts had Muckross House built between 1840 and 1843 and the place was considered grand enough for Queen Victoria to stay there when she visited Killarney in 1861. But the Herberts had over-extended their budget in the building of the house and in 1899 the property was sold to Lord Ardilaun, a member of the famous Guinness family. In 1910 the house and estate were bought by an American, W.B. Borne, as a wedding gift for his daughter whose family later donated all 11,000 acres of it to the Irish nation.

Available in Muckross House are booklets detailing the three nature trails, each one marked out with stopping points which explain what to observe. Particularly fascinating are the mossy woods walk and Arthur Young's walk. Muckross contains one of the finest yew woods in Europe and the grounds are particularly interesting because they include areas of both limestone alkaline soil and sandstone acid soil, so almost anything can, and does, grow here including many plants only seen in much warmer Mediterranean climates. The gardens should not be missed, particularly in the early summer when the azaleas and rhododendrons are in bloom.

A walk around the grounds of Muckross needs at least half a day. It is possible to walk for eight miles or more, never covering the same spot twice, and passing through a huge number of habitats. If the thought of all that trudging puts you off at least negotiate a jaunting car ride or hire a bicycle.

How to get there Muckross Estate is on the main road to Kenmare. The first entrance is about 2.5 miles/4 km along the road. There is a car park on the left noticeable by the jarveys parked there.

Muckross Friary

Also in the grounds of the park are the ruins of Muckross Friary near the shore of Lough Leane, founded around 1448 by the McCarthy Mór. The friary was an Observantine Franciscan foundation. Its ruins are considered the best preserved in Ireland of a building of this nature.

They include a mid fifteenth-century nave and choir, an unusually broad central tower and a south transept dating back to the sixteenth century. The style is Irish Gothic. The other buildings were used as dormitory, refectory and kitchens. Three of the Kerry poets are buried within the friary building while the fourth, Piaras Feiritéir, was hanged in Killarney and is buried somewhere in the graveyard.

Muckross House

The house itself, only 150 years old, has passed through various hands and was first opened to the public in 1964. Unlike visits to some grand old country houses, there is no sense here of wandering through the fossilised remains of a museum. The rumpled sheets, the accessibility of the interior to the visitor, and the general sense of a well-used home provides a vivid account of the lives of the inordinately rich people who once lived here.

Open to the public are the dining room, library, bedrooms, a ladies sitting room and the children's nursery. The children had a staircase of their own for, like the servants, they were kept well out of the way. The kitchens are still in working order and the cellars have been turned into display areas for the tools of local craftsmen and living workshops where pottery and bookbinding are still carried out. Muckross is developing as a supplier of hotel stationery items. There is plenty to see in the craft shop, which retails items made in the workshops.

Part of the exhibition at Muckross House shows the effect on the local habitats of the various industries which took place in the area at various times. Iron ore was discovered and mines were dug at Muckross Village in the eighteenth century. Part of the smelting process for iron ore involved the use of large quantities of charcoal. In order to make this about twenty acres of oak forest were cleared each year. Oak was also used to make barrel staves and the bark was used for tannin, so large areas of oak woods were lost. Entrance to the house is £3 (children £1.25, family £7.50) and it is open daily from 9 a.m. to 7 p.m. in summer and until 5.30 p.m. in winter. Joint tickets for the House and Muckross Traditional Farms are £1 extra.

How to get there Drive or cycle along the N71 road to Kenmare. At the first entrance there is a car park and pedestrian entrance. At the second entrance vehicles can be driven up. There is also a daily bus service from town. Enquire at the tourist office for confirmation of times of departure and return.

Muckross Traditional Farms

This is an imaginative heritage centre set in seventy acres of land beside Muckross House. Five farm buildings from the early years of this century have been recreated. A small farm with its outhouses adjoining, a farm worker's cottage, a larger farm with outbuildings built parallel to the house, a courtyard farm, a blacksmith's forge and a carpenter's workshop are all created with careful attention to detail. There is also a well and a limekiln. Admission is £3 (children £1.25, family £7.50). Joint tickets for admission to the Farms and Muckross House are an extra £1.

How to get there The traditional farm is next to Muckross House and well signposted.

Torc Waterfall

4.5 miles/7 km south of Killarney, off the N71 road between Kenmare and Killarney.

A pleasant scramble up a steep wide footpath leads to the Torc Waterfall, best seen early in the day before the tour buses hit the place. At the car park at the bottom of the waterfall is an information point. The waterfall has a fall of 60 feet/18 metres, and the footpath leading up to it offers excellent views over the lakes.

How to get there Leave town on the road to Kenmare and park in the space provided on the left side of the road by the tourist information office.

Crag Cave

The existence of caves in the area of Castleisland was first noted in a geological survey of 1859 but it wasn't until 1981 that anyone set out to explore them. What started off as an investigation of water pollution in the area turned into a major exploration. Three entrances were found, followed after a little clearing of boulders by the discovery of 2.4 miles/3.8 km of cave. Probably more remains to be surveyed. Like all caves, these are formed from carboniferous limestone which was deposited about 300 million years ago while Ireland lay at the bottom of a shallow sea. The limestone is made from the decayed and compressed bodies of millions of sea creatures. Later a major movement in the earth's crust, the one which created the mountains of Kerry, thrust the sea bed up. The limestone was fractured in places and this allowed water to flow into the cracks. As the water flowed it eroded and dissolved more and more rock until great underground tunnels were carved. As water dripped down through the limestone rock over the centuries it deposited tiny amounts of calcite on the ceilings and floors of the caves and so the stalactites, stalagmites and pillars of calcite came to exist.

The caves were opened to the public in 1989. A sophisticated light and music system follows you round your tour of the caves. Various parts of the caves have been named after characters and places out of *Lord of the Rings*.

Open 10 a.m.–6 p.m. daily (until 7 p.m. in July and August). It has a restaurant and craft shop. You can book guided tours at telephone 066–41244, fax 066–42352. Disabled friendly.

How to get there From Killarney or Tralee look for the sign on the right of the N21 after Castleisland. Coming from Limerick on the N21 the signposted turning is on the left at the top of the hill approaching Castleisland.

Kerry Woollen Mills

The older buildings date from the seventeenth century when the local river powered a wooden water turbine. This was replaced in 1928 by a steel turbine which is still used. As well as guided tours, there is a mill shop selling woollen goods and other Irish crafts. A tea-room is also available. Admission is £2 (children £3, students £1.50, family £5).

How to get there From Killarney take the Killorglin Road (R562) for 8 miles/13.6 km and turn right at the signpost. One mile further on, turn left for 100 yards, then right.

CYCLE TOURS

RETURN TRIP BACK TO KILLARNEY VIA GAP OF DUNLOE AND BLACK VALLEY HOSTEL

A round trip of approximately 16.7 miles/30 km. At least half a day

Ideally, this tour is best enjoyed outside the months of July and August. If this is unavoidable be prepared for heavy traffic on the first leg of the journey to Kate Kearney's Cottage and the last leg back to Killarney on the main road. Whatever the time of year this is an adventurous cycle that covers a variety of terrains: smoothly surfaced roads, small country lanes, rough tracks, bogland, wood, uphill and down through the dramatic ice-carved Gap of Dunloe. Make a day of it and bring a picnic.

Leave Killarney on Port Road heading for Killorglin and the Ring of Kerry. After passing through the village of Fossa it is 1 km to the first signpost left to the Gap of Dunloe. Turn left here and continue down this small road for 1.6 miles/2.6 km, crossing the River Laune that drains Lough Leane, until a T-junction is reached. Turn right at the junction and follow the sign, pointing to the left for the Gap, where the other road leads up to the Dunloe Castle hotel and Beaufort.

At Kate Kearney's Cottage — the beginning of the Gap — either rejoice in the splendid isolation or bemoan your fate while carefully negotiating the tour buses and visitors. Cycling to the head of the Gap, at 794 feet/242 metres, is not particularly demanding and it's made easier anyway by the constant wish to stop and admire the scenery. The first piece of water on the left is Goosaun Lough and then Black Lake appears on the other side of the road. The road follows alongside the river that connects this lake with the next one, Cushvally Lake. Very soon the road runs right alongside Auger Lake and then the steepest climb is up to the head of the Gap.

The view from the top is glorious and only good brakes are needed to facilitate the speedy descent into the Gearhameen Valley. Over to the left the Upper Lake can be seen, backed by Mangerton mountain (2,756 feet/838 metres), and on the other side the road heading into the Black Valley can be traced.

At the bottom do not turn right, which is marked as a cul-de-sac. This is the beginning of the second day's journey along the Kerry Way and it leads into the Black Valley. Turn to the left instead and pass by a church on the right, and the hostel which is almost immediately after it. There is a small shop at the hostel.

About 1.2 miles/2 km past the hostel there is a Y-junction. Take the left side, signposted for Gearhameen, Hillcrest B&B and Brandon's Cottage. After a hundred metres there is another Y-junction; this time bear right, signposted for Brandon's Cottage, and not left to the B&B.

Follow the Kerry Way signs across the bridge that leads to Brandon's Cottage on the left. Drink and light food is available here. Keeping Brandon's Cottage on the left continue past it and bear left at the pathway further down. Less than a hundred metres along here, by the side of a clogged stream cut into the bog, there is an iron and wooden gate. Go through the gate and turn right immediately and follow the path, leaving the path that goes along the stream.

After 150 metres cross a small bridge and follow the path that cuts its way through the bog and furze. The Upper Lake comes into view on the left. Once on the path in the woods of Derrycunnihy look for a walking sign that is signposted Derrycunnihy. This brings one out to the N71 where a left turn onto the main road allows a comfortable cycle back down into Killarney. If in the woods you had continued following the Kerry Way walk sign, you would have had to clamber uphill carrying your bike most of the way. This too, though, would bring you out on the N71 at the Derrycunnihy church.

RETURN TRIP TO KILLARNEY VIA LAKE ACOOSE AND MOLL'S GAP
A return trip of approximately 50 miles/80 km
This could be done in one day or, alternatively, you could spend a night at Glencar at the dilapidated but friendly *Climber's Inn* hostel (telephone 066-60101), or at a nearby B&B (telephone 066-60162).

Follow the instructions of the first cycle tour above until reaching the junction which points to the Gap of Dunloe and the Dunloe Castle

Hotel. Turn left for the Gap of Dunloe but after less than 1 mile/1.6 km turn right, signposted to the west to Glencar. For the next 10 miles/16 km the road continues through a series of crossroads — where you always go straight ahead — and then one T-junction where you turn left for Lake Acoose. Where there are signposts always follow the directions to Glencar. The landscape is terrific and cars are few and far between.

Just at the end of the lake, set below Beenkeragh, Carrauntoohil and Caher mountains, the road turns to the right and 2 miles/3.2 km further along the Climber's Inn pub/ hostel/ small shop/ garage/ post office is on the right. It is about another 1 mile/1.6 km to Bealalaw Bridge but just before reaching it turn left and then, almost immediately, turn to the right. After another 1.5 miles/2.4 km turn right again. The road straight on here will eventually come to an end, so you will have to come back to this junction if you miss the turning.

After turning right, as just directed, follow the rising road that leads through the Bellaghbeama Gap and then down to a T-junction. From Glencar this is a distance of about 10 miles/16 km. At the T-junction turn left and continue to the east, climbing along the R568 for 6 miles/10 km, until reaching Moll's Gap. The hard work is now over and it's an easy 14 miles/22 km back down to Killarney.

DAYTIME ACTIVITIES AND SPORTS

FISHING

Fishing licences can be obtained from O'Neill's at 6 Plunkett Street, telephone 064–31970. Licences are needed for fishing for sea trout and salmon. They cost between £3 and £25. If fishing in a privately owned lake or river a permit is also required from the owner. O'Neill's also arranges boats and gillies and supplies tackle and bait. Fishing trips also arranged through Castlelough Tours at O'Connor's Pub in High Street, telephone 064–32496.

The *River Flesk* drains the West Cork mountains and runs into Lough Leane. It has trout and spring salmon. All methods of fishing are allowed. The *River Laune* drains the Killarney lakes and is excellent for salmon, sea trout and brown trout.

Barfinny Lake is about 10 miles/17 km south of Killarney on the road to Sneem. Take the Kenmare Road out of Killarney and look for a left turn at Moll's Gap. It is stocked annually with rainbow trout. Worms, spinners and flies are allowed. *Lough Leane*, *Muckross Lake* and *Upper Lake* have both salmon and trout and trolling for salmon is popular. A boat and gillie would cost about £50 for a day.

There is no coarse fishing in the region.

AQUA SPORTS

Kerry Country Rambles, 53 High Street, telephone 064–35277 organises rafting through the three lakes including a tiny piece of rapids. Paragliding can also be arranged.

GOLF

Killarney Golf Club, telephone 064–31034. Two championship courses. Visitors can pay to become members for the day and also enjoy the clubhouse facilities.
Dunloe Golf Range Complex. On the road to the Gap of Dunloe near the Dunloe Castle Hotel. Telephone 064–44578. Thirty indoor/outdoor bays with artificial grass mats; 18-hole putting area. Open from 9 a.m. to 9 p.m.

HORSE RIDING

Rocklands Stables Riding School, Tralee Road, telephone 064–32592, fax 064–34003. Lessons for beginners and advanced riders. Trekking trips through woodlands. Open June–October from 9 a.m.–7 p.m.; October–June 9 a.m.–6 p.m. Advance booking advised.
Killarney Riding Stables (Sullivan's). Ballydowney, telephone 064–31686, fax 064–34119. Hacking, trekking, 1–3 hour trips, three- and six-day rides. Open from 8 a.m. AM, AE, DE, VB.

RIDE IN A JAUNTING CAR

There are several possible rides you can take in a jaunting car. At the first entrance to Muckross House, on the road to Kenmare, are jaunting cars which will take up to four passengers on a variety of tours around the grounds. They vary in price. It costs about £20 for a long ride, seeing most of the grounds plus stops at the friary, gardens and house. A short trip into the estate and back is around £7. The drivers are there from about 9 a.m. to about 7 p.m.

Other rides to be had are into the Gap of Dunloe (see page 144). Rides can also be arranged from the stretch of road between the tourist office and the roundabout.

PITCH AND PUTT

Gleneagle Hotel. Day membership of sports facilities for non-residents includes a 36-hole course. Clubs and balls for hire. Contact the Destination Killarney desk in Scott's Gardens, telephone 064–32638.

SWIMMING

Gleneagle Hotel. Special day membership for non-residents. Enquiries to Destination Killarney, Scott's Gardens, telephone 064–32638. Free bus to hotel from Scott's Gardens.

TENNIS

Day membership at the Gleneagle Hotel includes two hard surface courts. Racquets for hire and lessons available. Contact the Destination Killarney desk in Scott's Gardens, telephone 064–32638.

OTHER SPORTS

Kerry Country Rambles, 53 High Street, telephone 064–35277. Mountaineering and abseiling, rafting, boating and paragliding can be arranged.

LAKE CRUISES

M.V. *Lily of Killarney.* Watercoach. Sailing times 10.30 a.m., 12 noon, 1.45 p.m., 3.15 p.m., 4.30 p.m., 5.45 p.m. The departure point is Ross Castle. Contact: Watercoach Cruises, 3 High Street, telephone 064–31068.
M.V. *Pride of the Lakes.* Destination Killarney, Scott's Gardens, telephone 064–32638. Sailing 11 a.m., 12.30 p.m., 2.30 p.m., 4.00 p.m., 5 p.m.

WALKING TOURS

Tracks and Trails, 53 High Street, telephone 064–35277. Night walks are also available.

Jaunting cars in Killarney National Park, Co. Kerry

HORSE RACING

At the Racecourse, Ross Road. Meetings during May and, especially, July.

GUIDED TOURS

Killarney and Kerry Tours, Inisfallen Mall, Main Street, telephone 064–33880. Gap of Dunloe, boat and coach trips, Ring of Kerry coach trip, local circuit coach trip, trips on the lakes.
Castlelough Tours, O'Connor's Pub, High Street, telephone 064–32496, fax 064–35088. Gap of Dunloe, lakeland tours and boat tours.
The Cloghereen Trail for the Visually Impaired is a marked out trail which goes around the blue pool area. A cassette machine and tape describing the walk can be collected from Muckross House for a deposit of £5.
Deros Tours, Main Street, opposite the tourist office. Local tours, Ring of Kerry, Gap of Dunloe, Dingle and Slea Head, Cork and Blarney, Glengarriff.
Killarney Boating & Tour Centre. High Street, telephone 064–31068, fax 064–34525. Gap of Dunloe, boat tours on the lake, Ring of Kerry and Dingle coach tours.

EVENING ACTIVITIES

During the summer there are not many pubs or hotel lounges in Killarney that don't provide some sort of musical entertainment. (The problem, in fact, is to find a pub for a quiet drink.) The type of music ranges from traditional Irish music to country and western and popular. Some of the places that can be relied on for regular and lively sessions are listed below.

Buckley's Bar, College Street. Music on Monday, Tuesday and Friday nights.
Eviston House Hotel, New Street. The Danny Mann lounge bar is always crowded for the musical sessions and afterwards the Scoundrels disco continues the fun.

Great Southern Hotel. Evenings of traditional music on Thursday, Friday, Saturday and Sunday from 9 p.m. Admission charge.

Gleneagle Hotel. Cabaret evenings most nights through July and August followed by a disco.

Hannigan's Bar, International Hotel, Kenmare Place. Entertainment nightly from 10 p.m. from April to October.

Kate Kearney's Cottage, Gap of Dunloe. Traditional music and ballads on Sunday, Wednesday and Friday nights.

Killarney Manor Banquet. An evening of traditional music, song and dance with or without a meal. Dinner starts at 8 p.m. and the entertainment at 8.45 p.m. Telephone 064–31551, fax 064–33366. Reservations are recommended.

The Laurels, Main Street, with the music pub at the back and reached by a side alley. Very touristy but good fun. A nightly show from around 10 p.m. with a cover charge.

O'Connor's Pub, High Street. Popular with young people.

Scott's Hotel, College Street. Piano music in the bar, traditional music in the lounge and open air song, weather permitting, in the beer garden.

Tatler Jack, Plunkett Street. Ballad sessions most nights from 10 p.m. during the summer.

WHERE TO STAY

HOTELS

The following hotels are categorised according to the cost per person sharing a double room. The descending scale is similar to that in earlier sections of this book. The grade accompanying each listing is the grade given by Bord Failte and is based on the facilities the hotel has to offer.

High

Great Southern Hotel. Opposite railway station, telephone 064–31262, fax 064–31642. Constructed in 1854 and set in large grounds, the hotel has one of the best lobbies in town and an attractive Victorian-style bar. Facilities include a heated pool, gym and jacuzzi. Breakfast not included in room rates. Open all year. Five Star. AM, AE, DE, VB.

Aghadoe Heights Hotel. Telephone 064–31766, fax 064–31345. Modern building in large grounds, own salmon river, swimming pool. Open all year. Four Star. AM, AE, DE, VB.

Cahernane Hotel. Muckross Road, telephone 064–31895, fax 064–34340. Built in 1877, recently refurbished, and once the home of the earls of Pembroke. Another fine lobby, full of Victorian character, and rooms which vary in character. There are no televisions — blessing or blight? — in the rooms. The dozen rooms in the main house are the most interesting. Open all year. Four Star. AM, AE, DE, VB.

Castlerosse. 1.2 miles/2 km out of town, telephone 064–31895, fax 064–34340. Facilities for pets. Open April to October. Three Star. AM, AE, DE, VB.

Dunloe Castle Hotel. West of Killarney in Beaufort. Telephone 064–44111, fax 064–44583. A modern building in large grounds, complete with ruined castle. Indoor pool and fitness track. Open May to September. Five Star. AM, AE, DE, VB.

Gleneagle Hotel, Muckross Road, telephone 064–31870, fax 064–32646. Modern building in extensive grounds; rooms in the new wing have lakeside views. Extensive leisure facilities and lively, noisy entertainment at night. A baby-sitting service is provided. Double rooms only. Open all year. Three Star. AE, AM, DE, VB.

Hotel Europe, Killorglin Road. On the shores of Lough Leane with excellent lakeside views from nearly all the rooms, though the hotel itself spoils the view when looking across the lake from other vantage points. Telephone 064–31900, fax 064–32118. A very big modern complex with an Olympic-size pool, horse riding and live entertainment in the evenings. Open April to October. Five Star. AM, AE, DE, VB.

Killarney Park Hotel, Kenmare Place, telephone 064–35555, fax 064–35266. A new and comfortable hotel in the town centre complete with satellite television, a leisure centre that includes an indoor pool and steam room. All the rooms are tastefully decorated and some are specially designed for needs of handicapped. Baby-sitting available. Open all year. Four Star. AM, AE, VB.

Muckross Park Hotel, Muckross Village, telephone 064–31938, fax 064–31965. Comfortable modernised rooms with a very popular pub attached. Open March to December. Four Star. AM, AE, DE, VB.

Moderate

Eviston House Hotel, New Street, telephone 064–31640, fax 064–33685. Satellite TV, tea and coffee making facility, baby-sitting service. Nightclub attached. Open all year. Three Star. AE, AM, DE, VB.

International Hotel, Kenmare Place, telephone 064–31816, fax 064–31837. TV, baby-sitting service, nightly entertainment. Breakfast not included in room rate. Closed January and February. Two Star. AE, AM, DE, VB.

Killarney Ryan Hotel, Park Road, telephone 064–31555, fax 064–32438. Modern. Set in large grounds. Leisure centre with indoor pool. Open March to November. Three Star. AE, AM, DE, VB.

Killarney Towers Hotel, College Square, telephone 064–31038, fax 064–31755. Situated in the centre of town. Tea and coffee facilities in the rooms. Open March to October. Three Star. AM, AE, VB.

Lake Hotel, Muckross Road, telephone 064–31035, fax 064–31902. Old mansion first turned into a hotel in the nineteenth century. Games room, baby-sitting, facilities for pets, wheelchair access. Closed November to mid-March. Three Star.

Randles Court Hotel, Muckross Road, telephone 064–35333, fax 064–35206. Open all year. Four Star. AM, VB.

Three Lakes Hotel, Kenmare Place, telephone 064–31479, fax 064–33217. Satellite TV, tea making, baby-sitting. Open all year. Three Star. AE, AM, DE, VB.

Budget

Arbutus Hotel, College Street, telephone 064–31037, fax 064–34033. Small, recently modernised and friendly family hotel. A baby-sitting service. Closed over Christmas. Three Star. AM, DE, VB.

East Avenue Hotel, East Avenue, telephone 064–32522, fax 064–33707. Small family-run hotel. Lively nightlife with a nightclub and cabaret. Closed November and February. Two Star. AM, AE, VB.

Belvedere Hotel, New Street, telephone 064–31133. Tea and coffee making facilities, live music twice a week, snooker tables, baby-sitting service. One Star. AM, AE, DE, VB.

Killeen House Hotel, Aghadoe, telephone 064–31711, fax 064–431811. Large gardens around this small renovated nineteenth-century house, baby-sitting. Closed January and February. Three Star. AM, AE, DE, VB.

Ross Hotel, Kenmare Place, telephone 064–31855, fax 064–31139. Guests have use of the extensive leisure facilities across the street in the Killarney Park Hotel. Open all year. Three Star. AM, AE, VB.

Royal Hotel, College Street, telephone 064–31853, fax 064–34001. Out of season price reductions for senior citizens, centrally located, facilities for pets. Closed during the Christmas week. Three Star. AE, AM, VB.

Torc Great Southern, 0.8 miles/1 km from town, telephone 064–31611, fax 064–31824. Swimming pool and tennis court. Open 9 April to 17 October. Three Star. AM, AE, DE, VB.

Whitegates Hotel, Muckross Road, telephone 064–31164, fax 064–34850. Children's playroom, baby-sitting, games room. Three Star. AM, VB.

Economy

Failte Family Inn, College Street, telephone 064–31893, fax 064–33404. Open all year. One Star. AE, DE, VB.

Grand Hotel, Main Street, telephone 064–31159. Facilities for pets. Open all year. One Star. AM, AE.

Linden House Hotel, New Road, telephone 064–31379, fax 064–31196. Family hotel offering functional but good value accommodation. Open February to November. Two

Star. AM, VB.

McSweeney Arms Hotel, College Street, telephone 064–31211, fax 064–34553. Bar downstairs. Open March to December. Two Star. AM, VB.

Park Place Hotel, High Street, telephone 064–31058, fax 064–3445. Open all year. One Star. AM, VB.

Scott's, College Street, telephone 064–31060, fax 064–32646. Open all year. Two Star. AM, VB.

GUEST HOUSES/BED AND BREAKFAST

There are too many to list and the most convenient way to arrange a night's stay is to contact the tourist office in Killarney. For a small booking charge they will telephone for an available B&B or guest house.

SELF-CATERING

There are very many self-catering houses or apartments available in Kerry and individual houses for rent are not listed below. The places below usually include facilities such as washing machine, dishwasher, central heating, bed linen and TV. It is advisable to book as early as is possible and a computer booking service is available for most of them through the Cork City Tourist Information Office, Grand Parade, Cork, telephone 021–273251, fax 021–273504. Expect to pay between £400 and £500 during July and August.

Forest Lake Cottages. Some 3 miles/5 km from town on the Killorglin Road. Forest Lake Cottages, Fossa, Killarney, telephone 064–31554, fax 064–35058. Sleeps 6.

Killarney Holiday Village, Beaufort. Enquiries and bookings to Dagmar Willms, c/o Killarney Travel, Market Cross, Killarney, telephone 064–35166, fax 064–35171. Three-bedroomed bungalows, 6 miles/10km from Killarney. Sleeps 5–6.

Killarney Holiday Villas. Semi-detached villas, 2 miles/3 km from town. Baradi Sales Services, Kenmare, telephone 064–41170, fax 064–41839.

Accommodation Killarney. Town houses in the centre of Killarney. Contact Frances Russell, Accommodation Killarney, 52 High Street, Killarney, telephone 064–31787/021–273251, fax 064–35238/ 021–273504. Stone-built houses on street. Sleeps 4–5.

Killarney Country Club. Courtyard buildings, 6 miles/9.5 km from town. Contact Pat Henderson, Killarney Country Club, Faha, Killarney, telephone 064–44655, fax 064–44657. Sleeps 5–8.

Killarney Lakeland Cottages. Cottages at Muckross. Contact Brian O'Shea, Muckross, Killarney, telephone 064–31538/021–273251, fax 064–34113/021–273504. Three-bedroomed cottages set in parkland, tennis, games room, children's playroom. No washing machine but laundry on site. TV can be hired. Sleeps 6–8.

Parkland Holiday Homes. Less than one km from town. Parkland Holiday Homes, Port Road, Killarney, telephone 064–35366, fax 064–35358. Sleeps 6.

Ross Castle Holiday Homes. New bungalows, ten minutes walk from town. Contact Limerick Travel, Bedford Row, Limerick, telephone 061–413844, fax 061–416336. Sleeps 6.

HOSTELS

All hostels offer dormitory accommodation for around £6, hot showers and kitchen facilities. Some have double rooms.

The Sugan, Michael Collins Place in College Street, telephone 064–33104. Open all year. At night the kitchen services the mostly vegetarian restaurant downstairs and is not available to residents. There is, however, a discount on the restaurant meals. Bikes can be hired and there's a free pick-up service from the train and bus station.

Four Winds, 43 New Street, telephone 064–33094. Two kitchens, video library, TV room, free transport to and from station. Open all year.

Bunrower House Hostel, Ross Road, telephone 064–33914. Set in woodlands on

shore of Lough Leane on the road that leads down to Ross Castle. Bikes for hire, wheelchair friendly. Under the same management as The Sugan. Open all year.
Neptune's Killarney Town Hostel, New Street, telephone 064–35255, fax 064–32310. Purpose built, centrally heated, open all year, kitchens, laundry room, en suite family rooms, wheelchair friendly, smoke-free areas. Courtesy bus, luggage store, baby-sitting, games, TV rooms.
An Óige, Aghadoe House, Fossa, telephone 064–31240, fax 064–34300. Very large youth hostel in old country house. Two kitchens, TV room, lounge area, family rooms. Advance booking essential July and August. Membership card for An Óige essential but these can be bought at the hostel and will last for one year. Open all year, bicycle hire at hostel. Open all day.

CAMPING AND CARAVAN SITES

Fossa Camping and Caravanning Park. About 3.5 miles/5.6 km west of town at Fossa on the Ring of Kerry road towards Killorglin. Telephone 064–31497, fax 064–34459. Site caravans, dormitory accommodation, takeaway food, restaurant, shop, playground, TV lounge, electric hook-up, laundry, hire cycles. Dogs welcome. Open Easter–October. Four-star rating by Bord Failte.
Beech Grove. Same location as above. Telephone 064–31727. Site caravans, electric hook-up, games room, playground, TV, shop. open March–October. Two-star.
Fleming's Whitebridge Caravan and Camping Park. 3 miles/5 km west of Killarney on the Ring of Kerry road towards Killorglin. Telephone 064–31590. Good shelter, landscaped, site caravans, laundry, shop, television room. Four-star rating.
White Villa Farm Caravan & Camping Park. 2 miles/3 km east of Killarney on the main N22 road to Cork. Only twelve pitches for tents. Two-star rating.

WHERE TO EAT

There is no shortage of food in Killarney. What follows is a selective list of the eating places in town and around it organised into ascending price categories for an evening meal.

KILLARNEY TOWN

Economy
Busy Bee's Bistro. Italian food, sandwiches, soups. Wine bar open till 3 a.m. Serves breakfast all day. Situated in New Street near junction with High Street.
Allegro Fast Food. Takeaway and eat in. Chip dominated menu.
Charlie Chan Chinese. Standard Chinese dishes.
Burgerland. High Street, but it could be anywhere from Valparaiso to Wagga Wagga.

Budget
Caragh Café. Chips again. Functional decor. Children's menu. Serves house wine. New Street.
Stella, Main Street. Children's menu. Tourist dinner menu. Cafe style.
Laune. A pub/restaurant. Competitive prices.
Sceilig Restaurant. Nice place, does basic meals such as Irish stew, grilled trout, pizza. Vegetarian dishes. High Street.
Sheila's, High Street. Set dinner or a la carte. Interesting starters. Unpretentious, reliable good Irish food.
Sugan. By day this is an independent hostel while at night its kitchen converts to a mainly vegetarian restaurant.
An Taelan. Vegetarian only. Closed in winter. Bridewell Lane.
Colleen Bawn, New Street. Upstairs in Eviston Hotel. Art nouveauish decor, coachloads of tourists in summer. Good value tourist set meal. AM, AE, DE, VB.

Café Chinos. Downstairs in Eviston Hotel. Trendy sort of place, little shelves to sit at and hard rock café-type food. AM, AE, DE, VB.

Pat's Restaurant, College Street. In Arbutus Hotel. Does a three-course evening meal at a competitive price. Open from 6–9 p.m., 12–3 p.m. for lunch. AM, DE, VB.

Moderate

Picasso's. A wine bar/restaurant. Lifestyle atmosphere, lots of prints on walls, white piano plus player in window. AM, AE, DE, VB. Open from 10 a.m. to 10 p.m. but closed on Sunday. Telephone 064–31329.

The Laurels, Main Street, telephone 064–31149. Open April–October. Evenings only, 6–10.15 p.m. Reservations appreciated. Wine bar style, tiles and wood, vegetarian choices, wine list. AM, AE, DE, VB.

Kiwi's, St. Anthony's Place, off College Street, good food and you can bring your own wine.

High

Foley's, High Street. Edwardian gentleman style. Open fires. Seafood and steak dishes. Choice of vegetarian dishes. One of the best wine lists in town. Telephone 064–31217. Reservations recommended. AM, AE, DE, VB.

Gaby's, High Street, telephone 064–32519. Tiled floors and wooden booths. Highly rated seafood restaurant, specialising in lobster. Extensive wine list. Open from 6 to 10 p.m. Mondays to Saturday, and from 12.30 to 2.30 p.m. Tuesday to Saturday. AM, AE, DE, VB.

The Strawberry Tree. In Plunkett Street, this restaurant is open evenings only from 6.30 p.m. AM, AE, DE, VB..

Failte Family Inn, College Street. Some vegetarian food. AM, AE, DE, VB.

Dingle's Restaurant, New Street. Some vegetarian food. Evenings from 6–10 p.m. AM, AE, DE, VB.

Robertino's is a relatively new Italian restaurant at the top of High Street. Telephone 064–34966. AM, AE, DE, VB.

OUTSIDE KILLARNEY

Kate Kearney's Cottage, Gap of Dunloe, telephone 064–44146. The restaurant is open all day during the summer and dinner is from 6.30 to 9 p.m. Bar food is always available.

Molly Darcy's Pub & Restaurant. On the N71 road to Kenmare, beside the Muckross Park Hotel. A thatched roof pub with bar food all day and meals at the Molly restaurant. Very popular, with an atmosphere of people on holiday enjoying themselves.

Killarney Manor Banquet, Loretto Road, telephone 064–31551, fax 064–33366. Open from April to October. Confirm availability by telephone. Dinner starts at 8.00 p.m., followed by music, song and dance.

SHOPPING FOR GIFTS AND SOUVENIRS

There is no shortage of tourist oriented shops in Killarney, particularly the leprechaun and teatowel type. Standard items include woollen and Aran jumpers, embroidery and tweeds. Several jewellers do Claddagh rings and other jewellery based on Celtic designs. These are very pretty but expensive. What follows is a necessarily selective listing.

Kerry Glass Studio, Fossa, 5 miles/8 km from town on the road to Killorglin. Open from February to December, until 9 p.m. between June and September. Watch the glass being made in the studio, with free tours between 11 a.m. and 4 p.m., and visit the show room. A tearoom is attached and an international mail order service available.

Bricin, High Street. Open all year. Crafts made in Cork and Kerry: pottery, paintings, prints and books.

Quill's Woollen Mills, High Street. Well-established store with the whole range of tourist paraphernalia as well as some nice Celtic jewellery, Aran jumpers, patchwork quilts, wax jackets and Donegal tweed jackets.

Keane's Jewellers, High Street. Standard items plus Claddagh rings and Celtic designs. AM, AE, DE, VB.

Brian De Staic Jewellers, High Street. Some Claddagh and Celtic designs and also a pendant in which you can have your name inscribed in Ogham script.

The Kilkenny Shop, Main Street. Quality clothes, china and crystal.

Muckross House. Three craft workshops in the basement, the products of which are on sale in the shop upstairs. Fine pottery and weaving work and excellent bookbinding service. Open all year, 7 days a week until 5.30 p.m.

The Emerald Collection, Main Street. Leading brands of crystal and china.

Sweater Company. New Street. Sweaters for both sexes.

Macken of Ireland, Fossa. 3 miles/6 km west of Killarney. The store has a large range of tourist items, including pottery, crystal, china and jewellery. Jackets and skirts in cashmere, tweed and lambswool. There is a car park and coffee shop too.

Killarney Bookshop, High Street. Excellent bookshop with full range of stock. Especially good on tourist literature. Knowledgeable staff. Mail order service overseas.

Kate Kearney's Cottage, Gap of Dunloe. A range of souvenir and gifts available at the most touristy spot in Killarney.

Moriarty's, Gap of Dunloe. Tweeds, linen, Aran sweaters, souvenirs and crafts.

CHILDREN'S ACTIVITIES

- Visit the Transport Museum (see page 143)
- Take a pony ride through the Gap of Dunloe (see page 144)
- Hire a rowing boat from outside Ross Castle and row over to Inishfallen Island with your parents.
- Go horse riding (see page 152)
- Visit a swimming pool (see page 152)
- *Churchtown Country Park,* Beaufort, telephone 064–44440. Family farm, adventure playground, flower gardens. Open May–September. Monday–Saturday from 10 a.m.–6 p.m. Sunday 1–6 p.m. The park is 7 miles/11.2 km out of Killarney on the Ring of Kerry road to Killorglin.

RAINY DAY ACTIVITIES

- Pay a visit to the cinema, located next to the Killarney Park hotel near the roundabout where the N71 road to Kenmare begins. Three films each evening and late night shows on Fridays and Saturdays.
- Visit the Transport Museum (see page 143)
- Drive to Crag Cave for a visit underground (see page 148)
- Visit the *Kerry Glass Studio* (see page 158) for a free tour of the studio.
- Get organised with raingear and go for a walk through the Gap of Dunloe or around Ross Castle.
- Visit Muckross House
- Visit Kerry Woollen Mills

ECOTOUR

This tour explores the ecology of the Killarney lakes and the immediate areas around them, while trying to avoid some of the inconvenient aspects of the Killarney phenomenon. The town of Killarney is really very small and the large number of tourists milling around can easily create the impression that the surrounding countryside is going to be equally busy. This is not at all the case. As in all the ecotours, driving is an essential feature but there are plenty of opportunities for long walks in places that, even in the height of the visitor season, will be almost deserted. Stout walking shoes, wet gear and a pair of binoculars are needed.

The first stage of the tour involves a short drive out of town to the west side of Lough Leane in Tomies Wood.

Link Killarney to Killorglin. 12.5 miles/20 km.

After leaving Killarney and passing through the village of Fossa, turn left at the first signpost to the Gap of Dunloe. After 2.6 kilometres down this road a T-junction appears. Take the left turn signposted to Lough Leane (right is for the Gap of Dunloe). A single track leads down towards the lough. Where the road takes a left-hand turn at a small bridge, find a place to park in front of the gates which warn that the road is a right of way for walkers only. If there is insufficient space here carry on down the road to the left to where it ends on the shore of the lough. There is more ample space here for parking.

Walk The walk begins at the gates and carries along the pedestrians-only path that leads up to and through a farm.

The first part of the tour takes you through a modern farm. New outbuildings and machinery can be seen, milk production has been joined by sheep rearing and in a field on the left bee hives can be seen. In days gone by the keeping of bees not only provided a valuable source of food; the beeswax was used to make candles, absolutely essential items in any household. Nowadays, in many parts of the country, the number of bee hives that can be maintained is limited by the increasing difficulty bees have in finding sources for their honeymaking. The destruction of ditches and hedgerows, as fields are made larger and larger — plus the effect of modern chemicals ladled out by farmers — is reducing the amount and variety of flowers that bees can visit. West Cork and Kerry is probably one of the best remaining habitats for the noble and ancient art of bee keeping.

The scale of this farmer's dairy operation is small compared to farming in some other parts of Ireland and most of Europe, there being a score of cows here at the most. Not that many years ago, and certainly within the living memory of most farmers in West Cork and Kerry, rearing and milking twenty cows would have been considered a prosperous undertaking. Nowadays, reduced milk subsidies are increasing the optimum number of cows that farmers need to keep. Another factor working against the small farmer in this part of Ireland is the 'rationalisation' of the creamery system. Up until fairly recently farmers would deliver their milk on a daily basis to their local creamery where the milk was tested and separated. Small, local creameries no longer do this; instead, a milk lorry collects the milk three times a week and farmers have no choice but to invest in expensive cooling equipment to keep their daily milk collection at the right temperature on the days when the milk lorry is not calling. For a small farmer with less than a score of cows there is an economic pressure to give up dairy farming altogether, or sell out to a larger farmer.

Further along this road, past the farm, the road enters forested land, at first a plantation of spruce. This tree has been introduced in planting programmes although remains of spruce pollen have been found in Ireland going back 200,000 years. It can be distinguished from other conifer trees by the long narrow cone with toothed scales. If you look about the ground where you are walking you should see some. Beyond the spruce, a locked gate with a stile leads to a wooden bridge giving way to the indigenous woodland of Kerry. To get a picture of the ecology of the woodland needs only a journey of a few hundred yards into the wood proper, but an undemanding and very beautiful circular walk of about 4 miles/6.5 km can be made, bringing you back to this spot.

After the wooden bridge a green road on the left takes you into the wood, crossing a precarious wooden bridge. The wood is typical of this area, mainly oak forming the top canopy of leaves in the summer with another layer of birch, beech and holly beneath. These woods may be as much as 800 years old. The evergreen holly makes use of the bare branches of the oaks during the winter months. Early flowering plants such as bluebells also make use of the extra daylight before the oak is fully in leaf, while other woodland plants such as foxgloves are abundant. The flowers have adapted to the woodland habitat and need less light to grow. The floor of the forest is relatively bare and all available space is covered by mosses which take their nourishment from the exceptionally pure but humid air. In spring every available puddle fills with frogspawn and other wildlife is easily spotted. This includes of course the infamous Kerry slug, a gaily spotted grey creature only to be found in this area.

If you are lucky you may see a large red deer hurrying across the path after being alerted by the sound of your approach. This herd of red deer is the only surviving native herd in Ireland, the others having been wiped out by hunting many years ago. Fallow and Sika deer also

Ladies View, Killarney, Co. Kerry

live in the woods but these are introduced species. There are about 350 red deer in the woods, both in the national park and outside it. They are a protected species, even on private land. Their mating season is in October, with calves born from June to July. Stags lose their antlers in late spring and spend the summer growing new ones. It is thought that one reason for the scratch marks they make on the trunks of trees is part of the process of growing new horns. Antlers can have up to fourteen points.

The Sika deer were brought to Killarney in 1865 and have flourished here ever since. There are about 1,000 of them in the area and their numbers are beginning to threaten the woodland since they graze on the herbiage of the forest floor and kill tree seedlings. They can be recognised by their antlers which are smaller than those of red deer and only have about eight points.

Encroaching on this delicately balanced ecology is the invasive rhododendron, an introduced plant whose ability to cover the ground beneath the trees and its evergreen nature is damaging the forest's ability to reproduce itself. Seedling oaks and birch are smothered by the bushy, purple-flowered plant. An ironic part of the story of the rhododendron is that thousands of years before the Victorians introduced it to their gardens the rhododendron flourished here only be driven back to warmer parts of Europe during the Ice Age.

Another introduced tree that can be noticed in the wood is the larch, which is unusual in that it is a deciduous conifer. It produces tiny cones in bunches on its branches. Its deciduous nature makes it a suitable companion tree for natural oakwoods. In early spring it is easily spotted because it is sprouting bright green new leaves.

As the walk carries on out of the wood and high up along the side of Lough Leane, excellent views over the lough and Killarney can be seen. You are standing at this point on what was probably, thousands of years ago, the final resting place of a great glacier, a terminal moraine made up of all the material the glacier was carrying when the temperature caught up with it and it stopped. The moraine blocked the valley and helped create Lough Leane out of the hollow made by the tail-end of the glacier as it sat in the valley below.

Kerry escaped the worst of the Ice Age. The ice sheets stopped north of Kerry but the mountains of the region were high enough to carry ice caps.

Looking at the soil on the path you will notice that it is mainly made up of very regular shaped red blocks of stone, the basic building blocks of Kerry. This was laid down at an even earlier period as great rivers carried debris of sand and grit from the central plain of Ireland westwards and deposited it around what is now Cork and Kerry. This is old red sandstone and forms the bulk of the mountains of Kerry. For a time the sandstone was under water as was all of Ireland and then, about 300 million years ago, a massive earth movement thrust these one-time deposits of grit and sand up into gigantic folds which broke and shifted, forming the mountains seen today. Three hundred million years ago the sandstone was covered in deposits of coal from a previous carboniferous time but this was all eroded away leaving the sandstone exposed. The Ice Age did the rest.

The walk circles round, reaching a higher point of the mountain and returns towards your starting point, crossing the stream by means of stepping stones this time.

Link Return to Killarney and the roundabout near the cinema where the N71 road to Kenmare begins. Almost immediately turn right at the Shell garage on the road signposted to Ross Castle. Continue down this road to where it stops at Ross Castle and park your vehicle.

The ecotour continues in the grounds of Ross Castle and explores in more detail the ecology of Lough Leane.

Walk down towards the shore of Lough Leane. As you pass through the woods most of the plants around you are not naturally occurring but have been planted by the parks department or by the earls of Kenmare whose estate this was until 1956 when the last earl died. There are many pretty walks around the estate and the lakeshore but any point along the shore will bring you to a spot where you can consider the ecology of the lake.

This lake — like the other two Killarney lakes — represents places where parts of great glaciers rested, quarrying out the ground beneath them as the ice alternately melted and froze over. Lough Leane itself is dammed by glacial deposits scored out of the lake bed by the glacier. After the glaciers left, loughs Leane and Muckross continued to be deepened by the action of water on their limestone base. The limestone dissolved, making the lake look very blue and also providing a great source of food for animal life. The lakes drain an area of land amounting to 650 square kilometres and are in turn drained by the River Laune. At its deepest point Lough Leane is probably about 65-70 metres deep. In addition to the limestone in the water, material from the town finds its way into the lake as do effluents such as excess fertiliser put on to the fields around Killarney. In some ways this is an advantage, since the materials are mostly an excellent source of nutrition for the lake life, but particularly because of over fertilisation of the soil, the lake becomes depleted of oxygen on hot summer days.

Lough Leane forms part of a system with the two lakes above it, Muckross Lake and the Upper Lake. The Upper Lake lies on sandstone and so the water flowing down from it is acid and high in oxygen. As it passes through Muckross Lake it gains nutrients and becomes neutral and finally meets the mildly polluted and calcium rich waters of Lough Leane. Still the lake is rich in wildlife. Brown trout, the native trout of the rivers and streams of Kerry, grow large here where they have a lot less fighting to do in order to find food. Salmon still find their way up here along the Laune. Perch and eels also live here, feeding on salmon and trout fry. The Irish char, which only exists in Kerry and Wicklow, is also present in this lake. Another very local fish is the Killarney shad, a kind of freshwater herring which would normally spend part of its life cycle in the sea but in this case is completely freshwater dependant. Many other species of fish also live in the lake — tench, flounder, lamprey, minnows and sticklebacks. They in turn provide rich pickings for the birdlife that lives around the shores. Cormorant can be seen gliding over the surface of the lake on the lookout for dinner, while herons also breed here. Living on the lake's plant food are ducks and mute swans. Otters live along the shores feeding on fish. The great crested grebe, little grebes, tufted ducks, red breasted merganser, moorhens, coots, common sandpipers, kingfishers and dippers have also been seen here.

The lake also supports several species of birds escaping from harsher winters further to the north of Ireland. The Greenland white fronted goose, which has a world population of about 12,000, spend most of their winter in Ireland and about 150 of them come to Killarney. The wigeon, pochard and curlew also overwinter here.

Return to your car for the next part of the ecotour.

Link Ross Castle to Muckross House. 3.7 miles/6 km.

Return to the Shell garage and turn right, out on to the Kenmare road. Leave your vehicle at the first car park for Muckross House, on the left of the road. It is usually easy to find because of the jaunting cars waiting there for visitors.

This part of the tour explores Muckross peninsula, the strip of land that separates Lough Leane from Muckross Lake. The plant life of the peninsula is examined and the effects on it of the sandstone soil being interrupted by a strip of limestone in this area.

Walk Cross the road from the car park and walk through the gates to Muckross and along the main drive towards the house.

When you come to an iron bridge over a stream head off to the right and walk along the shores of Lough Leane. The trees you are walking through bear all the signs of having been planted for their architectural use rather than being part of a naturally occurring system, although all of them are in fact native trees. As their wild shapes indicate, they have developed unsurrounded by other trees. Their shade supports considerable woodland plant life and several parasitic plants have found homes in their branches. Beside the lake you will notice the fallout from the many boat trips that ply the lakes. Bits of plastic and sweet wrappers lie alongside the more natural flotsam and jetsam.

Standing under the shade of the trees it is noticeable that the plant life here is of the woodland type. It is also vegetation which can survive quite damp conditions, since there is evidence of the lake rising and falling here. The trees along the shoreline are mostly alder, which can tolerate damp conditions. The alder is a broad-leaved tree but it produces cones — similar to those of conifers — which stay on for much of the winter. The alder is able to survive in these damp acid conditions by taking in atmospheric nitrogen via tiny bacteria which live in its roots. This is a case of symbiosis; both the bacteria and the alder tree benefitting from the relationship.

In summer tall swathes of purple loosestrife will fill this area. They are perennial plants and their leaves and stems die off completely during the winter to re-emerge quite late in spring. This leaves the ground bare for some time in spring, allowing other plants to flourish before they take over the available space. In spring the ground is littered with wood anemones, primroses, bluebells, speedwell and yellow celandines, all plants that can tolerate shade and damp and fairly acid conditions. The soil here is laid down over red sandstone although as you carry on along the walk you will see a clear break in this, as the limestone cuts in. Other summer plants in evidence are sneezewort and water mint with its bunches of tiny purple flowers and strong minty smell. Again these are plants that can tolerate damp conditions.

As you walk along, natural oak woodland — with its ability to support an enormous range of plant and animal life — builds up to your left. If you stand still long enough and gaze upwards you might be lucky enough to see some of the woodland birds which usually stay high up in the canopy, seeking out butterflies and berries. Bluetits and jays are difficult to miss while robins are always near to holly trees. Other birds common in this area are spotted fly catchers, siskins, long tailed tits, wrens, tree creepers, which live on the insects that inhabit the bark of the trees, and wood pigeons. The pigeons are present in huge numbers in autumn when acorns provide their winter diet. On the ground the deeper shade allows plants such as woodrush to survive.

As you carry on, the change from sandstone to limestone gradually becomes obvious with whitish pitted rocks standing up out of the ground and weirdly-shaped pinnacles of limestone that have somehow survived out in the water. This area supports a great deal of animal life besides the birds you hear high up in the trees. Deer inhabit these woods and are now so numerous that they threaten them. The marks of their antlers can be seen scratched into the bark of the trees, particularly the yews further on. Along the shores of the lake are many small caves hollowed out of the limestone rock. These provide homes for otters who leave tell-tale spraints, or droppings, on the rocks along the shore. Badgers also live in the wood, although like the otters, they are nocturnal animals and are rarely seen except at night, although their sets can be spotted fairly easily. Red squirrels also live in these woods, though as yet the aggressive grey squirrel has not found a home here. There are also three species of bats, again to be seen at night, pigmy shrews and stoats live in the woods and there have been reports of bank voles — an introduced species since 1964 — and pinemartens, but mistakes are easily made with brief sightings of these tiny woodland creatures.

When you reach a wall, break off to your left until you reach a tarred road. This will take you to a crossroads from where Muckross House is visible. Do not head for the House but instead take the right turn which leads to a path going out onto the Muckross peninsula. Follow the signs for Dinish Cottage and the Meeting of the Waters. You are now walking through some woods with plenty of ferns of many different species at your feet.

Keep walking along this road and take another right fork, still on a tarred road. This leads you to Reenadinna Wood. The road will have markers on it, numbers 20 to 18, part of the Arthur Young Walk, laid out by the National Parks Service. (Arthur Young, the eighteenth-century agricultural improver, was a guest at Muckross.) At marker number 18 you will be in yew woodland, a very rare type of wood and probably the biggest now surviving in Europe. The yews are growing on a tiny veneer of soil laid down over the highly fertile limestone rock which is quite deeply laid here — so much so that when some rough land near this area was being cleared of rocks in the nineteenth century the effort had to be abandoned in this spot when it was realised they weren't rocks at all but the underlying surface. Under the yew trees very little plant life survives but the whole area is covered in moss which survives by taking its nutrients from the damp air. The roots of the yews burrow deep into the limestone in search of a good grip and most of them seem to be anchored quite securely. In autumn and winter the yew trees produce red berries which provide winter food for many birds, especially flocks of fieldfares which arrive in Ireland from Scandinavia; Ireland being the first place on their journey south which does not have a snow covering for the winter. Other birds common in the yew woods are coal tits, blue tits and chaffinches, all seed eaters.

On this limestone section of the peninsula, even where there are no yew trees, the rhododendron does not grow. It cannot tolerate the alkaline soil, preferring the acid soil of the oakwoods. Although the oakland areas of Muckross were cleared extensively of rhododendron over a decade ago, it seeds prolifically and within a few years will soon be threatening the regeneration of the oakwoods again.

If you care to carry on with the walk by following the signs of the Arthur Young Walk backwards, you can see a naturally occurring arbutus tree at stop number 8, at the other side of the peninsula. These trees are part of the Lusitanian flora of this area, plants which naturally occur in much warmer Mediterranean climates. Pollen analysis of bogland in the area, though, shows that the arbutus trees have existed in Ireland for the last 5,000 years. Also at this stop are the remains of a marble quarry, developed by the Herbert family. The marble exists because the original limestone containing tiny flakes of shale and chert has been put under enormous pressure some time in the geological past, probably from rock folding and faulting, and metamorphosed into marble. Green, red, white, and brown marbles were taken out of this quarry.

As the little peninsula of Muckross juts out further into the lake the red sandstone reappears, so that the limestone is a slice cut into the peninsula supporting completely different vegetation. The oak and holly return and at the end of the peninsula are the remains of copper mines. There is evidence that the copper from this area was mined by Bronze Age people. The chief period of their exploitation was between 1749 and 1754 and it is estimated that at current rates, about £8-£10 million of ore was taken out of here. This explains the lavishness of Muckross House which was built on the proceeds. The ore was taken to Bristol for smelting.

From the very end of the peninsula Eagles Point can be seen, a cliff

The interior of Muckross House, near Killarney, Co. Kerry

overlooking the Long Range stretch of water which connects Muckross Lake with the Upper Lake. Golden eagles, now extinct in Ireland, once nested here and in the last century tourists would discharge firearms as they sailed down this part of the river to watch the eagles fly out from the cliffs.

At this point head back to your vehicle by retracing the route. Some time can be saved by keeping to the tarred road all the way out of the grounds and this way will pass the ruins of Muckross Friary.

Link Drive south on the N71 road towards Kenmare for a few hundred yards and turn left at the signpost for Mangerton. A few hundred yards up the road turn left again into a car park and leave your vehicle here.

This is a marked-out nature trail laid out by the National Parks and Forestry Commission and there are references below to numbered points clearly visibly along the easy-to-follow trail. The ropeway that is seen along part of the walk is intended for the visually handicapped and a cassette to accompany the blind is available from Muckross House.

Walk back towards the pool. This is an example of a completely unnatural environment. The pool was made some time in the past by man and requires periodic dredging in order to prevent it silting up. It was used in earlier times as a mill pond and later as a fish hatchery. The woods around it consist of some naturally occurring oaks, pines laid in when this was administered by the Forestry Commission, beech trees planted more recently, and some willow, birch and alder which have found homes in the damp soil around the pool. There are also the ubiquitous rhododendrons which have been cleared but are now threatening the young trees again.

Unnatural though it is, the area survives quite well with a bit of help. Follow the obvious trail by crossing over the bridge and bearing to the right.

The oak trees surrounding the pool are naturally occurring. Otters breed in the pool and can be spotted swimming about and then dashing for the bank when alarmed by the sound of people in the vicinity. As in any deciduous wood there is a great diversity of plant life on the forest floor, particularly plants that flower early, such as marsh marigolds, violets and wood anemones. They flower around March, with bluebells appearing in May. There are also many ferns and a huge amount of woodrush with its grass-like leaves and delicate flowers.

At stop number 2 vertical scars on the trunk of the spruce tree to the left of the marker can be noticed. This indicates that deer inhabit these woods. Sika deer, another introduced species, use the trunks of the trees to scratch marks, perhaps as some kind of territorial behaviour. If you look at the vegetation around the edges of this area you will see that it has been grazed quite heavily. With no predators except man, the deer threaten to disturb the balance that rests on this unnatural collection of plant and animal life.

The trees around this spot are mostly spruce, planted around the same time and too close together for their natural shape to emerge. On the ground are the remains of the plant life that existed before the forest floor became too dark to support it. Rotting black humps are all that is left of the once flourishing sedge, a water-loving plant which builds up islands in the bog.

As you move around the pool the beginnings of the beech planting can be seen. The area around marker number 3 is very boggy and sitting happily in the water are alder trees. In early spring these bear male and female catkins before the leaves appear and in autumn have fruit looking a little like tiny pine cones. On the surface of the water are many water-loving plants, including the water mint with its distinctive smell. Deeper in can be seen living examples of sedge, forming huge grassy tussocks. Sedge supports much insect and water life and as the pond is dredged the park attendants are careful to leave islands of sedge in the water to provide shelter for coots and moorhen.

As you pass marker number 3 and start to climb the hill the woods turn back to spruce with beech trees interspersed, again too close together to form anything but spindly shapes as they try to find enough light. The ground cover is thin except under the oak trees to your right over the wall. In among all the spruce and beech are sycamores with their smooth grey bark and maple-shaped leaves, forcing them back and making a good job of getting their share of the light. Sycamore trees are very effective at seed dispersal and can often become weeds themselves, preventing other trees from seeding.

Further on between markers 3 and 4 larch trees have been planted. They are a deciduous pine tree and so are able to support more plant life beneath them. Ivy is climbing up the trunks of the trees but has been grazed by deer up to about five feet. Unlike the floor of Tomies Wood, visited above in the first part of the ecotour, the trees and ground here are not covered by mosses since there is too much light here.

After marker number 4, four birch trees have been planted, and quite recently since they are small. Passing marker 5 can be seen the remains of a gravel pit. The gravel was laid down during the Ice Age as meltwater, or perhaps a sheet of ice itself dumped tons of ground-up material here. From this spot the walk leads into more natural woodland, chiefly holly. In winter, only some of the bushes carry berries, for holly has male and female trees and only the female carry the berries.

After marker 6 the path turns off the green road and goes down to the edge of the pool. Here, by the edge of the water, careful observation will show deer tracks. The pool is blue because it is fed by a stream carrying limestone, although most of the natural woodland here is that typical of a sandstone base. Besides the moorhens and ducks that inhabit this area the heron may be seen or, if lucky, the dazzling blue flash of a kingfisher. The more elusive birdlife of the woodland include goldcrests, robins, wrens, chaffinches and greenfinches. The typical birdlife would be berry gatherers feeding on holly berries.

The path leaves the pool with its encroaching rhododendrons and passes through ranks of boring conifers, planted when this was a cash crop forest. Little life exists within this part of the wood. The needles take many years to decay in the poor light of the forest floor and they add to the problem of lack of light to prevent anything from growing there. Approaching the end of the walk more signs of human habitation occur. Elder bushes are interspersed with chestnut trees where once a hedge was planted. The walk continues back to the car park.

Link Continue along the Kenmare Road, past another entrance to Muckross House, and look for a road branching left and signposted for Torc Mountain. Follow the road to its end at a car park and leave your vehicle here.

The ecotour concludes with a visit to a viewpoint that provides an opportunity for an overview of the area.

Walk From the car park a path goes up to the peak of Torc Mountain giving excellent views over Killarney and the lakes. The walk covers easy terrain for about 2.5 miles/4 km to the top. Otherwise a quick walk brings you to Torc waterfall, with almost equally pretty views.

Even from the car park the views are very good and give an overview of the geology of the area: the three lakes now standing in what were once the beds of great glaciers and the old red sandstone of the mountains beyond, smoothed and flattened by the ice caps that sat on them. Looking down on the lakes it is possible to make out the boundary between the old red sandstone to the south and west of Muckross Lake, including the area you are standing on, and the limestone belt to the north and east of Muckross Lake, including a part of the Muckross peninsula itself.

During the Carboniferous era there occurred a period of mountain building. The same earth movements which created the Alps also thrust up the surface limestone and the old red sandstone lying underneath. The fold formed on an east-west axis and can be seen in the peninsulas to the south of here — the Beara and the Sheep's Head — and the Dingle peninsula to the north. At the top of the folds, the weathering and the effects of the Ice Age removed all the limestone and other carboniferous material, leaving the sandstone exposed. In the lowland parts, between the mountains, the limestone remained and in the area of Killarney forms an extensive field stretching northwards. Within this field of limestone, metamorphic changes occurred, creating the Killarney marble which was quarried in the past. The copper ore also occurs in the limestone field. The basin of Lough Leane and Muckross Lake are in the limestone area and because of the process of dissolution strangely shaped caves have been formed along the shores of the lakes.

Two thousand years ago the last ice sheets moved in a north-easterly direction across this area. The valleys already made by the earth movements of an earlier period were deepened and smoothed by glaciers. All these glaciers converged on the gap west of Torc mountain. High above the glaciers frost eroded the slopes and carved out horseshoe shaped bowls or corries such as the Devil's Punchbowl on the slopes of Mangerton mountain behind you.

DINGLE PENINSULA
INTRODUCTION

The windmill at Blennerville, Co. Kerry

The Dingle peninsula, with its high central ridges running up to Mount Brandon, the starting point for the first transatlantic crossing ever made, is the most northerly of the series of mountain ranges of Kerry. Its scenery is clearly created by the glaciers of the last Ice Age: rounded, sloping valleys with coombs cut into them filled at their bottom with ice-cut lakes. If people lived here in prehistoric times they have left few remains except for middens dotted about the peninsula, at Inch Strand and at Clogher Head. But the early Christian period is difficult to ignore even from the enclosed confines of a car. No one has ever counted the number of oratories, beehive huts, megalithic tombs, high crosses, cup and circle stones, promontory forts or ogham stones that literally and generously litter the landscape. The work of archaeologists is made more difficult by the fact that up until very recent times ancient beehive huts were still in use and newer ones were being made by farmers as toolsheds and storerooms.

It is believed that tenth-century Norsemen may have had a settlement in the far west of the peninsula, based on the etymological evidence of Smerwick from 'smoer' (butter) and 'vik' (harbour). Blaskets may also be a word of Norse origin. By the thirteenth century the peninsula had attracted the attention of Anglo-Normans and it became part of the territory of the earls of Desmond. In the following century Spanish traders began to settle in Dingle.

There have been various attempts by foreign forces to aid Irish rebellions and the first occurrence was at Smerwick in 1580. Some 600 men, Italians and Spaniards with a few Irish, met a disastrous end at Dún an Óir (Irish for Fort del Oro; the Golden fort) at the hands of Lord Grey who put them all to death. People at nearby Ballyferriter still tell the story of the Dún an Óir massacre, and workmen collecting stones at a nearby beach once refused to go on working when they discovered that this was the famous beach of the heads; where the heads of those massacred, cut off by English troops, washed up on shore and were buried by local people.

This is the least tourist-developed Kerry peninsula and consequently the most rewarding if one takes the time to discover it. There is a real sense here that history, all the way back to the Ice Age, is a living part of the landscape and that if you just look and listen carefully enough all the activities of man and beast that ever took place here would be available to you. Rare plants and rarer birdlife are to be seen and the nearest pollution is hundreds of miles away. In the shops and pubs of the west you will hear Irish spoken and the visitor to Ireland should make the trip if only for that reason.

ESSENTIAL INFORMATION

BANKS

Banking hours around the peninsula are 10 a.m. to 1 p.m. and 2 to 3 p.m. Late opening is usually on Wednesdays till 4 p.m.

Dingle
There are two banks, the *AIB*, telephone 066–51400, and the *Bank of Ireland*, telephone 066–51100, on Main Street opposite one another. The regular banking hours apply.

Tralee

AIB banks are on Castle Street, telephone 066–21045, and Denny Street, telephone 066–22611. The *ACC* bank, telephone 066–23200, is at 3 Denny Street. The *Bank of Ireland* has branches in Denny Street and Lower Castle Street with the same telephone number, 066–21177.

BICYCLE HIRE

Dingle Bike Hire, a few doors down from Supervalu car park
Moriarty's, Main Street, Dingle, telephone 066–51316. Raleigh rent-a-bike scheme.
Tralee Gas and Bicycle Supplies, Strand Street, telephone 066–22108.
E Caball, Ashe Street, Tralee, telephone 066–22231
Lynch's Hostel and Foodstore, Castlegregory.
Connor Pass Hostel, Stradbally.
Vincent O'Gorman, Ballydavid, telephone 066–55162.

BUREAUX DE CHANGE

All the banks have bureaux de change which operate during banking hours.
Dolphin Gift Shop, Strand Street, Dingle.
First Rate, Castle Street, Tralee
Lynch's Hostel, Castlegregory.

CAR HIRE/REPAIRS/24-HOUR PETROL

Hertz Car Hire, Mount Brandon Hotel, Tralee, telephone 066–23635.
O'Donoghue's Garage, Tralee, telephone 066–24993.
Kerry Motor Works, Edward Street, Tralee, telephone 066–21555.
Practical Rental, Duggan's Garage, Ashe Street, Tralee, telephone 066–27527.
Moran's Garage, Dingle, telephone 066–51155.

GARDAÍ (POLICE)

Anascaul: telephone 066–57102.
Ballyferriter: telephone 066–56111.
Castlegregory: telephone 066–39122.
Dingle: at the junction of Bridge Street and the Mall, telephone 066–51222.
Tralee: telephone 066–22022.

LAUNDERETTES

Green Lane Courtyard, Dingle, open Monday, Wednesday, Friday 9 a.m.–5 p.m. Closed for lunch 1–2 p.m.

PHARMACIES

Dingle

J. O'Keeffe, Strand Street, telephone 066–51310.
J. Walsh, Green Street, telephone 066–51365.

Tralee

C.H. Chemists, 31, The Mall, telephone 066–13331.
Kelly's, The Mall, telephone 066–21302.

POST OFFICES

Dingle

Main Street, at junction of Green Street. Open 9 a.m.–5 p.m, lunch 1–2 p.m. Half day Saturday. Telephone 066–51661
There are sub-post offices in the following villages which keep the same hours as Dingle:

Anascaul: telephone 066–57101.
Ballyferriter: telephone 066–56110
Brandon: telephone 066–38126
Castlegregory: telephone 066–39131
Inch: telephone 066–58151
Ventry: telephone 066–59060

Tralee
General Post Office, telephone 066–21013.

TAXIS
Dingle
Flannery, Cooleen, telephone 066–51163, Kathleen Curran, telephone 066–51229.

Tralee
Kingdom Cabs, 48 Boherbee, telephone 066–27828.

TRAVEL AGENTS
Tralee
Courihan's Travel Agency, 32 Castle Street, telephone 066–22833
Kingdom Travel, 14 Lower Castle Street, telephone 066–22588
Slattery's Travel, 1 Russell Street, telephone 066–21722

TOURIST OFFICES
Dingle
The tourist office is in Main Street, telephone 066–51188/51175, open from April to September. Outside these months use the tourist offices in Tralee or Killarney.

Tralee
Ashe Memorial Hall, off Denny Street, telephone 066–21288. Open all year.
Local tourist information is available at the shop in Castlegregory.

FESTIVALS AND SPECIAL EVENTS

Festival of Kerry/Rose of Tralee Held in Tralee at the end of August. The festival focuses on a kind of sanitised beauty contest involving a large number of young women from all over the world who claim Irish descent. Held over several days and widely televised, it is based on the song written by William Mulchineck. The story goes that William, the son of a wealthy family which lived at Clogher House in nearby Ballymullen, fell in love with a servant girl. Denied permission to marry her he wed another, emigrated to the US and pined for his love. Determined to find her again he left his wife and family, returned to Tralee and discovered that she had died of a broken heart. This spurred him to write the song. The Festival started in 1959 as a tourist-promotion venture and is the biggest thing of its kind in the country. Other events, including the Tralee races, also take place in Festival week. As for the Rose of Tralee herself, she is judged mainly on her personality and charm. This is Ireland, so the more obvious physical vulgarities are not emphasised. Tickets for the competition itself can be booked at Hurley's bookshop in Castle Street, telephone 066–21322.

Listowel Races. Four days of hilarity, drinking and gambling. End September.
Dúcas An Daingean. Dingle mid-July cultural festival.
Dingle Races. Usually early August.
Dingle Regatta. August.

WHAT TO SEE

TRALEE

Not the cutest Irish town to visit, Tralee is the county town, partly tuned in to tourism and partly industrialised. The town you see today is largely a nineteenth-century creation, with a classical courthouse and neo-Gothic churches. The Dominican Church of the Holy Cross was designed by Pugin and built by George Ashlin and has some stained glass and five paintings by Michael Healy. Beside it is a priory which contains sculpted stones from the old Dominican Holy Cross abbey. One of the carvings seems to be of a knight or perhaps a gallowglass, a mercenary soldier, while another is of a dragon. The graves of John of Callan and his son lie here as do many of the earls of Desmond. The priory was destroyed by Cromwell's forces in 1652.

Just outside of town on the road to Killarney is Ratass Church, a very early sandstone building. The nave of this building is thought to be part of a seventh- or eighth-century church. The building material is unusual — sandstone — although the major rock type around Tralee is limestone. It still retains some interesting fine details such as the moulding inside the window of the Romanesque east window and the huge stone lintel over the west door. The church was probably burned in the twelfth century — cracks probably caused by fire can be seen in the stonework. Before this the church had been an important ecclesiastical centre, the seat of a bishop, but after the fire it never rcovered its former importance and became just an ordinary parish church.

Tralee still has a rail link with Cork and Dublin which once extended all the way to Castlegregory and Dingle. Ships came into Blennerville bay and up into Tralee by a now disused ship canal, built in 1830. The ships carried coal and timber into Tralee and grain and people out. Many emigrants had their last sight of Irish life in this town.

Further back in history the town was the chief seat of the earls of Desmond, the Munster branch of the great Hiberno-Norman family, the FitzGeralds, who were the supreme rulers of West Munster in the late Middle Ages. Indeed, the word Desmond is itself an anglicised form of the Irish 'Deas Mumhan' meaning West Munster. The last Desmond was captured in 1583 and murdered nearby at Glenageenty and his head taken to London and displayed on London Bridge. This followed a futile rebellion against the ever-encroaching power of the English crown. The estate was given to loyal English men, the Dennys, who took over the castle which stood at what is now the junction of Denny Street and the Mall. In 1691 the castle was held against William of Orange's forces by supporters of the Catholic James II.

Blennerville Windmill and craft centre. Telephone 066-21064. A little west of Tralee, this is the largest working windmill in the British Isles. It was built at the end of the eighteenth century and milled wheat and other grains. After almost a hundred years as a working mill it fell into disuse at the end of the nineteenth century. It has now been restored and is fully functional. Visitors can take home flour milled here. The exhibit also includes an audio visual show explaining the windmill's history and guided tours of the working mill. Also at the mill is a restaurant serving snacks and full meals, a working pottery and craft shop selling Irish crafts as well as an exhibition about the area's role as a major embarkation point for emigrants. As a part of the renovation programme of this area part of the *Tralee–Dingle Narrow-Gauge Railway* was also restored. The line was originally opened as a passenger railway in 1891 and stretched 31 miles to Dingle with a branch line to Castlegregory. It was very slow because of some steep gradients and lasted in all only sixty two years before being closed in 1953. Somehow one of the original engines found its way to the US from where it was brought back and restored to its former glory.

How to get there Take the main road out of Tralee to Dingle and stop when you see the sails. The steam railway connects Tralee with the windmill and reduced rates can be had by buying combined tickets. The windmill is open from 10 a.m till 6 p.m., (later in August), six days a week (seven from March to November). Entrance is £2.50 for adults (£1.50 children) or a family ticket costs £6.50. From Tralee the trains run out of Tralee on the hour from 10 a.m. to 6 p.m. (later in August) and on the half-hour from Blennerville. Train fares are the same as for the windmill. A combined family ticket for both can be bought at the station.

Kerry The Kingdom, Ashe Memorial Hall, Denny Street, Tralee. A good half day out for the children, this consists of an exhibition of the history of Ireland from a Kerry point of view while downstairs is a recreated medieval Tralee including town walls and various scenes of city life. Visitors are transported around in small cars. Open during the summer months from 9.30 a.m. to 6 p.m. Admission is £2.50 (children £1.50).

Lynch Farm, Kilflynn, telephone 066-32100. A real working farm using modern dairying techniques as well as a farm in the old style of Kerry farming with all the variety of animals that farms used to have and a few more thrown in. Rabbits, goats, pigs, hens, sheep, peacocks, ducks and geese, a donkey and a pony. The farm is well organised with a video show about milk production, a guided tour around the modern dairy farm, relics of the past set in a genuine country farmhouse and lots

Geraldine medieval experience in Tralee, Co. Kerry

of walks around the farm lands. Lots of things to occupy children young and old including sheltered play areas for rainy days. There is also a café or picnic tables are laid out if you want to take a picnic. Well worth the investment if you have children who love to bounce about in the hay or pet all manner of creatures. The farm is open from June to August Monday to Friday 11.30 a.m. to 5.30 p.m.

How to get there Take the road to Listowel and after 6 miles/9.6 km take the left turning signposted for Kilflynn. The farm is signposted from there.

Memory Lane Museum, Coom, Cordal, Castleisland, telephone 066-42158. An interesting afternoon's wander around old farm machinery, cars and other antiques. It is open 10 a.m. till 5.30 p.m. Admission £3 adults (children £2)

How to get there From Tralee take the main road to Castleisland and follow the one-way road through Castleisland to the library at the top end of the town. From here it is clearly signposted. It is 15 miles/24 km from Tralee.

DINGLE

Fungie the dolphin Since Fungie the friendly dolphin turned up in Dingle harbour a few years ago an entire industry has developed around him and the efforts of those people who seem to need closer communion with him. At first the chirpy little chap flirted and frolicked with the hundreds of people who each year doggie-paddled in the water hoping for a meaningful relationship. Now he's grown older and less frolicky, perhaps even a little bored by the frogsuited and earnest acolytes.

Dolphins are naturally gregarious creatures living in large communities. Herds of around twenty females of several generations of the same family live together following shoals of fish and hunting them collectively. When a shoal is spotted the dolphins surround it and take turns eating while the others keep the shoal trapped. Female dolphins act as midwives for each other, helping to bring the air-breathing baby mammal to the surface for its first breath of air and protecting both mother and child while they are in this vulnerable state. They look after one another when they are injured and when the herd is threatened by sharks form a circle around the young or even attack the sharks. Dolphins are capable of breaking a shark's back or ramming a hole in its side with their snout.

A male dolphin like Fungie will have lived for the first two years of his life close by his mother suckling from her. After that she would allow him to hunt with the herd. Dolphins spend a lot of time touching each other, especially in courtship. Male dolphins often leave their own herd and go in packs in search of female dolphins whose herds they may then join. So there is something a little odd about this solitary animal, who rarely allows anyone to touch him and seems to have no need of other dolphinkind. But, weather permitting, each day boats go out into the harbour mouth and hang around hoping he will repeat the tricks he used to perform. Fungie is still there but rarely bothers to play any more and there is something faintly ludicrous about the wetsuited visitors waiting for a frolic.

How to get there Boats take visitors out to see Fungie if the weather is calm and charge about £5 per person, and about £6 extra to hire a wetsuit and swim with him. It's just as easy to watch Fungie from the shore. From Dingle take the road to Tralee and turn right down a lane about 0.9 miles/1.5 km from the Shell garage. The turning is easy to miss so look for a set of whitish gateposts beside the lane. Coming from Tralee look for the Ballytaggart hostel on the right hand side and further on a blue sign for Pax House nursing home on the left. About 100 metres further on are the whitish gateposts and the lane going down to the left. At the bottom of the lane is a tiny parking space and if you walk along the sea wall towards the old tower you will come to the mouth of the harbour where people wade out in wetsuits in the hope of an experience. When parking bear in mind that this land is owned by someone who needs access to his fields. Wetsuits can be hired from *Flannery's* (telephone 066-51163), a two-storey house near the pier, or from *Seventh Wave* (telephone 066-51548), just by the bridge on the road out of town going west. This last place has children's wetsuits.

Dingle Heritage Centre, at the junction of Main Street and Green Street. Exhibitions on the flora of the peninsula, the Dingle railway and the history of the town. Link this visit with a trip to the library which has some interesting material on Thomas Ashe, a martyr of the Easter Rising, and Thomas Crean who travelled with Scott on his journey to the Antarctic. Also a good collection of books on topics of local interest, especially the Blasket Islands. The library is open from 10.30 a.m.-5 p.m., Tuesday to Saturday, closed 1.30-2.30 p.m. for lunch. The Heritage Centre is open 1 July-31 August.

A Walk Around Dingle

The Irish form of Dingle is An Daingean, the fortress, which suggests that Dingle was involved in defensive wars from the very earliest times. As a town it evolved after the arrival of the Hiberno-Normans as a fishing and trading port, chiefly with Spain. Many of the buildings in town have signs of Spanish settlers and Spanish blood is said to still be noticeable in the dark hair and eyes of the inhabitants. During the sixteenth century Dingle became involved in the Desmond rebellions against the English crown until in 1585 Elizabeth I was reconciled with the townspeople and gave a grant of £300 to restore the town's walls and gave the town a charter.

Begin at the pier, first constructed in the late eighteenth century. In the late 1980s it was extended and a marina was begun. The developments are largely tourist orientated since the local fishing industry is in decline. Walking back into town towards Green Street there is a series of terraced houses known as the Colony which legend says were built by Protestants during the Famine years for Catholic families that were willing to convert. In Green Street are plaques set above the doors of houses indicating that Spanish families lived there. The Spanish were considered dangerous so their homes lay outside the city walls and the plaques stood as a warning to newcomers.

Also in Green Street is the church, typically neo-Gothic and designed by a student of Pugin, J.J. McCarthy. The stone is local red sandstone. As you go up Green Street the old wall on your left contains part of the original town walls. The house at the top of Green Street stands on the site of a house which once was prepared to offer a home to Marie Antoinette, the doomed Queen of France. James Rice, who owned the house, served in the French army and planned to rescue her from her prison in Paris and bring her here. When she discovered that her children were not to come with her she declined the offer and met her end on the guillotine.

Turn right down Main Street and you will find the Anglican Church on your left. It seems to spend a lot of its time locked up and its tower is no longer with us. It was built in 1804 on the site of a medieval church rebuilt in the fifteenth century by Spaniards who dedicated it to St James. The graveyard has some interesting inscriptions: the tomb slab of the Fitzgeralds dated 1504, the Rice slab dated 1622, and the Mullins slab of 1695. Inside, if you can get in, is a black marble slab dedicated to the Knights of Kerry. The stone font is thought to be medieval.

WEST OF DINGLE
The Blasket Islands
Off the coast near Dunquin. A visit to the biggest island would be a

whole day trip. There are seven islands in the group, the largest being Great Blasket. Great Blasket has some excellent walks and one glorious sheltered beach (see Ecotour). It is about to be taken over by the government by compulsory purchase so within the next few years interpretative centres and who knows what horrors might spring up there but right now it is pristine. People lived on the Blaskets for centuries, most of them knowing little English and rarely visiting the mainland.

The interesting history and lifestyle of the islands' inhabitants have survived through the writings of some of their residents. Visiting scholars encouraged the islanders, who experienced storytelling and poetry as a part of their everyday life, to write their stories and record their memories. These were published and are widely available, not least in all the bookshops in Dingle. The most famous and readable is *Peig* by Peig Sayers while *The Islandman* by Thomas O Crohan and *Twenty Years A-Growing* by Maurice O'Sullivan are also popular.

Earliest records show that a few families lived on Great Blasket around 1700 and were very healthy indeed, only falling sick if they left

The corry at Brandon, Co. Kerry

the island to go to the mainland. There was only ever one village on the island, at the eastern end, closest to the mainland. It was well sheltered, had good natural springs, and was surrounded by the only arable patch of land on the island. Local parish records, begun in 1808, tell of there being 128 people on Great Blasket in 1821; by 1841 there were 153. The islanders suffered fewer losses than the mainland during the Famine. Tradition says that the potato blight never reached the island and that the islanders relied less on potatoes anyway. Fish, shellfish, seaweed, rabbits, seabirds and their eggs supplemented their diet. There was also salvage from three major sea wrecks around their shores during the early 1850s. During the Famine years a school was built by Protestant missionaries and some families became converts but by the end of the crisis in 1851, the school was closed and the families had returned to their own church.

The island is inaccessible by boat except for one small harbour, created out of an offshore rock with a wall built across to the shore. Only one shallow boat can land there at a time even now and this inaccessibility was very useful to the islanders during the times of the land wars. The villagers could see boats approaching the island long before they arrived there and could easily hide livestock and other goods and chattels before the bailiffs could land and take them in lieu of rent. Stories have been told of how the women of the island bombarded the landing bailiffs with rocks from the cliffs above as they tried to get ashore. J.M. Synge, who visited the island in 1904, tells of a story he was told about how some fifty years earlier a bailiff had had a stone tied round his neck and was thrown off the cliffs.

But the Blaskets were never really a viable proposition. They could never support much more than 150 people and this was too small a figure to make schools, shops, pubs, doctors or nurses a possibility on the island. Regular, yet frequently dangerous, trips to the mainland had to be made to sell produce and buy necessities. In the early twentieth century a national school was set up and in the 1930s a post office and telephone were built. Perhaps the fate of the island was sealed by its very proximity to the mainland. If it were further away there might have been more incentive to survive without contact.

There is no graveyard on the Blaskets, except for the burying ground for unbaptised babies and shipwrecked foreigners. After independence the feeling of the islanders seemed to be that they had no future there. Only two couples from the island marrying after 1920 actually settled there. The rest went to the mainland. By 1947 there were only forty seven inhabitants and by 1953 only twenty two. The school was closed in the 1940s and the island's children boarded on the mainland if they wanted an education. The final blow came in 1952 when a young man died because he could not be brought quickly enough to a hospital in bad weather. The four remaining families who were tenants, not land owners, were offered new homes on the mainland overlooking the island. Ironically, on the day they were to be evacuated the sea was so rough that the fishing boat sent to collect them could not land and their belongings and the post office's telephone equipment had to be left behind.

What happens to the islands now is anybody's guess. There are plans to partially restore some of the more historic houses on the island; and regular ferry trips are planned. This may remove much needed income from some local boat owners and concern has been expressed about continued sheep grazing rights on the island. If the island were turned into a nature reserve and building prohibited it might be spared the indignity of tasteless tourist developments. The government is currently issuing compulsory purchase orders on the tenancy rights of the descendants of the islanders.

How to get there At present, boats to Great Blasket leave from Dunquin harbour starting at around 10 a.m. till around 3 p.m. The journey costs about £8 return (telephone 066-56188 for details).

Blasket Island Interpretative Centre

Located at Dunquin, the centre introduces the visitor to the heritage of the Great Blasket Island, with particular reference to the Irish language and the extraordinary body of literature which the island has produced. It has an exhibition, video presentations and a research room, together with car/coach parking, coffee shop and conference facilities. Guided tours are available on request.

Open every day from 10 a.m. to 6 p.m. from Easter to September, admission is £2 adults, £1.50 OAPs, £1 children/students, £5 family, £20 group. A Heritage Card giving unlimited admission to OPW sites for one year may be bought at most interpretative centres for: Adult £10, OAP £7, Child or Student £4.

Brandon Creek

This is the inlet from which legend has it that the first transatlantic crossing was made by St Brendan in the sixth century. Brendan was the son of Finnlug and Cara, descendants of Fergus McRory, the high king of Ireland in the first century. He was born in 484 in supernatural circumstances: on the night of his birth the whole countryside lit up. Similar oddities surrounded his baptism. As was the custom he was fostered out to St Ita at a convent in Co. Limerick. He returned to his family at the age of six and began to study the scriptures. As a young man he travelled all over Ireland visiting other monasteries. He took holy orders back in Kerry in 510, founded a monastery at Ardfert, and built an oratory on Mount Brandon. Many people travelled to the area to pray with him. But the wanderlust remained with him and, being told about a wonderful island far to the west of Ireland, he decided to go in search of it and bring his religion to its inhabitants.

Taking fourteen monks, he set off in a curragh or its like and probably arrived at the Hebrides. His next port of call was an island which turned out to be the back of a whale which must have been fast asleep at the time. Next, they drifted south to Madeira where they waited for the spring. The story tells that it took Brendan seven years in all — with stops at what are probably Greenland, Iceland and Newfoundland — until he finally reached America. He returned safely to Ireland and continued his mission there, dying in 578. With the exception of the whale, the story is not as improbable as it seems. In 1976, Tim Severin and a group of friends built a similar boat and safely reached Newfoundland in it. It took him thirteen months to travel 3,000 miles.

How to get there From Dingle take the road north before the bridge at the west end of town. Brandon Creek is 6 miles/10 km.

Ballyferriter village, Heritage Centre and Dún an Óir promontory fort

This tiny village is interesting for several reasons. It is named after the Ferriter family whose most famous son was Piaras Feiritéir, a poet and military leader who fought in the rebellion of 1641 and held out against Cromwell's forces against all the odds. He was executed in 1653 in Killarney and is thought to be buried in the grounds of Muckross Friary. In the village is another of Ireland's many heritage centres with exhibitions, local history and other points of interest. The church opposite was built in 1855 and is worth a few moments' perusal. It has some pretty stained glass and a well-used atmosphere. The parish of Ballyferriter, which includes the Blaskets, is unusual in that over the past sixty years at least sixty books have been published by its residents. Considering the tiny numbers in the parish that is quite remarkable.

About 3.5 miles/5.5 km away is Dún an Óir promontory fort which has a very bloody history. It was built in 1578 by Piers Rice as a stronghold against the English in the Desmond wars. Promise of help from Spain encouraged the rebels to fortify the stronghold and wait it out inside for help from the sea. It came a year later on 13 September 1580 in the form of 600 mixed Spanish, Italian and Irish with cannons and arms, led by Sebastioano di San Giuseppe of Bologna. The space they perched on was about 350 feet by 100 feet and all those men stayed on in the fort waiting for more reinforcements from the sea. This was a bad move because although the fort was walled it was vulnerable to a seige and had no fresh water or means of escape. On 7 November the English forces arrived at this tiny headland looking for a fight. The force included Lord Grey, the Lord Deputy, Edmund Spenser, the poet who was his secretary, Sir Walter Raleigh, and Edward Denny who was later to be rewarded with confiscated lands at Tralee. Ships came round from Smerwick Harbour and landed big guns here, a trench was dug around the fort, cutting off any hope of escape, and the men inside were besieged. By the next day the defenders' guns had stopped returning fire. Another trench was dug closer to the fort so that the cannons could be pulled up closer. Two days later the besieged defenders surrendered, and it seems that they were given reason to think they would be spared. It was not to be. What followed was the massacre of six hundred men and women who had laid down their arms. Some fifty Irish people, including pregnant women, were hanged and six particularly responsible men had their arms and legs broken in three places before they too were hanged.

The fort earned its name before the massacre when a ship laden with iron pyrites, fool's gold, was driven aground and forced to shed its load. The pyrites lay in the water around the promontory and led to the name Dún an Óir, fort of gold.

How to get there From Dingle go north on the R559 road towards the Gallarus Oratory. At the Y-junction 2.4 miles/4 km from Dingle take the left fork. After 1.8 miles/3 km take a left turn at a T-junction just after an iron bridge. After about 300 metres/yards turn right at a brown sign for the An Óige hostel and the Golf Links Hotel. Ballyferriter is 1 km further on. For Dún an Óir leave Ballyferriter in the opposite direction — going west. After 0.6 miles/1 km turn right at a brown sign to Smerwick Harbour. 0.9 miles/1.5 km further on take the right fork at a Y-junction. After 1.6 miles/2.6 km turn right at a T-junction and after 300 yards/metres the fort is signposted left on a poorly surfaced road.

Reasc Pillar Stones
This site, 1.25 miles/2 km north-east of Ballyferriter, was excavated in the early 1980s and revealed, besides the pillar stone, a whole series of foundations of an early monastic settlement. There are foundations of several beehive huts, a boat-shaped oratory, several incised cross pillars, and a wall separating the consecrated part of the monastery from the rest. The biggest pillar stone is inscribed with a cross and curling patterns typical of La Tène art although it is very late La Tène since this site is early Christian and La Tène decoration is mainly pre-Christian Celtic. The excavations show that the early Christian monastery was built over an earlier site, dating back to A.D. 400. This must have been a very large and significant settlement of monks. Traces of iron slag have been found, suggesting that the monks smelted iron here and some of the foundations suggest quite large buildings, probably thatched.

How to get there Follow the directions to Ballyferriter but just before the iron bridge and T-junction turn left along a little sign-posted lane just before a petrol pump. Almost immediately turn right.

Gallarus Oratory

This beautifully crafted little hut, which has stood intact on this site without the aid of mortar for twelve centuries, is one of the glories of the Dingle Peninsula. Similar in style to the beehive huts but boat shaped, it is a seamless dry stone wall which turns into roof without even noticing it is doing it. The method is called corbelling, with each stone supporting another above it which juts out (or in this case in) beyond the perpendicular of the wall. As each stone also slopes slightly downwards rain is kept out of the building by just running off, as if on a tiled roof. There must have been many other such buildings in ancient times, indeed a couple of fields away there is another but it has collapsed. Monks would have used this little hut for private prayer.

How to get there From Dingle cross the bridge west of town, take a right turning just after Seventh Wave (noticeable because of its dolphin murals), and travel on the amazingly straight road towards Ballyferriter. At the Y-junction approximately 2.5 miles/4 km out of Dingle take the left fork and almost immediately bear right (this is not signposted). Half a mile along that road the car park for the oratory appears on the right.

The beautiful strand at Inch, Co. Kerry

Kilmalkedar Church

This Romanesque church marks the transitional point in architecture between the corbelled stones of the oratory and the development of tiled roofs. It is thought to be twelfth century in origin and stands on a much older site. Part of the roof remains and can be seen to be similar in style to the oratory. It is part of a whole complex of buildings. Close by on the other side of the road is *Brendan's House,* a two-storey medieval building probably once the home of a priest. South of the church is the *Chancellor's House,* once the home of the chancellor of the diocese of Ardfert. Interesting architectural features of the church are the blind arcading in the nave and the design over the doorway of a tympanum with a head on one side and an imaginary animal on the other.

In the church graveyard there is an ogham stone while inside the church itself there is an alphabet stone. The road between the church and St Brendan's house is the beginning of the Pilgrim's Way, the traditional route up to the summit of Mount Brandon.

How to get there From Dingle cross the bridge west of town and turn right just after Seventh Wave. Head north towards Ballyferriter. After 3 miles/4.7 km bear right at the Y-junction. Continue on for 1.4 miles/2.1 km. The church is on the right.

NORTH OF TRALEE
Ardfert Cathedral, churches and priory

This is one of the most important religious sites in Kerry. Bishop Erc, an assistant of St Patrick, established a missionary post here in the mid fifth century. St Brendan was educated here in about A.D. 500 and set up a monastery here. For several centuries Ardfert vied with Ratass as the seat of the bishop of Kerry until in 1660 Ardfert was linked with Limerick. When the Catholic episcopacy was restored in 1720 the bishopric was established first at Dingle and then at Killarney. Three churches stand side by side at Ardfert. The cathedral itself was erected about 1250 in the early English style of the Hiberno-Normans. Later additions in the fifteenth century were the south transept and the north-east chapel. They are in a different style of architecture — the late Irish Gothic. Sixteenth-century additions are a pointed ogee arch in the north-side of the cathedral and the battlements. The cathedral was destroyed in 1640.

In a niche in the north-west corner of the cathedral is an interesting effigy. It is supposedly the figure of fifteenth-century Bishop Stack. But on closer inspection the crozier that the figure holds is turned inwards: this is normally the symbol of an abbot rather than a bishop. This suggests that perhaps the figure is actually St Brendan who was an abbot here in the first century. The carving is thought to be late thirteenth century. The size of the cathedral ruins gives some indication of just how large a congregation this area provided.

The southern transept has been restored by the Office of Public Works and now houses an exhibition and model of the site. Open from June to September 9.30 a.m. to 6.30 p.m. every day, admission is £1.50 adults, £1 OAP, 60p children/students, £4 family. Guided tours are given on request.

North-west of the cathedral is Temple na Hoe or church of the virgin. This represents the next stage of Norman architecture — Romanesque. It has columns on the external corners and carved flowers bordering the south window. North-west again is Temple na Griffin, named mistakenly after two carved wyverns in a window jamb in the north wall. They represent evil devouring itself. The church is fifteenth century.

Across the road in the grounds of Ardfert House are the remains of Ardfert Friary, founded in 1253 for the Franciscans. They were ejected in the sixteenth century and the buildings were used as a barracks but were later taken over by the Church of Ireland bishop who again used the chancel for religious services.

How to get there From Tralee take the road to Ballyheigue which passes through Ardfert.

Banna Strand

A glorious eight-mile stretch of beach where in 1916 Roger Casement landed from a German submarine having organised a shipment of arms for the Easter Rising. Unfortunately a passing farmer spotted something suspicious and alerted the authorities. Casement was arrested; the submarine made a quick getaway; the accompanying arms ship was captured. He was taken to London and tried for treason and executed, but many years later his body was returned to Ireland. There is a memorial to him close by the beach, signposted to the left on the road down to the beach.

CYCLE TOURS

DINGLE TO BALLYFERRITER RETURNING via VENTRY
approximately 18.6 miles/30 km

Head west out of Dingle and take the main R559 road by turning right, signposted, just after crossing Milltown Bridge. After just under 3 miles/5 km bear left at the Y-junction and immediately after take the right fork where the road divides. There is no signpost here.

Pass the lane on the right to Gallarus Oratory after 0.3 miles/ 0.5 km and take the first turning left about 0.4 miles/0.7 km after this. The road is dead straight for 0.6 miles/1 km until a T-junction is reached. Turn right at this junction.

After 1.2 miles/2 km the road bends to the left over a painted green and yellow bridge, with a pub on the left. Just before the pub, on the same side of the road, a lane leads up to the Reasc early Christian site.

At the bridge ignore the smaller road that heads off to the right; it leads to Wine Strand and holiday cottages. Stay on the main road, bearing left, for 0.2 miles/0.3 km and then turn right following the brown sign for the An Óige hostel and the Golf Links Hotel. From the sign it is just over 1 km to the village of Ballyferriter, with shops, a pub and heritage centre.

Continue on the R559 west of the village for about 1 km and turn right at the brown sign that points to Smerwick harbour. After about 0.9 miles/1.5 km a Y-junction is reached and a choice can be made between turning right for a place of historical interest or left for scenic views.

The right turn leads to Dún an Óir, passing huge windbreaker stakes on the right of the road before coming to a T-junction where a right turn leads, after 0.2 miles/0.3 km to a sign on the left for the fort. The road here is poorly surfaced and from the car park go on foot along the footpath to the site of the fort. See page 184 for the bloody and tragic history of this site.

Back at the Y-junction the turning to the left leads to Doon Point, passing the small beach at Ferriter's Cove and holiday homes. The road heads out to Sybil Point, uphill all the way until a signal tower is reached at the end of the path at 206 feet (62 metres) above sea level.

Whichever route is taken, return to the village of Ballyferriter and beyond it to the T-junction where the brown sign to the An Óige hostel and the Golf Links Hotel was encountered earlier. This time turn right at the junction, signposted for Ceann Tra, for the road to Ventry which is about 3 miles/5 km to the south-east.

The first kilometre of the road to Ventry passes a windmill on the left — all the way from Beatrice, Nebraska, USA — and then a ruined church on the right just before the road crosses a stream. The road now climbs gently until Ventry harbour comes into view with the ruins of Rahinnane castle on the right.

Just before Ventry the road meets the main R559 at a T-junction. Turn left for the 3.7 miles/6 km back to Dingle.

NORTH OF DINGLE
Circular Tour. 12.4 miles/20 km round trip
The tour involves many changes of direction and it helps to have the new 1:50,000 Dingle Ordnance Survey map.

The tour begins and ends at Milltown Bridge, just out of town where the two roads heading west meet.

From the bridge take the road east back into town, the one that leads to the hospital and main street, not the road that runs alongside the quayside and harbour. Just before the hospital, 0.4 miles/0.7 km from the bridge, turn left at the white sign that reads Staisiún Doiteain (Fire Station). Go up this road for 0.9 miles/1.5 km where it bends to the left

189

and forms a T-junction with a main road, with a pretty little house directly in front.

Turn right and immediately cross a stone bridge over the Ballyheabought River. The road heads north in a long straight line, with Brandon Peak coming into view after 1.8 miles/3 km — just after passing a small school on the right of the road — tucked behind the hills to the right.

After another 1.1 miles/1.8 km, cross a stone bridge over the Milltown River and pass a turn off for a road on the left. The road ahead begins a gradual ascent for about one mile until it bends to the left and the sea comes into view. It is only just over 3.7 miles/6 km since leaving Dingle Bay to the south and already the Atlantic ocean to the north of the peninsula is visible.

The road now begins its descent, passing Ballinloghig lake on the left. After the lake take the next turning on the left and follow it down until it comes to an end after 0.4 miles/0.8 km. Leave your bike here for a while and head up on foot for a hundred metres between the two homes on the left — an old two-storey house and a modern bungalow — where an early seventh-century site can be appreciated. A stone with a cross is easily found; the stone broke in two and the bottom half was repositioned upside down. Facing the stone to the right is a semicircle of stones and the entrance to a souterrain.

Back on your bike, continue westwards along the unsurfaced road for about 1 mile/1.6 km. Be careful of the potholes and be prepared for some splashing if the ground is wet. Before reaching a surfaced road again a number of farmhouses are passed on both sides of the road.

At the end of the 0.9 miles/1.5 km unsurfaced road a junction is reached with a surfaced road going to the right. Ignore this and continue straight on — also now surfaced — and pass a house with the gable painted green. After about 0.3 miles/0.5 km take the turning on the left (the first one since passing the green gable) and carry along this straight road for 0.7 miles/1.2 km. Turn left at the next junction — there is a church and hostel on the left — and travel south along this main road for about 0.9 miles/1.5 km, passing houses and farms until a signposted junction is reached, with the inviting beach of Murreagh straight in front. Follow the road to the left, signposted in white for Ballyferriter, and ignore the brown sign pointing right to Ballydavid harbour.

After 0.9 miles/1.5 km a road is signposted to the right for Slea Head. Ignore this and travel uphill, passing the Gallarus Oratory sign, until a wide T-junction is reached. Go left here and after a hundred metres the main road is joined. Turn right at the main road.

After a couple of wide turns in the road there is a dead straight run for a few kilometres until another T-junction is reached. A left turn brings one to the stone Milltown Bridge where the tour began.

DAYTIME ACTIVITIES AND SPORTS

BEACH GUIDE

The beaches of the Dingle peninsula are listed here in an arc from Tralee west and then back along the southern coast. Few of them have any facilities or lifeguards and where wheelchair access is noted it is usually a rough bump down a rocky slope.

Derrymore Strand. 9 miles/14 km west of Tralee.

Very large car park, no facilities, difficult wheelchair access. The most pleasant part of the beach is a good walk east of the car park.

How to get there Take the main road west from Tralee to Dingle and after 8 miles/13 km a road is signposted to the right.

Trá Áth Na Chaisle. 11 miles/17 km west of Tralee.

This is a continuation of Derrymore Strand. Car parking but no facilities and difficult access for wheelchairs.

How to get there Follow the instructions for Derrymore Strand. Along the stretch of road from Derrymore to Castlegregory there are many small roads going down to this same stretch of beach. There are no facilities and no lifeguard but local people will assure you that it is safe for swimming.

Castlegregory Beach

No car park, facilities or lifeguard but safe to swim. Wheelchair access. Miles of yellow sand with sand dunes and wildlife reserve behind.

How to get there The beach is just east of Castlegregory and is signposted from the village.

Stradbally Strand. 13 miles/22 km west of Tralee.

This beach is on the other side of the spit of land that stands out into Tralee Bay. No facilities or lifeguard, wheelchair access, nice sandy beach.

How to get there From Tralee follow the coast road to the Connor Pass as far as Stradbally village, about 13 miles/22 km. The beach is signposted from the main road at the village and there are other roads down to the beach further west. All have parking space but no facilities and are safe to swim and provide wheelchair access.

Fermoyle Beach, an extension of Stradbally Strand.

Good parking, no facilities but good access for wheelchairs. Cars can and do go down on to the beach. Excellent sandy beach, safe for swimming.

How to get there At Kilcummin/Hillville take the right fork for Fermoyle (Fhormaoile). The beach is signposted to the right. The road goes down to the beach crossing a three-arched bridge on the way. This and the others mentioned above form one of the longest beaches in Ireland and are rarely crowded.

Cappagh Beach. 11 miles/18 km north east of Dingle.

Huge beach with a river flowing through it. Wheelchair access. Not really a sandcastle beach but it has interesting purple sand. No facilities.

How to get there Coming from the east, continue on the main road towards Cloghane from Fermoyle. Continue through Cloghane village on the road to Brandon. At a crossroads, 1.8 miles/3 km beyond the village, turn right down to the beach. The road is not signposted. From Dingle it is 10.5 miles/17 km to the crossroads, via the Connor Pass, taking a left fork signposted to Clogher after 7 miles/12 km, and a left at a T-junction after another 1.2 miles/2 km, signposted *An Cloghan*.

Brandon Beach. 13 miles/21 km north of Dingle.

An excellent beach for children. Big waves, fine sand. Good for sandcastles, and dunes behind the beach offer shelter for picnics. No facilities but there is a pub behind beach. Wheelchair access difficult.

How to get there From Dingle or Tralee follow directions to Cappagh Beach. At crossroads continue on road to Brandon, taking a left fork just under 1 mile/1.6 km further on. In Brandon village at the post office take a right for the beach. Parking space at the beach is limited but parking is possible up on the road.

Ballydavid Beach. 5 miles/8 km north of Dingle.

Two small sandy beaches in a sheltered bay. No facilities on the beach but there are two pubs and a post office/shop close by. Good fishing from the beach while the children make the sandcastles.

How to get there From the west end of Dingle take the north road before the bridge (not the road to Ballyferriter which is after the bridge). Ballydavid is signposted.

Murreagh Strand. 4 miles/6.5 km north west of Dingle.

The north end of this beach is good clean sand.

How to get there From Dingle take the R559 road to the Gallarus Oratory and Kilmalkedar. At Kilmalkedar keep straight on towards Murreagh village. In the village a side road leads down to the beach.

Wine Strand Beach. 5 miles/8 km west of Dingle.

A very popular beach because of its shelter from the wind and safe swimming. Parking is limited and it gets crowded in high summer. No facilities. Wheelchair access. Back on the road to Ballyferriter is a small pub, Tig Ohric. Look out for the ogham stone in the dunes behind the beach.

How to get there From Dingle take the road towards Bellyferiter (R559). At the Y-junction 2.4 miles/4 km out of Dingle take the turn left for Gallarus and Ballyferiter and keep straight on, ignoring another right-hand turn that appears almost immediately. Likewise, ignore another right-hand turn about 1.5 miles/2.4 km later signposted for Gallarus. At the next T-junction, signposted for the Wine Strand Cottages, turn right and go through the holiday village (Wine Strand Cottages.) The beach is at the end of the lane.

Dún an Óir, on the Dingle peninsula, Co. Kerry

Bal Bán Strand. 5 miles/8 km west of Dingle.

Less sheltered but safe since the water is very shallow. No facilities, access for wheelchairs.

How to get there Follow the same route as for Wine Strand but park alongside the holiday cottages and go off to the left where the road turns into track.

Clogher Strand. 13 miles/20 km west of Dingle.

A wild and dangerous beach, safe enough to sit on but not to swim. Several people have drowned here. Very pretty but windy with fine white sand. In rocks around beach look for fossils. Car park, no facilities.

How to get there Follow the route from Dingle to Ballyferriter. It is the same as that for Wine Strand beach (above) except that you turn left at the T-junction toward Ballyferriter. In the village, carry straight on for about 1.2 miles/2 km to the townland of Clogher. Here there is a 90° left-hand bend in the road, where a stone-built house stands on the opposite corner. Cross the road on the bend and go down the narrow lane to the beach. If you go past Louis Mulcahy's Pottery you have missed your turning.

Coumeenoole Strand. 11 miles/18 km west of Dingle.

Another tiny beach but with fine white sand. Parking space and wheelchair access but no facilities. Famous for the fact that Robert Mitchum almost drowned there while filming *Ryan's Daughter*.

How to get there Follow the R559 west (not north) out of Dingle. The beach is signposted at Coumeenole, just past Slea Head.

An Trág Bhán. Great Blasket Island.

The best and least accessible beach on the Dingle peninsula. Clean, sheltered, safe for swimming. Needless to say no facilities and only for the very adventurous wheelchair user.

How to get there Boats go to the Blaskets at the moment from Dunquin harbour on the hour from 11 a.m. to 5 p.m. from May to September.

Inch Strand. 10 miles/16 km east of Dingle.

Vast stretches of smooth yellow sand with interesting sheltering sand dunes behind. Cars are allowed on the beach but be careful as vehicles regularly get stuck in wet sand. Shop, toilets, wheelchair access. If you are prepared to walk far enough along the strand you can be quite alone even in the peak season.

How to get there From Dingle take the main Tralee road, take the right fork just before Anascaul, signposted to Castlemaine. About 4 miles/6 km further on you arrive at the car park for Inch Strand. From Tralee take the main road to Dingle till the junction just beyond Anascaul and then turn sharp left for Castlemaine. Follow the instructions above from there.

FISHING

Most fishing on the Dingle peninsula revolves around shore or deep sea fishing but there are places where game fishing is possible. *The Owenascaul River* flowing through Anascaul and the lough itself are good for grilse and sea trout from June onwards. No licence is necessary. *Lough Gill* at Castlegregory has brown trout. Fishing is from a boat which can be hired from Mrs Kelleher, the Guesthouse, Loubeg, Castlegregory. *Lough Eagle* is also said to be excellent for brown trout. There is no coarse fishing on the peninsula.

Shore Fishing

Fishing from the shore is the most common means of angling on the Dingle peninsula and along the 62 miles/100 km of shoreline there are many places where this is possible. Starting from the north-east near Tralee and working westwards along the north shore and then back eastwards along the south shore, there are twenty or so good spots.

The first of the many spots is around *Blennerville*, good for bass and flatfish. Along

Tralee Bay, where streams empty on to the shore, there are good spots at *Derrymore, Camp* and *Aughacasla*. Lugworm is the preferred bait here. Surf fishing here will provide bass and flatfish. At the mouth of *Lough Gill* bass and flatfish can be got by spinning and bottom fishing, especially at high tide. On the end of that spit of land, the *Magharees* are good places again for bottom fishing and spinning. Along the western shore of the Magharees there is good fishing all along the beach especially at *Fermoyle, Kilcummin* and *Stradbally*. Surf fishing will provide bass, flatfish and the occasional tope. At *Blackrock,* conditions are good for spinning for bass, and surf fishing on the beach.

Further west at *Cloghane estuary* there are bass in the river channel as the tide turns to early flood and from *Lady's Island* into the channel, spinning for bass and sea trout is possible. At the beach in front of the parking lot at Lady's Island at high water there are bass and flatfish (bottom fishing). At *Brandon* bass and flatfish can be caught on the north-facing beach. Travelling west *Smerwick* harbour has three beaches where bass and flatfish can be got by surf fishing while from the rocks at the centre of the bay spinning for bass is possible. *Ferriter's Cove* offers possibilities for surf fishing as does *Ventry* harbour. From *Dingle* pier, mullet and flounders, can be got; arrangements can be made for deep sea and inshore fishing. Along the south shore, *Benbane* and *Reenbeg* in the mouth of the harbour are good spots for spinning for bass while further east *Trabeg, Anascaul* and *Inch* can provide spinning for bass and flounders and surf fishing for flatfish and occasional tope.

Deep-Sea Fishing

For deep sea fishing, including tuna and shark, contact *Sea Ventures* in Milltown outside Dingle, telephone 066–51552. Alternatively at *Dingle Bay Angling Centre* is George Burgum, telephone 066–51337. His boat is Tourist Board approved, has lots of safety gadgets and can take 8 to 10 passangers depending on what you want to catch. At *Angler's Rest Angling Centre,* Dingle, telephone 066–59947, is Nicholas O'Connor. Similar boat, rates and equipment. At *Brandon Pier* is John Young, The Curlews, Lower Tier, telephone 066–38246. Slightly cheaper with slightly larger boat. All have equipment for hire and will offer a weekly or individual rate. Deep sea fishing is usually available between April and October.

AQUA SPORTS

Wine Strand Cottages, Ballyferriter, telephone 061–53582, fax 061–326450. Holiday cottages that cater to diving parties. Compressor, tank trough, drying room, showers, changing room. Experienced divers only.

SURFING

Good beaches to surf are Inch, Slea Head, Brandon Bay. Good all year round condition, waves average 1–3 metres. Bring your own equipment.

TEN-PIN BOWLING

Superbowl, Godfrey Place, Tralee, telephone 066–22311, fax 066–22120. Open from 10a.m., 7 days. Prices include shoe hire.

GOLF

Golf Driving Range, Tralee Rugby Football Ground, Ballyard, telephone 066–21984. Open 11 a.m.–9.30 p.m.
Castlegregory Golf Course, telephone 066–39444. Eighteen holes on sand dunes at Castlegregory. Green fee £10.
Cean Sibeal, Ballyferriter, telephone 066–56133. Eighteen-hole course on dunes.
Tralee Golf Club, West Barrow, Ardfert, Tralee, telephone 066–36379.

GUIDED WALKS AND CLIMBS

Horgern Bergwandern Walking and Climbing Holidays, 2 Ballymullen, Tralee, telephone 066–23174. Contact Michael Horgern.

Walking the Best of Kerry, Curragraigue, Blennerville, telephone 066–24467. Contact Margaret Ryle.

GREYHOUND RACING

Greyhound Stadium, Brewery Road, Tralee.

HORSE RIDING

El Rancho Riding School, Tralee, telephone 066–21840. The school also organises trail riding.
Eagle Lodge Equestrian Centre, Gortatlea, Tralee, telephone 066–37266.
Thompson's, Carhoo, Dunquin, telephone 066–56144.

HORSE RACING

Ballybeggan Racecourse, Tralee.

SNOOKER

Superbowl, Godfrey Place, Tralee, telephone 066–22311. Snooker and American pool tables.

SWIMMING

Indoor pools at *Dingle Skellig Hotel*, telephone 066–51144; *Brandon Hotel*, Tralee, telephone 066–23333.

BOAT RIDES

Trips to see the Dingle dolphin can be arranged with any of the boatmen at Dingle pier. To the Blasket Islands boats leave Dunquin pier from 11 a.m. to 5 p.m. May to September.

TRAIN RIDES

Tralee and Dingle Light Railway, Ballyard, telephone 066–28888. Departures on the hour from Tralee, April–Sept. Last train departs 6 p.m. During winter season telephone for timetable. Ride goes to Blennerville and recreates a tiny part of the old Tralee–Dingle narrow-gauge railway. Passengers enjoy reductions on price of entry to Blennerville Windmill Visitors Centre.

EVENING ACTIVITIES

Tralee
Watch *Siamsa Tíre*, the National Folk Theatre of Ireland, telephone 066–23055. Purpose-built theatre next door to the tourist office. Superb song, dance and mime show recreating aspects of Gaelic culture. Every evening in the summer 8.30 p.m. Not to be missed.

There are several good pubs in Tralee where a good evening's entertainment can be had. All have music regularly. *Paddy Mac's*, *Bailey's Corner*, *The Abbey Inn*, *Val O'Shea* and the *Brogue Inn* all have music regularly, not necessarily aimed at tourists so it can be quite interesting.
Keane's Bar, Curraheen, Tralee. Four miles out of Tralee on road to Dingle. Bar food all day, restaurant, music — check locally for dates.

Dingle
The main evening activity on the Dingle peninsula is, of course, visiting pubs. Many of them have regular traditional music or ballad sessions. Look locally for details of what

In Dingle, Co. Kerry

is on. They often serve coffee and some do bar food. Many are also prepared to allow children in if they are fairly restrained. The following are pubs which regularly have music.

Máire de Barra, Strand Street. Opposite the new pier. Evening meals, cocktails. Traditional music every weekend and nightly from June to September.
Star Bar, Strand Street, Dingle. Open fire, bar food all day, ballads from June to mid-September nightly, 9–11.30 p.m.
Murphy's Pub, Strand Street. Open fire, bar food all day, music of some kind nightly from April to October, 9.30–11.30 p.m.

West of Dingle
Tigh T P, Ballydavid. Overlooks the pier beach and harbour, bar food, music.
Kruger's at Dunquin is as close as you can be to the Blasket Islands and still have a drink. The story of one particular member of the Kruger family is told on one of the pub's walls, alongside photographs from the making of two films in the area: *Ryan's Daughter* and *Far and Away*.
An Bother is a friendly pub, perfectly located for anyone who has just descended Mount Brandon. To get there, go past the Tigh an Phoist Hostel at Bothar Bui village and turn right at the next junction (left goes to Brandon Creek). The pub is half a kilometre along the road to Dingle. From Dingle head out of town but turn right or carry on straight (depending on which road out of Dingle was taken) before crossing the bridge over the river.
Tigh Pheig is the main pub in the village of Ballyferriter.
In Anascaul, there are two pubs of note. *Dan Foley's* has one of the more colourful proprietors one is likely to meet, while the *South Pole Inn* at the end of the village was originally the property of Tom Crean, a local man who was a member of Scott's ill-fated Antarctic expedition of 1912. He survived and later accompanied Sir Ernest Shackleton on a similar expedition. He bought the pub when he finally came home and gave it the name it still bears.
In general, there are excellent pubs dotted all over the peninsula. The best advice is to follow your instincts! You won't go far wrong.

WHERE TO STAY

HOTELS

Dingle and the West
The Dingle peninsula's supply of places to stay is fairly limited. Some hotels close for the winter and all of them will negotiate terms if the season is a bad one.

Dingle Skellig Hotel. Telephone 066–51144, fax 066–51501. Satellite TV, indoor pool, sauna, sunbeds, children's play areas, snooker, tennis. Closed January to March. Three Star. Rating: moderate-high. AM, AE, DE, VM.
Dún an Óir Golf Hotel, Ballyferriter, telephone 066–56133, fax 066–56153. TV, outdoor heated pool, sunbeds, tennis, safe beach for swimming. Two Star. Rating: budget. AM, AE, DE, VM.
Benner's Hotel, Main Street, Dingle, telephone 066–51638. TV, gardens, tennis. An old hotel with a long history. Three Star. Rating: moderate. AM, AE, DE, VM.
Doyle's Seafood Bar and Townhouse, John Street, Dingle, telephone 066–51174, fax 066–51816. More a guest house than a hotel. TV, cosy atmosphere. Four Star guest house. Rating: budget. AM, DE, VM.
Crutch's Country House Hotel, Fermoyle Beach, Castlegregory, telephone 066–38118, fax 066–38159. Small converted hunting lodge, open fires, home cooking, baby-sitting, gardens, children's meals. Closed January and February. Nearby — golf, horse riding. Two Star. Rating: budget. AM, AE, DE, VM.
Alpine House, Mail Road, Dingle, telephone 066–51250. TV lounge, gardens. Closed Dec–Feb. Three Star guest house. Rating: economy. AM, VB.
Hillgrove Hotel, Spa Road, Dingle, telephone 066–51131. TV, gardens, baby-sitting service. One Star. Rating: economy. AM, AE, DE, VM.

Tralee
Brandon Hotel, Prince's Street, telephone 066–23333, fax 066–25019. TV, indoor pool, sauna, gym. Baby-sitting, children's menu. Open all year. AM, AE, DE, VB. Three Star. Rating: moderate.
Ballyseede Castle Hotel, Telephone 066–25799, fax 066–25287. Fifteenth-century castle. TV, children's menu, baby-sitting, facilities for pets. Extensive grounds. Open all year. AM, VB. Three Star. Rating: moderate.
Earl of Desmond Hotel, Killarney Road, telephone 066–21299, fax 066–21976. TV, tennis, large grounds, children's play area, baby-sitting, facilities for pets, wheelchair friendly. Closed Dec–Feb. AM, AE, DE, VB. Three Star. Rating: budget to moderate.
Imperial Hotel, 27 Denny Street, telephone 066–24242, fax 066–27800. TV. Open all year. Friendly and comfortable. AM, AE, DE, VB. Two Star. Rating: budget.
Ballyroe Hotel, Ballyroe, telephone 066–26796, fax 066–25066. 1.2 miles/2 km out of Tralee on the Ardfert Road. TV, tea maker, family rooms, baby-sitting service, pet friendly, children's meals, wheelchair friendly, gardens. Closed Nov–March. AM, AE VB. One Star. Rating: economy.
Ballygarry House Hotel, Leebrook, telephone 066–21233, fax 066–27630. TV, tea maker, playground, children's meals, pet friendly, gardens. Open all year. AM, AE,VB. Rating: Budget.
Grand Hotel, Denny Street, telephone 066–21499, fax 066–22877. TV, baby-sitting, children's meals. Open all year, AM, AE, VB. Three Star. Rating: economy–budget.

BED AND BREAKFAST

Dotted around everywhere on the peninsula. Tralee has a fair number and there are many strung along the main road heading west to Dingle. In Dingle itself they are not difficult to find and again they are dotted along the road heading out to Ventry. Consult the tourist office in Dingle or Tralee if necessary.

SELF-CATERING

Self-catering holidays are probably the best value of the various types of holiday available in Ireland if you are going in a large party, or as a family, and intend to keep one area as a base. The tourist information service has a reservations scheme in Cork city, telephone 021–273251, fax 021–273504. Many places fill up very early in the year so if you intend to stay in self-catering accommodation book as early as possible. Bord Failte publishes a complete list of self-catering accommodation in the south-west. Rates rocket skywards in July and August and are more reasonable in spring. Listed here are the holiday villages.

Dingle Wine Strand Cottages. Mr B. Houlihan, Geraldville, North Circular Road, Limerick, telephone 061–53582, fax 061–326450. Reasonably priced accommodation compared to some of the competition. The houses sleep eight and have been comprehensively equipped with lots of amenities, including washing machine and satellite TV. There is a children's playground and tennis facilities. The houses are close to a sheltered sandy beach and interesting antiquities. Golf course close by.
Ventry Holiday Cottages. Mr J. Moore, Green Street, Dingle, telephone 066–51588, fax 066–51591. Three-bedroomed cottages, sleeps six, overlooking Ventry Harbour.
Dun an Oir Cottages, telephone 066–56133, fax 066–56153. Attached to Dun An Oir Hotel, near Ballyferriter. Use of hotel facilities.
Kerry Cottages, Castlegregory. R. Marshall, 37 Dalkey Park, Dalkey, Co. Dublin, telephone 01–2853851, fax 01–2854354. All mod cons, children's play area, close to Tralee and sandy beach.
Mountain Lodge Cottages, Dingle Road, Annagh, near Tralee, telephone 066–22461, fax 066–27150. Three bedrooms, sleeps six, reasonable rates, TV, washing machine.

HOSTELS

Hostels offer super budget but very basic accommodation — usually a bed in a dormitory. Their advantage, besides being cheap, is that they all have kitchens and many have common rooms where most hostel travellers do most of their socialising. Beds are usually around £6 a night but some hostels have single or double rooms which will cost more.

Lisnagree Hostel. Ballinorig Road, Tralee, telephone 066–27133. Private rooms, en suite rooms, open all year. Meals are available and there are laundry facilities and bikes for hire.
Finnegan's Holiday Hostel, 17 Denny Street, Tralee, telephone 066–27610. Open all year with dormitory accommodation and private rooms. Meals are available, there are laundry facilities and bikes can be hired.
Bog View Hostel, Luachair, Inch, telephone 066–58125, fax 066–23870. Open from March to 5 January. Meals are available, including vegetarian. Laundry facilities, bike hire, wheelchair friendly. Shiatsu massage also available.
Fuchsia Lodge Hostel, telephone 066–57150. Between Inch and Lispole, well signposted.
Seacrest Hostel, Kinard West, Lispole, telephone/fax 066–51390. Showers are 50p extra. Camping is available with use of hostel facilities. Meals available, including vegetarian, and there's a laundry.
Tigh a Phóist. Next to Carrigh church, Ballydavid, Dingle, telephone 066–55109. 7 miles/10 km west of Dingle. Open from March to November. Laundry facilities and shop.
Connor Pass Hostel, Stradbally, Castlegregory, telephone 066–39179. Wheelchair friendly, sitting room.
Ballintaggart Hostel, telephone 066–51454. A few miles outside Tralee on the road to Dingle, free bus service, bike hire, bureau de change, pony trekking, resident ghost. Camping.

CAMPING AND CARAVAN SITES

Pricewise there seems to be little difference between the various sites so choice might be better made on how big the site is, whether there is loud music near at hand, the facilities for children and the location. A big site might be nice for children to find friends but bad if you like to go to bed early. A TV room/recreation area is well worth it in wet weather.

Tralee

Bayview Caravan and Camping Park, telephone 066–26140, fax 066–27468. 1 mile/1.6 km from town on Tralee/Ballybunion road. TV room, playground, 38 pitches. Open 31 March–31 October. Dogs allowed.

Fuschia Lodge Hostel and *Ballintaggart Hostel* both have camping space with use of hostel facilities.

Dingle

Campaill Theach an Aragail (Oratory House Camp), telephone 066–55143. 5 miles/8 km west of Dingle town (follow signs for Gallarus Oratory). Campsite is signposted. Playground, washing machines, campers' kitchen, sitting/dining area, dryer, Irish spoken. No dogs. 36 pitches. Open 1 May–15 September.

Reasc, an early Christian site, on the Dingle Peninsula

Anchor Caravan & Camping Park, Aughacasla, Castlegregory, telephone 066–39157. Site 100 metres from beach at Aughacasla, 12 miles/ 9 km from Tralee. TV room, washing machines, playroom, playground, large site, 30 pitches. Open Easter Thursday to 30 September.

WHERE TO EAT

Dingle

In Dingle many of the restaurants close during the winter months, usually from late October/early November to Easter. One or two different establishments stay open each year on a rota system. Ratings are as previous sections and are based on dinner prices and most menus allow for more expensive choices; so regard these ratings as a guide only to minimum prices. Most places do inexpensive lunches.

Armada Restaurant, Strand Street, telephone 066–51505. Open for lunch and dinner, seafood a speciality, vegetarian and gluten free meals, closes 9.30 p.m. Does tourist meals. Nice atmosphere if you don't mind coach parties. AM, AE, DE, VB. Rating: moderate.
The Beginish Restaurant, Green Street, telephone 066–51588. Mostly seafood, some meat dishes, vegetarian choices if you phone in advance. One of the top restaurants in the town. A good wine list. AM, AE, DE, VB. Rating: high.
Lord Baker's Restaurant, Main Street, telephone 066–51277. Two seafood menus.

Good lunches. AM, AE, DE, VB. Rating: moderate to high.
Fenton's, Green Street, telephone 066–51209. Local seafood, Vegetarian and gluten free available. AM, AE, DE, VB. Rating: moderate to high.
Doyle's Seafood Restaurant, John Street, telephone 066–51174. Ranks with the Beginish as one of the best in town. Non-seafood choices. Closes 9 p.m. AM, DE, VB. Rating: high.
Half Door, John Street, next door to Doyle's. Another fine retaurant with a well balanced menu. AM, AE, DE, VB. Rating: high.
Cosan Rua, Benner's Hotel, Main Street, 066–51638. Varied menu, one vegetarian choice. AM, AE, DE, VB. Rating: high.
Dingle Bay Restaurant, Dykegate Street, telephone 066–51598, has a seafood emphasis to its menu. AM, AE, DE, VB. Rating: budget
The Islandman, Main Street, telephone 066–51803. A bookshop and restaurant combined. Range of dishes including vegetarian and gluten free. Good value tourist menu. AM, AE, DE, VB. Rating: moderate.
Smeara Dubha, Next to Westlodge Hostel, vegetarian. Rating: budget.
Greaney's Restaurant, Holy Ground, telephone 066–51694. Inexpensive restaurant serving café type food as well as good seafood main courses. Children's menu. Open till 11 p.m. AM, VB. Rating: budget.
The Forge, Holy Ground, telephone 066–51209. Steaks and seafood, tour group oriented, open till 11.30 p.m. AM, AE, DE, VB. Rating: budget.
Dingle Skellig Hotel, telephone 066–51144. Seafood. Vegetarian & gluten free dishes. AM, AE, DE, VB. Rating: high.
An Café Liteartha, Dykegate Street, bookshop/café, drinks and sandwiches. Rating: economy.
Weaver's Café. Craft village, lunch type meals. Rating: moderate.
Café Ceol/Culan Tí, Green Lane Courtyard. Upstairs is dinner, downstairs does lunches and snacks. Good vegetarian choices. Rating: moderate.
The Old Smokehouse, The Mall. Pizza, lasagne etc. Rating: economy.
The Shamrock, The Mall. Family type restaurant. Rating: economy.
The Singing Salmon. Opposite the pier, pizzas, steaks and seafood. Rating: moderate.
Tig an Portain, at the Tralee end of the town, is a café-style establishment. Mainly fish dishes, also does good sandwiches etc. Wine licence. Rating: budget.
Whelan's Restaurant, Main Street. Varied menu with emphasis on fish. AM, VB. Rating: moderate.
El Toro, Green Street, concentrates on seafood and pasta. AM, VB. Rating: moderate.
The Oven Door, Holy Ground, does good pizzas. Rating: economy.
Dingle Pub & Restaurant, Main Street, has a varied menu, competitively priced. Rating: budget.
Long's Restaurant, opposite the pier, has a solid, varied menu. Rating: economy.
The Waterside is a café, situated opposite the pier in a distinctive, conservatory-style premises. Closes 8 p.m.

Several pubs do good value lunches. *Máire de Barra* has a good menu including children's meals. The *Star Bar* does snacks and meals. *Benner's Hotel* bar is comfortable and has good snacks all day. *Murphy's Bar* also does food all day and *An Droichead Beag* in Lower Main Street does soup and sandwiches at lunchtime.

Around Dingle
Sheehy's Café and Pottery Shop, at Ventry does light meals and snacks.
Dun Chaoin pottery shop and cafe just before Clogher on the Slea Head road is similar.
An Bracan Feasa is a self-service restaurant 8 miles/13 km east of Dunquin on the Slea head coast road.
O'Shea's Bar at Brandon does pub food as does *An Bother* pub.
Gallery Restaurant at Ballyferriter does a three-course meal at all times. Rating: economy
Tig Ohric at Wine Strand beach does sandwiches.

Tralee

The Heritage, Imperial Hotel, Denny Street, solid dinner menu, good starters. AM, AE, DE, VB. Rating: moderate to high.

The Skillet, Barrack Lane, telephone 066–24561. Extensive interesting menu including several vegetarian choices. Olde worlde, nice photos of the owner's mountaineering trips. Don't even think about it if you're in a wheelchair. AM, AE, DE, VB. Rating: moderate.

The Grand Hotel, Denny Street, telephone 066–21499. Traditional food cooked and presented in comfortable surroundings. AM, AE, VB. Rating: high.

Benner's Hotel, Castle Street, telephone 066–21422. All faded charm and Irish cooking. Popular with locals for Sunday lunches. Rating: moderate.

Maura's Restaurant. Unpretentious, good value. Rating: moderate.

Allegro. Corner of Denny Street and the Mall. Not easily missed, large, very public, very busy at lunch time but not exactly *grand chic*. Wine list. Rating: moderate.

Brogue's Kirby Inn. Spacious, olde worlde pub with stone floor. Music every night with restaurant upstairs. Make a night of it. Rating: moderate.

Paddy Mac's. Pub lunches, sawdust on floor, music nightly. Rating: economy.

Fred's, Castle Street. Open till 8 p.m., budget evening meals, children's portions. Better for lunches. Rating: budget.

Majella's Restaurant. Good inexpensive lunches. Rating: budget.

Ho Kee. Chinese takeaway and eat in. Set dinners. Rating: moderate. Deliveries 066–26685. Open evenings from around 5p.m–early hours.

Kelleli's Kebabs, Castle Street, burgers etc. To eat in. Rating: budget.

Frank's Takeaway, Castle Street. Room to eat inside. Curry and chips. Rating: budget.

Charlie Nelligan's, The Mall. Lunches, cakes, hot bread shop. Self-service, small and crowded at lunch time. Rating: economy.

The Flower Pot Café, The Square. Small, basic but quiet and roomy. Chips with everything. Rating: budget.

Pizza Time. Predictable pizzas, lasagne, soup. Cramped. Rating: budget — just!

Hobnobs Café, 4 The Square, Nothing over £4. Cluttered. Chips++. Rating: economy.

Sizzles, The Square, burger joint, lots of yellow plastic. Take sunglasses. Rating: economy.

The Kingdom, High Street. Mostly lunches, chips with everything. Rating: budget.

Town and Country, The Mall. Pub lunches. Smoky, lots of meat dishes. Rating: economy.

The Mall Tavern, the Mall. Next door to Town and Country but much larger. The no smoking area is actually separate so the term does have some meaning here. Similar prices to the Town and Country. Rating: economy.

Brats. Vegetarian restaurant, upstairs in the mostly empty Mall. Open from 12.30, Monday to Saturday. Rating: economy.

The Snackery. Ten ways to serve burgers and lasagne. Takeaway or eat in on bar stools. Rating: budget.

Smythies. On the ground floor of the tiny Tralee Shopping Centre. Large menu of junk food, the compulsory listening to radios from nearby shops, but decent coffee. Open Monday to Saturday 9.30 a.m. to 6 p.m. Rating: economy.

Bilko, Tralee Shopping Centre, burgers. Rating: economy.

Eats, Ashe Street, superior takeout — no burgers, no chips. Fish and sandwiches. Rating: economy.

Castlegregory

Fermoyle Restaurant, Crutch's Country House Hotel, telephone 066–38118, at junction of main Tralee-Dingle road and turn-off to Fermoyle. The hotel also does bar food. AM, AE, DE, VB. Rating: high.

Lobster Pot Restaurant, Tralee Bay Hotel, Tullaree, telephone 066–39138, unmissable on Tralee to Dingle road. Snacks all day. Rating: moderate.

Barry's. Pizzas and burgers. Eat in or take out. Rating: budget.

Spillane's Bar, Fahamore, at the end of the Castlegregory peninsula. Food served all day, charcoal grilled fish and steaks after 6 p.m.

SHOPPING

Dingle

Ceardlann na Coille, Craft village, The Wood. Beyond the marina on the road west of town. Six workshops making and selling their own crafts — leatherwork, knitwear, felt items, handweaving, cabinet making, woodturning.

Brian De Staic, The Wood. Opposite the craft village. There is a workshop here where you can watch traditional Celtic-designed artifacts being made and have your name carved in ogham script on a pendant. Outlet also in Green Street. Open 9 a.m.–6 p.m., six days (seven days June–August).

Lisbeth Mulcahy. Weaver's shop, Green Street. Sells hand-woven blankets, shawls, rugs and pottery by Louis Mulcahy.

Louis Mulcahy, Clogher. Beautiful huge pots, plates and other really useable items. Highly recommended. Watch the pots being made.

Commodum, Main Street. Nice collection of craft items, especially pretty Celtic design jewellery.

Simple Pleasures. Craft shop, The Mall. Craft shop and stripped pine gallery with some pretty pieces. Open afternoons only.

The cross at Kilmalkedar Church, on the Dingle Peninsula

Holden Leathergoods, Main Street. Leather goods, belts and bags. There is also a workshop in an old school house four miles from Dingle off the Dingle-Ventry road.

Brandon

Brandon Arts Gallery and Studio. Oil paintings, watercolours, pencil drawings by Michael Flaherty.

Tralee

Blennerville Art Gallery and Studio. By the windmill at Blennerville. Pottery and Crafts.

Tralee Gift Shop. Next to Slattery's Travel in Russell Street. Souvenir items like plates and handkerchiefs with shamrock designs.

Fielding's Court Antiques, The Mall.

The Well Spring, Denny Street, arts and crafts.

Antiques and Interiors, Princess Street.

CHILDREN'S ACTIVITIES

- *Tralee Snooker Club.* Arcade games and snooker tables for children; in fact no adults use this place.
- Swimming in the *Brandon Hotel* or *Dingle Skellig Hotel*
- *Blennerville Windmill* and train ride.
- Go looking for fossils around the rocks between Dunquin harbour and Clogher head. Bear in mind that the beach at Clogher Head is very unsafe for swimming.
- Build sandcastles. Dig tunnels in the sand and wait for the sea to flood them.

- Visit *Crag Cave* (see Killarney section)
- Visit Memory Lane Museum to look at the cars.
- Visit *Lynch's Farm* (see page 177)
- Make friends with Fungie the Dolphin.
- Go looking for interesting shells along the beaches in Brandon Bay.
- Hire bikes and helmets and go for a cycle. The dunes around Winestrand beach make a good BMX circuit.

RAINY DAY ACTIVITIES

- Visit *Memory Lane Museum,* Castleisland. See page 178
- Visit *Kerry the Kingdom* museum in Tralee. See page 177
- Drive around the Slea Head peninsula, taking in the *Dingle Heritage Centre, Dingle Library, Louis Mulcahy's pottery shop* at Clogher and the *Heritage Centre* at Ballyferriter.
- Go to the *Cinedrome* cinema in Upper Castle Street Tralee, telephone 066–21055 or the *Phoenix Cinema*, Dykegate Lane, Dingle, telephone 066–51222.
- Go swimming at the *Dingle Skellig Hotel*, telephone 066–51144 or the *Brandon Hotel,* Tralee, telephone 066–23333.
- Take a train ride and see the Blennerville windmill.
- Go to an afternoon performance of *Siamsa Tire* in Tralee. See page 195
- Visit the Blasket Islands Interpretive Centre at Dunquin. See page 183

ECOTOUR

CASTLEMAINE–TRALEE VIA INCH, ANASCAUL, DINGLE, SLEA HEAD, GREAT BLASKET, CONNOR PASS, CASTLEISLAND AND TRALEE BAY

The Dingle peninsula, like its southern sisters, had its basic building blocks — old red sandstone and its variations — built about 420 million years ago when the first true jawed fish were nosing their way around the shallow seas that then made up this area. Over a period of some 30 million years sand and grit settled in these seas, sometimes burying the remains of the first fish or the huge fern-like leaves that were washed down into the seas by the rivers carrying debris from the north. The Dingle peninsula, being perhaps a little closer to the source of the rivers, has a more complex geology than the other peninsulas; having large areas of conglomerate rocks, bearing large boulders of earlier material rather than the smooth evenly-grained material of the mountains around Killarney. At its southern tip it also has volcanic material and some beautiful fossils can be seen in the much younger limestone rock around Clogher Head.

Occasionally lush and verdant — and more often bare and almost unearthly in its appearance — this peninsula seems to hold its flora and fauna reluctantly in tiny niches of survival. This tour begins at the south-eastern end of the peninsula, travels west and returns by way of the magnificent Connor Pass and the northern beaches.

Link Castlemaine to Inch Strand. 11.5 miles/19 km.

The southern coast road from Castlemaine to Inch Strand is littered with houses in a thin band. Behind them the deep red of the bare mountain looms and the land around them forms a fertile strip between the mountains and the sea. The houses are quite old and traditional in design, not modern holiday homes, indicating that this area was able to support quite a dense population. Over the centuries the soil was created by the people who lived here, carrying sand and seaweed up from the beach to create a living humus on the dead podsoil and scree of the mountainsides.

Stop Inch Strand, in the car park below the old Strand Hotel.

Walk down on to the beach and back into the sand dunes above. Inch sits on an exposed section of relatively young rock, carboniferous limestone. This type of rock covers the whole of Castlemaine Bay, a drowned valley. The strand and the two opposite on the Iveragh Peninsula — Rossbeigh and Cromane — are gradually building up until eventually Castlemaine Bay will be enclosed.

You see before you a vast area of apparently empty sand, the few day trippers petering out after a mile or so. On the beach behind the washed-up seaweed are straggling grasses that seem to be fighting to keep hold of a soil that is shifting even as you watch it. But this is an important and fast-disappearing habitat, particularly since golf has become such a tourist attraction in Ireland.

The sea inside the spits is shallow and provides a home to many sea and wading birds. This open, shallow sea provides food for diving seabirds such as gannets and shag searching for fish or shellfish. The beach itself is littered with the remains of the plentiful marine life which supplies the birds with food. The rotting debris on the beach attracts flies and sand hoppers which in turn provide food for shore birds such as ringed plovers and turnstones. These last birds can be seen on the foreshore turning stones and weed with their bills searching for food. They are distinctively small and black and white birds with white legs and are non-breeding visitors to the shores of Ireland.

Within the dunes themselves a complex system of land reclamation is going on as the marram grass gradually takes hold of the shifting sand. As new sand is thrown up over the grass it puts out new roots so that a cross section of the dune would show the grass's roots penetrating deep into the sand and forming the framework which allows more demanding plants to put down roots. The dunes are crowded with plants which cannot survive in any other conditions and whose future is in doubt. Lady's tresses is a rare white-flowered orchid which grows here. It is thought to produce seed once every decade so a careless foot or flower-gathering child may one day ensure that the plant no longer grows here. Other plants less rare but no less worthy of note are sea holly, with roots capable of supporting itself on salty sandy soils and spiked leaves which protect it from rabbits and other browsing animals which make their homes here. Sea holly in turn attracts butterflies which provide food for the birds of the dunes. Native wild bees find the dunes a good place to build nests and so the dunes help ensure that the process of pollination carries on well beyond the confines of this habitat.

The dunes themselves once provided shelter and a livelihood for our ancestors. Remains of their middens have been found here and it has been possible to determine their food sources and aspects of their way of life. Remains of charcoal fires have been found with hammer stones and tools for rubbing grain, sandstone knives, axes and bones as well as traces of iron smelting. Most of all, huge numbers of shells are discarded in the middens from the shelled fish that the primitive people cooked and ate.

Behind the dunes, inside the curve of Castlemaine Bay, are tidal mud flats which are a protected site for many migrant birds. The winter is the best time to be here if you are a keen birdwatcher because then thousands of geese, wading birds, swans and ducks come here from northern countries. The birds spend their summers in the vast uninhabited areas of Greenland, the Arctic, Siberia and Scandinavia and come to Ireland because it is the most northerly country where lakes are unlikely to freeze in winter and where there will be a plentiful supply of food. Brent Geese are particularly attracted to one plant, eelgrass, which grows in abundance in this estuary.

If you decide to walk any distance along this beach take a look at the abandoned shells which litter the sand. Many of them will have small holes in them. This is not some damage caused during their time in the ocean but the indication that this particular creature met its end by becoming a meal for one of the mollusc-eating estuary birds.

Link Inch Strand to Anascaul Lake. 5 miles/8 km.

After Inch Strand the houses thin out a little as the road draws closer to the shore and is at times cut out of the rock. About 4 miles/6 km from Inch Strand on the Dingle road a T-junction is reached; signposted left for Dingle (11 miles/18 km) and right for Anascaul. Take the right hand turn. After 0.7 miles/1.2 km further on the road for Anascaul turns to the right, just outside the village and before a bridge, while the next stop, Anascaul Lake, is signposted to the left. Notice how around Anascaul village evidence of modern human habitation can be found in the bright green of the fields; artificially induced with fertiliser. Shelter trees have been planted around houses and there are a few pine trees scattered about. Travel up a narrow road for about 2 miles/3.5 km, following the signs for the lake. A gate at the end of this road should be closed after passing through. Follow the narrow track up to the lake.

Stop Anascaul Lake, at the parking space provided.

You are standing at the bottom of a glacier-carved valley, the lough itself having been carved out by the base of the glacier. The scree slopes you can see across the lake on the slopes of Dromavalla have been broken off the top of the mountain by centuries of weathering. The lake itself is fed by typical acid mountain streams, low in nutrients and brown in colour. As the streams get closer to the lake that they feed, more and more sandy, silty patches will appear as the eroding effect of the water on the rocks gradually grinds them into silt.

The mountains surrounding the lake are made of 400-million-year-old Dunquin group sandstones; pale brown, red and yellow rocks. As rain falls on the higher reaches of the mountains it finds few nutrients. In its passage through the boglands higher up the mountains any nutrients in the form of lime it may have collected are taken up and it leaves the boglands brown in colour and nutrient free.

The green road leading away from the lough leads up the valley following the course of the River Garrivagh. The river is typical of upland rivers, slightly acid and fast moving because of the heights it falls from, and supporting only those creatures which can find a safe anchorage and food in its oligotrophic waters. Where pools form in the water the larvae of creatures such as mayfly, stonefly and caddisfly can survive. The caddisfly larva makes a small tube out of leaves or fragments of stone and uses it as anchorage and protection as it waits out the winter. This creature provides food for tiny brown trout, carnivorous fish which can now make a living on water fleas, flies, the caddis larvae, and even the occasional slug or snail that might fall in. The trout needs gravel in order to lay its eggs so it will be present in the type of pool which has sand and where the flow of the current is weak enough to allow it to swim against the stream. The trout is able to take bubbles of oxygen from the fast moving water and absorb dissolved oxygen.

Algae find a home on the rocks which are kept wet by spray as the water tumbles. They can collect nitrogen from the air and so do not need nutrients in the water. They, in their turn, provide food for other creatures such as the larval stages of midges. At the banks of the stream, or in any sandy spots that may have formed, plants such as water mint, moss, liverwort or clubrush will be clinging tenaciously to their anchorage in the silt. Some of these plants are able to take dissolved carbon dioxide from the water to use as sustenance.

Back down in the lough, the variety of life increases even more. Constantly fed by oxygen-rich water, the lake can support a whole range of life in a complex ecosystem. There is little chance of plants or animals being swept away, as there is in the stream, so a large amount of algal plants can flourish here. They in turn provide food for insects which bring trout — much bigger than those struggling to stay in one place upstream — to the surface. Around the banks, reeds, pond weed, water millfoil, pondweed and starwort provide food and cover for other creatures. One plant which grows here is water lobelia, more common in southern and western parts of Europe. Its leaves lie below the surface of the water and it sends up whitish lilac flowers in July and August.

In the marshy ground around the edge of the lake can easily be spotted the common flag, putting up its yellow flower from June to August. Also here are two species of butterwort, the famous insectivorous plant which has adapted to life in the nutrient-free boggy land around the lake by finding its food in the insects which land on its surface and are dissolved. Its leaves are a distinctive bright green and its flowers deep purple.

Link Anascaul Lake to Trabeg Beach. 7.5 miles/12 km.

Return to the main Dingle road heading towards Lispole and on to Dingle. Once again the land becomes more hospitable to the eye, with fewer rocks protruding from the soil and more hedgerow plants surviving the driving winds which bend them into odd shapes. After 5 miles/9 km the little village of Lispole sits on the road and 1 mile/1.7 km further on a left turn, signposted for the beach (*trá*) and the Seacrest Hotel, takes you down through high reed beds to Trabeg, an excellent

A mountain stream near the Connor Pass, Dingle peninsula

beach with a fascinating display of the geological history of the peninsula.

Stop at Trabeg Beach.

The boreen runs down to end on the beach. To your left as you look at the sea quite high cliffs rear up behind the beach with shallow caves worn into the rock. Inset in the rock are veins of quartz laid down as the rocks cracked and shifted. The quartz was once part of a layer of limestone which lay above the sandstone rocks. As the rocks cracked and shifted the limestone dissolved and filled the cracks and gradually under pressure metamorphosed into the crystals you see today. In the meantime the layer of limestone eroded away leaving only the quartz crystals as any sign that it was ever there. The rock also shows the complex pattern of shifting that took place in the rocks as the mountains behind you were formed. To the right of the road you can see the brilliantly coloured red and blue sandstones known as the Dingle group of conglomerate rock. It contains small pebbles of siltstone, some volcanic rock and some limestone, all of which must once have been swept down to this point in the enormous river which deposited the sand here. Around the curve of the bay you can see the seastack known as *An Searrach* (the foal).

Link Trabeg Beach to Dingle Harbour. 6.5 miles/10 km.

Back on the road to Dingle signs of human habitation are everywhere. Having left the higher peaks of Croaghskearda and Gowlanabeg behind, the valley widens out with low marshy land along this part of the coast, leading down to the salt marshes of Short Strand. The hedgerows are looking a little scantier while willow, the typical plant of wet land, grows everywhere. The stunted trees are created not by the force of the wind bending them backwards but by the icy winds of early spring which destroy the buds on the windward side, thus allowing one side to develop more than the other. Fishing ponds between the road and the sea provide a living for one family here.

Continue on this road to Dingle town where the harbour is an excellent place to stop to watch the local birdlife.

The waters of Dingle Bay cover rock known as Silurian because of its age, about 435 million years. One theory is that Dingle Bay was once on the coast of a continent, named Atlantis, now completely disappeared. The sandstones and conglomerates of Dingle Bay are thought to be 6,000 feet thick and represent the washed-down debris of ancient rivers.

As the road approaches the town the shape of Dingle harbour comes into view. In medieval times this was the most important harbour in Kerry and provided a living for many traders and fishermen. The town became less important as a port after the crushing of the earls of Desmond at the end of the sixteenth century. In the eighteenth century smuggling provided a living for many people. It seems to be a quirk of history that created in this peninsula a place where the Irish language could survive intact through all the years of its eradication in other parts. If Dingle had remained a vital port, it would almost certainly have been anglicised. Remoteness was the saving of Irish.

Stop at Dingle harbour where the river enters the harbour. Limited parking space is available at the Brian De Staic workshop or at the Craft Village across the road.

A brief stop here allows one to admire the plentiful birdlife which these mudflats support. By the time this river arrives here, at the end of its journey from its sources on the slopes of Gearhane and Ballysitteragh mountains, it will be carrying lots of debris and able to support much animal and plant life. As it meets the tidal waters, it will be further enriched with warm marine water. Many plants that can survive in both salt and fresh water flourish here and provide the starting point of the food chain of this estuary. Typical birdlife here is redshanks and dunlin which feed on smaller marine creatures such as ragworm and a tiny shelled creature called hydrobia. In an average mudflat, 25,000 of these creatures can be found to each square metre of mud. Evidence of a past economic life is close by here across the road — the remains of a millwheel which gave this area its name — Milltown.

Link Dingle to Fahan. 8.5 miles/14 km.

As you travel westwards out of Dingle on the road to Ventry the spit of land that forms the south arm of Dingle harbour appears on your left. It was for a long time the home of the Lords Ventry. Inside the grounds of the house, now a girls' school, are several ogham stones. This spit of land is wooded, a sure sign that the gentry once owned it. A brief detour down the road will take you through lush woodland with montbretia and fuchsia dominating the hedgerows. Ash trees and pine dominate. Back on the main road to Ventry the road travels through almost continuous houses, few of them modern. Ventry was once an important seaport. During the Desmond wars Admiral Winter kept a fleet of ships here and many refugees driven before the conquering English found shelter in the town.

As the road goes on towards Slea Head the vegetation gets wilder, high grasses and reeds block the view and the signs pointing out beehive huts and ring forts become numerous. The land is poor here, only able to support a few sheep. The occasional house will be surrounded by planted vegetation as cover but it is scanty. Life here must have been difficult for the early people as the number of promontory forts suggests. Dún Beg is a particularly well-preserved promontory fort with two souterrains or escape tunnels and the remains of an inner house inside four earthen defensive rings.

Stop at any of the signposts for the Fahan group of remains.

Nearby, above the road is a clochan: a stretch of 3 miles/5 km of ancient huts, many with souterrains and what might be sentry boxes at their entrances. There are over 500 remains in all including cave dwellings, rock shelters, standing stones, inscribed stones, forts, cahers and a church, all stretched out along some long-lost roadway. There are many unanswered questions about this area but it is possible that this represents a late pagan/early Christian version of a town, the only one extant. The houses represented here show a development from cave dwellings to sophisticted, rectangular, stone-roofed and many-roomed houses. If this was once a town then the people who lived in it must have used the mountains behind them as defence and the sea as their transport system and source of food. They were small people as the size of the clochans indicates and yet they were able to manipulate large stones and had skills as masons.

Link Glenfahan to Dunquin (for Great Blasket). 4.2 miles/6.5 km.

Back on the road you will come upon a sudden bad bend where a small stream flows over the road and takes a little bit of it away each winter. To the far south on a good day can be seen Bray Head on Valentia Island and even farther beyond that Great Skellig. Towering above is Eagle Mountain. On a misty day this part of the tour can be positively eerie as you travel along with the sea below and the mountain above and never a sign of life. Just after an impossibly decorated house, covered in care bears and Disney flowers, on a sharp bend in the road are gardens built in the shelter of what must once have been a building. Inside, the soil has been built up into lazy beds. This system of cultivation goes back to Neolithic times and is well suited to the barren poorly drained soil of the west of Ireland. In areas such as this the soil itself would be made from sand and seaweed and deposited on the top of the existing soil each winter ready to rot down for the following spring. The lazy bed would be built up as a series of ridges which would drain far more effectively than the peaty soil beneath. They also characterised a culture which depended on spades for turning the earth as this peninsula did until fairly modern times. Ploughs came very late to this part of Kerry.

The road descends into Coumeenoule with views for the first time of the Blaskets and their many accompanying rocks. These are part of a very different rock formation to the Dingle group of sandstones which dominate the peninsula. They are older, part of a volcanic period in Ireland's history and are made up of yellow siltstones and volcanic materials. If you had been here in September 1588 you could have watched four Spanish ships fighting for their lives around the Blasket Sound. Two made it into shelter while the other two sank, one with all hands. On the slopes above Coumeenoule are behive huts or clochans, not quite as old as the Fahan group but signs of a now abandoned way of life. They were used in the system of booleying when the family moved up into the mountains with the cattle for the summer so that they could graze the higher land. They must have been under threat from wolves and even wilder creatures in early times but by the time the booleying tradition ended in the nineteenth century most of the peninsula's wolves were long gone.

In Dunquin harbour the Silurian rock, formed by volcanic activity 400 million years ago, can be seen quite clearly. Another slightly less ancient thing to see here are the curraghs; boats made from tarred canvas over a light wooden frame. The design dates back to St Brendan's time when they must have been made from hides stretched over wooden frames. They are called naomhogs here and are bigger than those used in other parts of Ireland with the stern standing higher out of the water.

Stop Dunquin Pier, south of the village, past Kruger's B&B.

Boats leave the pier every hour for Great Blasket from 11 a.m. to 5 p.m. from May to September. Bad weather may mean there are no boats so you can ring 066-56146 in advance to find out or just turn up hopefully. This part of the ecotour will take at least a half day and if you intend to get your money's worth a picnic might be in order and make it a day out.

Stop Great Blasket.

Great Blasket is four miles long and half a mile wide and it supported human life for centuries until 1953. The Great Blasket is a peak of the range of hills that run down the spine of the peninsula. Between it and Eagle Mountain would once have been dry land. It was the last of the Blasket islands to be inhabited. When the botanist Robert Lloyd Praeger visited the island in the 1930s he saw small patches of cultivation of potatoes and oats on the north-east end and sheep grazing elsewhere. Two hundred and eight species of plants have been identified on the island. Only St Patrick's Cabbage of the unusual Lusitania flora grows here. The common plants of the island are all low-lying salt tolerant ones as would be expected — thrift, field mouse ear, lesser tway blade, rock sea spurrey, plantains, common heather and rush. An interesting plant which grows abundantly here is scurvy grass, a plant which for centuries before the cause of scurvy became known was prescribed for that disease. Herb sellers would sell fresh and dried scurvy grass in the cities and sailors would take dried and bottled supplies with them to sea. The plant is indeed rich in vitamin C and is still in use among herbalists as a remedy. It is not always found in salty areas but is reputed to taste salty wherever it grows. It is a low- growing plant with thick flat leaves and small white flowers which bloom all summer and have an unpleasant smell.

Adder's-tongue is a fern which, unusually, grows abundantly on the ridge behind the village. It looks much like cuckoopint with its sword-shaped leaves and white whorl of spores. The damp climate and mild winters and well-drained slopes of the islands encourage many species of ferns such as this one.

A plant called tree mallow that is more commonly seen in gardens is actually an indigenous plant of Great Blasket and of several uninhabited islands of the area despite the fact that it grows to a height of three feet. It too enjoys a bare habitat close by the sea.

Like the Skelligs, the isolation and soaring cliffs of the island provide abundant habitats for thousands of sea birds to nest. From the cliff edge gannets can be seen skimming the surface of the water in search of food, while guillemots and razorbills can also be seen. The razorbills have white breasts which can be seen from a distance while close up the unusual flattened beak with white stripe stand out. The guillemots have white patches on the wings. Storm petrels nest on Inishvickillane and can be seen searching for food. They are small compared to other seabirds and look a little like housemartins, all black with a white rump.

Like Glenfahan, the island has the remains of many different periods in man's history. Dún Fort, about halfway along the island, is thought to be an iron age fort with two defensive walls in front and the cliffs behind. At the top of the hill behind the village is a signal tower put there to warn of possible attack by Napoleonic forces in the early nineteenth century. Clochans abound towards the far end of the island but these are fairly modern, having been built by the inhabitants to dry turf. And of course the village, abandoned only in 1953, remains with many of its houses almost dangerously reclaimable just waiting for someone with some EU money to decide to build a 'tourist paradise' here.

Animal life on the island is restricted to rabbits and sheep but in the surrounding waters seals are often to be seen. When the island was inhabited, donkeys were the chief means of transport but there are none left now. Considering the economic importance of donkeys to the nineteenth-century Irish farmer it is surprising to learn that donkeys first came to Ireland only in the eighteenth century.

Return to the mainland.

Link Dunquin to the Connor Pass. 13.6 miles/22 km.

The area north of Dunquin is full of fascinating archaeological remains and amazing scenery and should not be missed, but for this ecotour the route turns back towards Dingle and the Connor Pass. By way of return take the road inland which passes behind Eagle Mountain across stark moorland with only telecommunications masts for company, emerging back on the R559 to Ventry and Dingle. In Dingle take the Connor Hill road. It is a turning off Main Street and is well signposted. Travelling up the road to Connor Hill it is possible to see

The Great Blasket Island, off the Kerry coast

the Garfinny river gradually getting smaller and smaller as it draws nearer to its source. Behind you views of Dingle Bay open up. Although it looks sparse this area of boggy land is able to support a varied wildlife and hawks can be spotted soaring above the grass searching out small creatures.

Stop at the car park at the top of Connor Hill.

You are looking down a flat U-shaped valley. To the north-west is the peak of Mount Brandon, almost 1,000 metres in height. This ridge of mountains, Brandon to the north and the rest running the length of the peninsula to the east, is the last of the great mountain ranges thrown up by the earth movements of thousands of years ago. To the north lie the carboniferous limestones, sandstones and shales with occasional tiny seams of coal of north Kerry and the Lower Shannon estuary.

In a colder age than this, the east slopes of Mount Brandon trapped snow in tiny pockets which over long periods turned to ice disks which scoured out the patch of rock they sat on. As the ice disc grew it threw out tongues of ice which drifted downwards, carrying bits of debris with them. The tongues gradually filled this valley which would once have been V-shaped, carved by a river. The ice sheet again scoured out a rounded shape and travelled slowly towards the sea making the wide flat valley you see before you. The east slopes of the mountain are covered in these small coombs that were once the beds of great ice boulders. The valley floor is littered with the debris of stones, sand and silt that the ice carried away from the mountainside as it smoothed and fractured it. The ice sheets probably left here about 16,000 years ago. As you can see, the land in this valley is badly drained and boggy and the river meanders across it on its way to the sea.

Link Connor Pass to Castlegregory. 11.7 miles/19 km.

At the head of the Connor Pass Brandon Bay opens up before you, the eastern side of it formed by a tombolo of land formed by what would have been islands of limestone rock and drifts of sand which have built up between them and the mainland. North of the tombolo are the Magharee Islands, tiny points of limestone rock not yet eroded away by the action of the sea. The road runs along the shore of Brandon Bay with lanes running down to the vast stretches of beach. Castlegregory is signposted from the main road at Stradbally. The village itself is at the neck of the tombolo. It is named after a castle now long gone built here in 1550 by Gregory Hoare. His son Hugh entertained Lord Grey, Spencer and Raleigh for one night at the castle on their journey to the massacre at Dún an Óir. His wife, whose name is now lost, opened all the wine barrels and let them run dry rather than allow these Englishmen drink: Hoare murdered her in anger at her deed.

Stop At Lough Gill, 1 mile/1.6 km from the turn-off to Castlegregory.

Lough Gill is a shallow lagoon fed by rainwater and drained by a small stream to the shore east of the lake. It is quite shallow and the water is brackish because of its origins. It is home to a number of wild birds including the Bewick swan that migrates here from Siberia. The area around the lough with its mixture of sandy soil, lime and stagnant damp ground is also home to an unusual mix of plants. In the lough itself can be seen large yellow water lilies while around it are meadowsweet, asphodels, and irises. But there are also some unusual types of rush, whorled caraway, great burnet saxifrage, strawberry clover, squinancy wort, and an unusual variety of dodder, a semi-parasitic plant. Also in abundance is eelgrass which is food for many of the migrating birds that overwinter here.

Link Lough Gill to Fahamore at the end on the tombolo. 4 miles/6 km.

Stop at the pier at Fahamore.

From here the Magharee Islands are much clearer. Illauntannig has the remains of an early Christian settlement surrounded by an 18-feet thick cashel. Inside it are two oratories, three beehive huts and three burial stones. One of the huts has a cross of white stone set into it. The island is named after St Senan who founded the monastery here.

The landscape around this part of the coast is distinctively limestone. There is constant erosion as the sea dissolves the calcium carbonate in the rock. Wave action and the battering of tiny stones carried by the sea is also having an effect on the rocks which are rough, fluted and ridged. The weathering is more effective on lines of weakness in the rocks which are also being dissolved slowly by rainwater filtering down. Thus deep narrow inlets, often with a shallow cave at the end, are being formed both by the sea and by rainwater. In Irish these are called coos.

This area is famous for the family called Hartney who moved here from Clare in 1830 and brought with them the skill of making curraghs, or naomhogs, from canvas rather than animal skin.

Like the sand dunes at Inch these dunes have uncovered middens dating back to Mesolithic times including tools, and in one case a bear tooth and the bones of red deer.

Link Castlegregory to Tralee along Tralee Bay. 20 miles/31 km.

This last section of the ecotour follows the main road back along the shore of Tralee Bay. This is also an excellent spot for lovers of shore birds and waders which overwinter along here in large numbers. As the tour grows closer to Tralee the evidence of holidaymakers gets denser, with signs for caravan sites every few hundred yards and inns and pubs lining the road. Before Tralee is Blennerville, noticeable now because of the restored windmill. Much of the agricultural land along here was built up in the last century by basketloads of sand and seaweed which were often dumped into cowsheds first as litter. This added to the fertile quality of the sand and helped to desalinate it a little. Onion growing has been very successful in this area due to the creation of these fertile fields in past centuries.

FURTHER READING

MAPS

There is no shortage of quality maps. The Michelin Map of Ireland No. 405 (1:1,000,000) has the scenic roads highlighted in green.

The West map in the series of four that make up the Ordance Survey Holiday Map series is very useful for just Cork and Kerry. The scale, 1:250,000, is more detailed than the whole Ireland map. For greater detail the Ordnance Survey covers the whole island in 25 sheets with a 1:126,720 scale (half an inch to 1 mile). This series, however, is being replaced by an excellent new series of 89 maps with a 1:50,000 scale (2 cm to 1 km). At the time of writing the map for the Dingle peninsula has been published and in time the rest of Kerry and Cork will be available.

Special maps for the Kerry Way and the Dingle Way are available from tourist offices, and at a pinch they will do. See the walking guides section below for the Gill & Macmillan book that covers both walks in more detail.

CORK

Archaeological Inventory of County Cork, Vol. 1 — West Cork. Denis Power and others. Office of Public Works IR£20. Nearly 500 pages make up this archaeological inventory of West Cork and at IR£20 in hardback this is exceptional value. Maps locate every site recorded: megalithic tombs, stone circles, boulder-burials, standing stones, prehistoric copper mines, pit and urn burials, abbeys, post-medieval military and industrial sites and a lot more.

Hungry Hill. Daphne du Maurier. Penguin. This novel is based fairly closely on the history of the Puxley family who owned the once valuable copper mines at the end of the Beara peninsula. Daphne du Maurier had access to the family papers and blends fact with fiction. The book makes ideal holiday reading if visiting West Cork and the splendid remains of the Puxley mansion outside Castletownbere.

Some Experiences of an Irish R.M. and *Further Experiences of an Irish R.M.* by Edith Somerville and 'Martin Ross' (Violet Martin) are enjoyable to read but if a choice has to be made then *The Real Charlotte*, their novel, is by far the more interesting read. Its 'Big House' setting evokes the world of the Anglo-Irish Ascendancy and the novel has been called the least unselfconscious novel of the 'Big House' tradition. In the *R.M.* books the local Irish inhabitants — the 'natives' — are portrayed in a condescending and picturesque manner. In *The Real Charlotte* there is revealed a contempt for the Irish, born of an assumed sense of racial superiority.

Inside Cork. Alannah Hopkins. The Collins Press. Three of the twelve chapters give detailed comments on places to visit, restaurants and accommodation possibilities in West Cork.

KERRY

Discovering Kerry. T.J. Barrington. Blackwater Press (Dublin), 1976. Over 300 pages, in hardback, dealing with the history and topography of the county. The style and organisation of the book is off-putting at times but there's a wealth of detail to dip into.

A Country Diary: The Year in Kerry. Patrick O'Sullivan. Anvil. An entry for each day takes the reader through local history, folklore, poetry, and observations of life. Illustrated.

Peig, Peg Sayers; *The Islandman,* Thomas O Crohan; *Twenty Years a Growing,* Maurice O Sullivan are three books dealing with life on the Blasket Islands, written by islanders.

Skellig — Island Outpost of Europe. Des Lavelle. O'Brien Press.

The Blasket Islands — Next Parish to America. Joan and Ray Staghles. O'Brien Press.

WALKING GUIDES

New Irish Walk Guides: Southwest. Seán Ó Súilleabháin. Gill & Macmillan. Details and maps for 49 walks in Cork and Kerry, ranging from the easy walk to the strenuous climb. The Kerry Way and the Dingle Way are covered in detail.

West Cork Walks and *Kerry Walks.* Both by Kevin Corcoran. O'Brien Press. Excellent books, with maps, dealing with ecological and historical points of interest.

FISHING

Coarse Angling Guide. Central Fisheries Board. Gill & Macmillan.

Sea Angling Guide. Central Fisheries Board. Gill & Macmillan.

ECOLOGY

Bellamy's Ireland — The Wild Bogland. David Bellamy. Christopher Helm Publishers.

Irish Nature Companion — A Guide to Irish Flora and Fauna. Appletree.

Man and the Landscape Ireland. F.M.A. Aalen. Academic Press. Unfortunately out of print, but available in libraries. This study of how the present physical and cultural landscape evolved is an interesting blend of history and geography.

A Field Guide to the Flowers of Europe. Collins. London.

A Field Guide to the Birds of Europe. Collins. London. These two paperback guides, with colour illustrations, are highly recommended.

INDEX